THE BEST OF
CHARLES
BUCHAN'S
FOOTBALL
MONTHLY

In an alleyway behind *Football Monthly's* offices on the Strand, Charles Buchan, immaculately turned out as always, shows a few moves to 18 year old Steve 'Kalamazoo' Mokone from Pretoria. Together with the Wolves and England captain Billy Wright, Buchan was instrumental in arranging for the young international's visit to England, after the South African authorities had tried to block the move. 'This colour bar makes me mad,' fumed Buchan in the March 1956 edition. 'Though I am by nature a mild-tempered man, I got very angry when reading reports I received from South Africa, which made it painfully clear that the "colour bar" has crept into Soccer... the happy spirit of a game played throughout the world is being sullied by racial prejudice... the more I read about it the more nauseating it became.' Alas Mokone failed to make the grade in England, having a difficult season at Coventry City, where he was dismayed at the prejudice he encountered. But he did go on to stardom in Dutch and Italian football. *Football Monthly* columnist John Macadam wrote of Buchan's efforts, 'Charles is an incorrigible humanist and sentimentalist. He sees only the good in all men.'

When Stephen Mokone arrived in England from South Africa, to try his luck with Coventry City, the first person on whom he called was Charles Buchan. In this picture the old England captain and the lad from Africa stage a little demonstration in the alley behind the office of "Football Monthly," the magazine which helped Mokone to get his chance.

▲ October 1956

The Best of Charles Buchan's Football Monthly
© Malavan Media and Football Monthly Ltd 2008

Text by Simon Inglis
Design by Doug Cheeseman
Production by Jackie Spreckley
Additional imaging by Jörn Kröger

Malavan Media is a creative consultancy responsible for the Played in Britain series of books and events

www.playedinbritain.co.uk

Thanks to Deborah Benn and Lawrence Gosling at Football Monthly Ltd., Pat Collins and George Klepp. Boys Club badge courtesy of Martin Westby

ISBN: 978 0 9547445 88
Sixth reprint October 2008
Zrinski, Croatia

THE BEST OF
CHARLES
BUCHAN'S
FOOTBALL
MONTHLY

Edited by Simon Inglis

Published by Malavan Media

Nat Lofthouse, of Bolton Wanderers—the "Lion of Vienna"—is still an idol for every Bolton boy. And these cheering Burnden Park youngsters let him know that he is still secure in their admiration.

CHARLES BUCHAN'S
FOOTBALL
MONTHLY

Edited By . . . CHARLES BUCHAN
and JOHN THOMPSON

Associate Editor . . J. MAXWELL SARL

SEPTEMBER, 1951   No. 1

Contents:

Published by Charles Buchan's Publications, Ltd., 408, The Strand, London W.C.2.
Printed in Great Britain by Greycaines (Taylor Garnett Evans & Co., Ltd.) Watford.
Distributed by Thorpe and Porter, Ltd., Oadby, Leicester.

◄ October 1960

From the beginning....

AT first there was one chair in the office of "Football Monthly." I cannot remember why. We were hard-up for furniture for a long time. We would take it in turns to perch round a trestle table on orange boxes and would courteously leave the chair for any visitor who proved himself healthy enough to climb the steep stairs leading to our new home.

The trestle table was covered with a grey blanket and smelled of old apples. This was probably because Covent Garden was just round the corner.

Long before "Football Monthly" increased its tangible assets in any substantial way, Charles Buchan climbed the stairs with a purchase wrapped in brown paper. It was a splendidly expensive feather-duster.

Every morning Charles would whisk it energetically over the walls, the little pieces of furniture and the weary strips of linoleum.

Then he would look around as proudly as if he had just scored the winning goal against Scotland.

The moment he had finished, all the dust would settle down gracefully to await the next disturbance. The office overlooked the Strand, London . . . buses almost passed through the room, and it was difficult to keep clean for any time at all.

That first winter was singularly comfortless. In an unenviable spot, furthest from the windows, Joe Sarl would peer with a kind of hopeless determination at typescript and proofs and emerge at the end of the day with the lost look of a man who has been wandering through a thick fog.

He was, however, the warmest of our company.

To avoid frost-bite from the draughts that whistled through the room, Charles Buchan would wrap newspapers round his legs. The paper rustled disconcertingly whenever he moved.

LONG before winter fell, there had been the task of reading the first contributions to our first issue. There had been a fascinating incongruity in sitting on an orange box and studying the earliest article to arrive.

It came from that fine and kindly friend, the Marquess of Londonderry. He had been converted to Soccer by his friendship with miners in his father's pits.

There was a certain dream-like quality in reading Lord Londonderry's description of how he had become a director of Arsenal . . . because of a conversation over dinner at Buckingham Palace with the Master of the Horse, who happened to be Chairman of Arsenal.

Well, Buckingham Palace was only down the road from our office. And for a moment the bare electric light bulb was a candelabrum . . .

As this one hundredth edition of "Football Monthly" was being prepared, I glanced with nostalgia through that long-ago Number One.

The front cover picture was of Stanley Matthews, of Blackpool and England. **There could be no other choice, for Matthews has enriched the pleasures of us all and, in the years that have intervened, there has been no challenger for his place among the giants.**

Inside, were pictures of little Henry Cockburn, of Manchester United, and of Jimmy Dickinson, who has served Portsmouth with devoted loyalty through so many triumphs and disasters.

There, too, were bow-legged Joe Mercer and Mal Griffiths, the happy Welshman, and George Young leading out Scotland, and Jimmy Mason poised over the ball in the colours of Third Lanark. All were players remembered now with gratitude.

There, too, was Joe Harvey, telling with humility of the day Newcastle United won the F.A. Cup . . . *The King handed it to me and as he did so, I had the feeling that all the good people of Tyneside were with me . . . I felt that His Majesty was giving the Cup to me not as Joe Harvey, but as the representative of all those supporters, that I was getting it on their behalf.*

The Queen gave me my medal and I made my way down the steps, perhaps stumbling a little because I was near to tears . . .

TURN again the yellowing pages of that old "Football Monthly". Here is Raich Carter talking of bomb-battered Hull . . . *It was the success of Hull City Soccer team that helped to put Hull back on the map and restore the morale of people who had come to regard themselves as isolated and forgotten . . .*

Arthur Drewry, then Chairman of England's Selectors, told how *his imagination had been fired in Argentina and Brazil by the development of football grounds as first-class social centres; the centre-piece of the local community for every kind of recreative sport . . .*

Turn the pages . . . here is J. B. Priestley, capturing, as he did so well in "The Good Companions", the emotions of those who follow our greatest game . . . *It turned you into a member of a new community, all brothers together for an hour-and-a-half, for not only had you escaped from the clanking machinery of this less life, from work, wages, rent, doles, sick pay, insurance cards, nagging wives, ailing children, bad bosses, idle workmen, but you had escaped with most of your neighbours, with half the town, and there you were, cheering together, thumping one another on the shoulders, swopping judgments like lords of the earth, having pushed your way through a turnstile into another and altogether more splendid kind of life, hurtling with Conflict and yet passionate and beautiful in its Art . . .*

AND now, close the pages and consider for a moment how "Football Monthly" grew from its orange-box days into the voice of the greatest game man ever played, the game that spans frontiers with a handshake and knows no barriers of race or belief.

"Football Monthly" became a unique 'family affair'. Readers sent ideas and views on how to improve the magazine. Never had a publication received such friendly and loyal support.

The family was scattered, as the magic of football is scattered.

There was a boy in Brazil, a shoe-maker in Alaska, a judge's son in Yugoslavia, the skipper of a tug-boat who took two copies so that he could send one to an unknown kid in hospital.

There was a cinema manager in Australia, a cipher clerk in a British Embassy, a lance-corporal in the Malayan jungle.

The addresses from which they wrote ranged from Bolton to Burma. They came from destroyers and trawlers, factories and farms. Some were at village schools, others at Eton.

Thus did "Football Monthly" prosper because of the kindliness and understanding of its readers.

And it is the kindliness that will be remembered always— the gifts that readers asked us to send to sick children at Christmas, the gestures that helped old players down on their luck.

There were letters from prisons and mansions and there was the miracle of finding how blind people retain their love for football.

And the family grew and gained in strength and influence. It is loyal and sturdy, as it always was. We are very proud of it . . .

▲ December 1959

Introduction

'Our object is to provide a publication that will be worthy of our National game and the grand sportsmen who play and watch it.'

Cometh the hour, as it is written, cometh the man. Or, in this instance, the man and his magazine. *Charles Buchan's Football Monthly* was a true phenomenon of its time.

And what a time it was.

If the popularity of football is measured purely in terms of its attendances, rather than, for example, by grassroots participation or by commercial gain, the late 1940s and early 1950s represent the very zenith of the game.

At their peak in season 1948-49, attendances topped an astonishing 41 million in the Football League, plus 6.2 million in Scotland, as the war weary population embraced football, and indeed every other form of escape from the daily grind of rationing and austerity. (By comparison figures for the English and Scottish Leagues in 2005-06 were 29 million and 4.4 million respectively). Cricket and rugby grounds, cinemas and amusement parks experienced similar surges in popularity, the likes of which shall surely never be repeated in a television-dominated world.

Yet amid this extraordinary era, something was missing.

In his autobiography *A Lifetime in Football*, Charles Buchan wrote 'that soccer, unlike other sports, has not produced a mass of literature. There have been passages in novels by great authors like Arnold Bennett and JB Priestley, and mystery stories by various writers.'

In particular, he noted that since the closure in 1931 of *Athletic News* – the weekly 'bible of the game', established in Manchester in 1875 – no newspapers or magazines had been devoted exclusively to football.

'Surely,' argued Buchan, 'the game is popular enough to be worthy of the attention of our present leading writers.'

It was to test this assertion that in September 1951 *Football Monthly* was launched.

In fact there were plenty of publications around in post-war Britain that sought to feed the nation's football frenzy.

In addition to coverage in daily and Sunday newspapers – albeit less detailed than today, but still considerable in the popular press – hardly a town or city did not have its own Saturday night football special, a *Pink 'Un* or a *Green 'Un*.

Moreover, stimulated no doubt by London's staging of the 1948 Olympics, by 1950 some 80 sports related periodicals were on sale, around ten of which focused largely on football. Among these were such shortlived titles as *Sporting World*, *New Sports Pictorial, Weekly Sporting Review, All Football* and *Weekly Football Dispatch*. Hardier than most was *Sport* (later *Sport Weekly,* then *Sport Express*) which ran from 1938-57.

For more discerning football fans, however, all these titles were lacking in two fundamental respects.

Firstly, they covered other sports, particularly cricket, rugby, boxing and horse racing, while their football content was aimed mainly at pools punters, with snippets of gossip thrown in. Even *Sporting Record* ('best for pools'), which sold over 100,000 during the 1950s and carried articles by such luminaries as Neville Cardus, Harry Carpenter and Eamonn Andrews, resorted to crossword guides, show biz fillers and swim-suited pin-ups. In short, neither fish nor fowl.

Secondly, partly because good quality paper was in short supply after the war, and partly because few of the publishers could attract significant funding, the general sports magazines invariably appeared washed out and tired before they left the bookstands, particularly when compared with mass circulation women's titles. For

a nation that was now hungry for freedom and light, a nation that, if the proponents of the 1951 Festival of Britain were to be believed, was bursting with energy and invention, this was simply not good enough.

Above all, what football fans wanted, in their footballing world as well as in their living rooms and wardrobes, was colour.

And that is exactly what *Charles Buchan's Football Monthly* gave them. Not much at first, it is true. In the first issue on the cover only, and thereafter in small doses. Nor in the early years was it true colour photography, but black and white images, hand tinted by artists.

Other sports magazines had toyed with spot, or single colours, often crudely applied to team groups and action shots on front covers. But none turned it into full colour, high art, as did *Football Monthly*.

Crucially too, the magazine struck a chord with middle class fans, especially boys at rugby playing schools where soccer-worship had to be conducted under desks or under the bedsheets, after lights out. One such boy was the BBC football commentator John Motson, a boarder at Culford School, Suffolk, in the 1950s. Every Monday John and his pals took turns to pore over the latest *Green 'Un*, sent by the parents of a classmate, Gary Newbon (who followed Motson into television). For boys of this ilk *Football Monthly* was a godsend. At last, a publication that covered only football, was attractive, and at least aspired to intelligence, even if it did not always succeed.

It was also, as one early reader recalls, 'satisfyingly weighty', hence its cover price of 1s 6d, which put it out of reach of many a working class boy. But this only added to its allure. One did not simply read and then junk *Football Monthly*. Instead, it became an instant collectable, as all good magazines should be. John

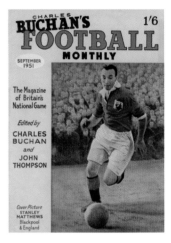

Motson, in common with many a former reader, still has his complete set, bound, in the attic.

The magazine had one other major advantage.

Charles Buchan's association with *Football Monthly* was no mere celebrity endorsement. Aged 61 at the time of the magazine's launch, Charlie was known to most readers as a broadcaster for BBC radio or as a journalist for the *News Chronicle*. He had long since retired from playing, in 1928. That said, his status would hardly have been so high had it not been for his reputation. As a player, Charles Buchan had been a class act.

The son of an Aberdonian blacksmith, based at the Woolwich Arsenal in south east London, Buchan was born in Plumstead in September 1891. His first ambition had been to teach, but in 1909 he signed as an amateur with his local club, Woolwich Arsenal. This arrangement ended when he asked for, but was refused, travel expenses, the first of many disputes with petty football officials that would shape his outlook.

From Woolwich he moved to Northfleet, then to Leyton, a Southern League club, and from there he progressed to First Division ▶

To millions of listeners during the 1950s, at home and overseas, Charles Buchan's measured tones – laced with his slight London drawl – were as familiar as the voices of Gilbert Harding, the Goons, the Archers, Mrs Dale or Henry Hall. He appeared in three slots on the BBC's Light Programme: previewing matches on Friday evenings and on Saturday lunchtime's *Sports Parade*, hosted by Eamonn Andrews. Or, he would battle through traffic after matches to deliver what the *Radio Times* called 'expert opinion' on *Sports Report* at 5.30pm. Though rarely controversial, he did once let his guard drop. During England's 7-1 drubbing in Budapest in 1954 he repeatedly lambasted the English players, wrongly assuming that his microphone was switched off. But Charlie escaped censure. England had, after all, been totally outclassed. His Friday evening chats always ended with this sign-off: '... and whether you are playing, watching or listening, here's to a good weekend's sport.'

▶ Sunderland, in March 1911. Six foot tall with long legs and a loping gait, Buchan developed into a gifted and prolific inside-forward, scoring 224 goals in 413 appearances for Sunderland (a club record which still stands). The tally would have been higher had it not been for the outbreak of war. Typical of his generation, in *A Lifetime in Football* (first serialised in *Football Monthly*, then published in 1955), he skirted over his experiences at the Somme and Passchendaele, preferring instead to recall matches played with his army chums.

Apparently unscathed, physically or emotionally, Buchan returned from the trenches to resume his scoring feats with Sunderland in 1918, whilst also teaching part-time and setting up a sports goods shop in the town in 1920. By then he was married to a Wearside girl, Ellen, and had two children. He also started contributing articles to the local press, unusually without the intercession of a ghost writer.

But stand out though he did, both on and off the pitch, regular England honours eluded Buchan. Perhaps because of his chippy manner, he won only six caps, to go with his one Championship medal and FA Cup Final loser's medal, both earned in 1913.

Then just as it appeared that his career was winding down, in 1925 Buchan gained a new lease of life. Out of the blue he was signed by Herbert Chapman, the newly appointed manager of his first club, Arsenal. Famously, rather than meet the £4,000 fee Sunderland demanded, Arsenal agreed to pay £2,000, plus £100 for each goal scored in his first season. As it transpired, Buchan netted 21.

But more than his goals, at a time when Arsenal were still trying to establish themselves at Highbury – having controversially moved from Plumstead in 1913 – Buchan's lasting contribution was to help mastermind a tactical revolution at the club. In 1925 the offside law was changed so that only two, rather than three defenders had to be goal-side of an attacker. While many a team struggled to adapt, Buchan's response was to suggest that Arsenal play with a deeper lying centre half. The ruse, known subsequently as the Third Back Game, proved an instant success, and was widely copied. Indeed its effect upon tactics was still being debated in early issues of *Football Monthly*, 26 years later. Some decried it as a negative influence. Buchan himself blamed its imitators for not understanding, or for lacking the skills to implement the system's attacking potential.

By now a respected veteran, Buchan thrived back in the capital. He settled his family in suburban Hendon, took up golf seriously, started writing for the *Daily News* and, on the eve of the 1927 Cup Final – in which he again ended up with a loser's medal – made his radio debut, broadcasting from the new BBC studios in Savoy Hill. This was also the year that outside broadcasts were first made from sporting events. Over two million radio sets were licensed in Britain by this time.

Too affable, and perhaps too canny to take up club management – he was, in his own words, 'not the worrying type' – in 1928, at the age of 36, Buchan accepted an offer to work full-time for the *Daily Chronicle* (which two years later became the *News Chronicle*).

By choice he never donned his boots again, not even for fun.

In today's media-saturated world it is common to hear former players air their dreary, predictable views on radio and television, though few make the transition to a newsroom or a sports desk. And in truth, Charlie was dependable rather than eloquent or innovative. Brian Glanville, who started contributing to *Football Monthly* as a young freelance in 1952, later described Buchan's prose as 'plodding' and his broadcasting as 'pedestrian'.

But he suited the needs of the BBC, and Glanville was the first to admit that a whole generation of fans, hungry for any media coverage at all, came to hang on his every utterance, laboured or not.

Charlie's watchword, in print and on the airwaves, was 'grand'. Matches were grand. The players were grand. Soccer itself – always with a capital S in *Football Monthly* – was forever grand. And almost certainly life too was grand for this gangling Plumstead boy-made-good. Football had brought him fame and financial security. Now it offered a passport to the world.

Buchan's first foreign assignment was in 1933, to cover England's international against Italy in Rome, where he immediately found himself cast adrift after his local minder was arrested by Fascist guards. Naturally he spoke no Italian, nor any other foreign language (a failing shared, unsurprisingly, by virtually every English football reporter of the day). He was also present at England's humbling defeat by the USA at the 1950 World Cup in Belo Horizonte, Brazil, an experience which fuelled much of the doom and gloom surrounding English football for most of *Football Monthly*'s early life.

Throughout his travels, as might be expected of a tall, former Guardsman and Arsenal captain, Buchan stood out among the press corps. Most notably, in 1947, returning from another England defeat – in Brussels – he was one of four reporters to set up the Football Writers' Association. One of the FWA's first decisions was to introduce an annual Footballer of the Year Award, decided by a vote amongst FWA members. The first winner, in 1948, was Stanley Matthews, whose image was also to grace – and help sell – the first *Football Monthly*.

Exactly whose idea the magazine had been in the first place will never be known for sure. But there were two main protagonists apart from Charlie. John Thompson, a tall, elegant and hugely respected reporter for the *Daily Mirror*, hailed from the north east, and was the magazine's de facto editor. He was joined by another former *Mirror* man, Joe Maxwell Sarl, who was more into racing but had a sound business instinct and apparently helped set up the business. This included not only the magazine but the annual *Charles Buchan Soccer Gift Book*, which soon became an essential item on schoolboys' Christmas wishlists.

Despite his advancing years and other commitments, Buchan played an active role in affairs. One reader, Bryan Horsnell of Reading, remembers visiting the Strand with his father in the early 1950s, on the off chance of meeting the great man. And sure enough there he was, at his desk, in an expensive dark suit, with stiff starched collar, Brylcreemed hair and, as ever, a pipe in hand. (Charlie had been encouraged to take up the pipe in his playing days, rather than smoke cigarettes, by the Sunderland trainer.) He signed a programme for young Bryan with a flourish of his fountain pen, as he did for all members of the magazine's Boys Club. He also personally signed hundreds of copies that readers sent in to be bound every year.

Buchan was similarly generous towards invalids, sending them free subscriptions, and towards readers serving in the army, of whom there were legions, at least until National Service ended in 1960. Over a thousand would not return from Korea between 1950-53. A further

It was a good kick-off for Queen's Park Rangers in the first floodlit match to be played on their ground. Spotlight was on stage star Pat Kirkwood, who is watched by Arsenal's Don Roper (left) and Joe Taylor, of Queen's Park Rangers.

'Charlie did a lot of things for charity that weren't broadcast. This here, this charity match at QPR (*December 1953*) was one of his. Jimmy Hill was on one line. Desmond Hackett, of the *Daily Express*, he was supposed to do the other. He always wore a Trilby as I remember. But he didn't turn up so I ran the line. I hadn't got any kit but I loved it. The next morning I walked into the office and Charlie said "Did you enjoy that?" I said I certainly did. He'd been sitting in the stand then afterwards gave this little cup to the winning team... He was a quiet chap, got on with his job. I mean Charlie, John and Joe used to laugh and joke in the main office but I never interfered. I was in the back room doing the adverts, the Boys Club page, that sort of thing. I never saw Charlie play, I was too young. But he was one of the old school, you could tell. He helped me, he helped everyone if he could. I felt very proud to work for him.'
David Stacey, office assistant at *Football Monthly*

100,000 servicemen were posted elsewhere, in Germany, the Far East and other outposts of the Empire.

Military life and war-time experiences inevitably created a real bond between the writers and a large proportion of its older readership. Players too were imbued with barrack humour and tales of battle. Blackpool's Stan Mortensen, featured on the cover of August 1952, told the story of how, as a wireless operator in the RAF, he had been the sole survivor of a Wellington bomber crew. His trainer at Blackpool, Johnny Lynas, survived a Japanese prisoner-of-war camp. Tom Finney of Preston drove a tank in Italy. And when Portsmouth were heading towards the First Division title in 1949, *Football Monthly* recalled, captain Reg Lewin had read out to the players a letter from the club president, Field Marshal Viscount Montgomery, urging them on to victory. 'What a game they played after that letter was received.'

Not that military life was all positive. A number of reports talked of how players often returned from National Service having put on weight and developed bad habits.

The source of these reports, more often than not, was Leslie Yates, *Football Monthly*'s longest serving contributor and compiler of the regular feature, Soccer Sideshow. Yates was 'a para man' – that is, he served up an endless diet of short paragraphs on footballers and managers, their moves, their mates and their off-the-field hobbies and sidelines. Several of these paras would appear in only a slightly amended form two or three times a year, and even pop up in other publications, such as *Soccer Star* (a weekly counterpoint to *Football Monthly*, set up by a rival publisher in 1952 and merged with *World Soccer* in 1970). A short, dapper man, Yates was a Spurs fan, ending up as the club's programme editor.

Feature writer and sub-editor Peter Morris was, by contrast, a dour Midlander who learnt his craft in Coventry and in 1960 wrote a history of Aston Villa, one of the first properly researched club histories of the modern period.

Another early contributor, as mentioned earlier, was that doyen of football writing, Brian Glanville. In 1952 the magazine serialised his mammoth Who's Who of over 1300 players. A year later, still aged barely 21, he was devastated when Thompson reneged on a deal to publish the series in book form. Even so, he continued to submit articles, but on the game abroad.

In those days that was no easy option, not only in practical terms.

British attitudes to Europe at this time were perhaps best summed up by the Labour politician Herbert Morrison's rejection of French and German overtures for a joint coal and steel community. 'It's no good,' he declared, 'the Durham miners won't wear it.'

Much the same insularity informed *Football Monthly's* approach. While Europeans were usually branded collectively as 'Continentals', Britain remained an intricate patchwork of communities and tradition. Durham had its miners, Sheffield had its Blades, Luton had the Hatters and Reading the Biscuitmen. Crewe, of course, were known as the Railwaymen.

Every reader knew that.

Our players had reassuring names too. Not only the usual Bills, Bobs and Berts but schoolboy favourites from the magazine such as Arthur Bottom (York), Grenville Hair (Leeds), Basil Acres (Ipswich), Gerald Cakebread (Brentford), and the unforgettable Clyde full back, Harry Haddock.

In contrast the 'Continentals' had unpronounceable names and unsavoury habits, even if their footballing prowess spoke for itself.

The antics of foreign spectators – rioting in Athens or firing guns in Brazil – were often highlighted. Next to an image of a heavily guarded moat and perimeter fence at a Buenos Aires stadium, John Thompson wrote sardonically, 'If some jackbooted policeman turned up with a carbine and a chestful of gas bombs at Goodison Park, White Hart Lane or St Andrew's, the paying customers would not do him the honour of even being angry. They would laugh at him.'

Similarly, in December 1954 the cover depicted a Uruguayan player receiving treatment after fainting during a World Cup match. It was, read the caption, 'an indication of the consuming fervour which fills so many foreign players. They are keyed up to a peak of mental and physical tension with almost fanatical zeal. Who has ever heard of an English player being so overcome with excitement at a goal that he needed the trainer's smelling salts?'

But then quirky tales of Johnny Foreigner were meat and drink to the popular press of the day, and *Football Monthly* was no different. It was, after all, the product of seasoned Fleet Street operators.

One such contributor from that hard school of reporting was Clifford Webb, a large, daunting Bristolian and bon viveur, editor of *Sporting Record* and a former *Daily Herald* man, while the magazine's amateur football correspondent – at a time when Amateur Cup Finals drew crowds of 100,000 to Wembley – was Norman Ackland, 'Pangloss' of the *News Chronicle*. One pictures an amateur soccer expert as a blazered gent in an old school tie. Instead, Ackland was a feckless, if amiable rogue. Thrown out of Trinity College, Dublin, for working as a bookie's runner, he survived Dunkirk to impregnate a succession of mistresses in Dublin, Poona and Maida Vale. One of his offspring is the actor, Joss Ackland.

In common with Norman Ackland, columnist John Macadam had always dreamt of becoming a great dramatist, but was happy in the end to help pay his bar bills by freelancing for Buchan. A diminutive, feisty Scottish bachelor, Macadam had worked his way up from the shipyards of Greenock to become a celebrated sportswriter for the *Daily Express* before the war. As described in his autobiography, *The Macadam Road*, he saw action with the RAF on D-Day, and in peacetime survived sundry dubious encounters, following prize fighters in the likes of New York and Chicago. On his death in 1964, ▶

Reporters in Rio! Charles Buchan (left), John Thompson, Roy Peskett, Clifford Webb and John Macadam with his ukelele.

IF HE'S IN THE SERVICES

Send him his favourite magazine. A year's supply of "Football Monthly" can be sent post free to anywhere in the world for £1. This ensures delivery of 12 issues. Just send postal order or cheque to Charles Buchan, 408 Strand, London, W.C.2

◀ November 1953 | June 1952 ▲

▶ John Thompson wrote that behind his outsized moustache Macadam had the 'melancholy of a man looking for something he could not hope to find.' His ukelele would be much missed on press trips.

Pat Collins, who joined the magazine's staff in July 1960, and who later took over as editor from John Thompson, was another Fleet Street veteran who had seen active service during the war. A scion of Bermondsey's Irish Catholic community, he had worked for the *Daily Mirror* before becoming the main football writer for *Reynolds News* during the 1950s.

A calm, easy going and popular man, Collins put immense effort into *Football Monthly*, recognising its worth in the game and in publishing circles. His son, also Pat, now a senior writer for the *Mail on Sunday*, used to contribute articles under the name of John Anthony, whilst still a schoolboy.

Then there were the short stories.

To modern tastes these appear tame and hackneyed, sub *Boy's Own* or *Hotspur*. And yet their themes, rarely heroic, often melancholy, reveal inner doubts and fears that may well have found echoes in dressing rooms and on the terraces of 1950s Britain.

A wizened old player hovers unrecognised outside the ground, unable to afford entry. Another veteran dies of a broken heart after his son is shot down over Germany. Kelton's Johnny Saunders hears his father speak to him from the grave as he scores the equaliser against Leasham City. Portcastle United are saved from bankruptcy by a mysterious pipe smoking stranger. Blackertown Rovers' new signing is lonely in his unfamiliar surroundings, until a waitress agrees to watch him in a reserve match. (She is, of course, the daughter of a Rovers' legend.)

Former Porchester Rangers centre

forward Clarrie Cartwright, now 'gaunt, unshaven and shabby,' holds up the grocery store of old Jerome Dunton. Dunton throws a cheese at him. Cartwright instinctively traps it with his foot. Dunton immediately recognises the player. Cartwright is offered a job, and redemption.

One regular author of these doleful tales was Ray Sonin, a Jewish East Ender who edited the music weekly *Melody Maker* and contributed comedy routines to the BBC hit show, *ITMA*. In 1950 Sonin won £5,000 on the pools, enough for him to retire to Suffolk and write whodunnits. Meanwhile he became chairman of the National Federation of Football Supporters' Clubs, whose profile he raised considerably. From 1952 until he emigrated to Canada in 1957 he edited *New Musical Express*.

Also contributing, during the 1960s, was the enigmatic Lesley Vernon, a bearded Hungarian refugee who worked as a bit-part actor. He once appeared in the BBC series *Dad's Army*.

Truly, *Football Monthly* attracted an eclectic bunch of scribblers.

And an immensely popular mix they provided. By 1958 circulation had grown to 107,000, at which point the magazine moved to new offices at 161-166 Fleet Street. By a curious coincidence, this was the site of the old Andertons Hotel, where the Football League was formed in 1888. Not only that but the new building, Hulton House, was owned by Hulton Newspapers, once publishers of *Athletic News*.

It was at Hulton House that Charles Buchan Publications Ltd expanded its interests. In 1958 it published *A Salute to Manchester United*, but also a book adaptation of a Marilyn Munro film, *Bus Stop*. Other magazine titles added were *Sporting Record, Sporting Cyclist, Cine Camera, Retail Gardening* and *Disc*, whose offices were apparently beseiged when Cliff Richard and the Beatles called by.

Football Monthly, meanwhile, went from strength to strength. A redesign in 1959 was rewarded by a spurt in circulation to 125,000, and all seemed well until in June 1960, Charles Buchan died while on holiday in France. He was 68.

Tributes poured into the offices, from Sir Stanley Rous, Matt Busby, Stan Cullis, Tom Finney, Stanley Matthews and many more. A memorial service at the journalists' church of St Bride, Fleet Street, was attended by leading sportswriters of the day.

But mourned though he was, Charlie's demise had no effect on sales. On the contrary, under new editor Pat Collins and riding high on England's victory in the 1966 World Cup, circulation exceeded the 200,000 mark for the first time in 1968, reaching an all-time peak of 254,000 the following year.

In the magazine's 200th edition in April 1968 it was also reported that membership of the Boys Club had topped 100,000.

The importance of the Boys Club and the magazine's open access pages cannot be overstated.

Members received a membership card, a badge, the right to enter competitions and, most importantly, the right to advertise in two of the magazine's most popular features, the programme and pen pal page, and the 'Fixtures Wanted' column.

Typical among the members was Southport grammar schoolboy David Howgate, who advertised in 1955 and wrote regularly to clubs begging for surplus programmes. Only three clubs ever failed to respond apparently. Football programmes were then a valuable form of currency to David and his network of pals around Britain. It was the magazine that brought them together, he recalls.

Barry Fry, a teenage autograph hunter from a Bedford pre-fab, advertised in March 1958. Even when he signed as an apprentice with Manchester United two years later he carried on pestering senior players for their signatures at the training ground. After a long career as player and manager, he is now the chairman of Peterborough.

Jim Rosenthal, the son of an Oxford antiquarian bookseller and a pupil at Magdalen College School – a rugger school – advertised in October 1963 for fixtures for his team, Wolvercote Wanderers. In November 1964 he also won a leather ball in the Square the Ball competition. He subsequently joined the *Oxford Mail* before starting his television career in 1980.

Keith Farnsworth of Sheffield was more interested in pen pals. Among several who replied was a lad in St Albans, whom Keith arranged to meet up with, only to discover that his friend was in fact 50 years old. Though his mother was furious, Keith escaped unscathed and went on to become sports editor on the *Sheffield Telegraph*.

Nor was he alone in finding inspiration from the magazine. In April 1959 it published a letter from

▲ February 1968

13 year old John Motson, whom we mentioned earlier, and although they misspelt the name of his school, he was so thrilled at seeing his name in print for the first time that five years later he embarked upon a career in journalism, starting work on the Barnet Press. He eventually joined BBC TV in 1971.

Similarly, Erland Clouston, a 16 year old pupil at Fettes College, Edinburgh, was flicking through the latest issue under his desk during a French lesson in April 1964 when he felt suddenly numb. *Football Monthly* had published his letter, and, even better, made it Letter of the Month. He showed his mates. He showed his teachers. At that point in his life it was the best thing that had ever happened (although the electric razor he won as a prize was hopeless). Three years later he was collecting film canisters from photographers behind the goals at Dens Park, Dundee, for DC Thompson Newspapers. From there he went to the *Liverpool Daily Post* at the height of the Shankly era.

Thirteen year old Sebastian Faulks, a pupil at Malvern College, was luckier. The prize for his Star Letter, published in September 1967, was three guineas in cash.

Another regular reader was Luton fan Nick Owen. After leaving Shrewsbury School to study Classics at Leeds University he was so desperate for funds to follow his beloved Hatters that he wrote to the My Team page in February 1967. His reward was one guinea (not his first freelance fee – that had been for a joke sent to *The Tiger*). As a result of the letter he also gained a pen pal, Terry, who worked on the line at Vauxhall Motors in Luton. Despite their different backgrounds the pair remain friends and still meet up occasionally in the Nick Owen Lounge at Kenilworth Road. Nick has worked in television since 1982.

Another Luton reader was John Hegley. His letter was published in September 1969, though he never received the fee. John recalls sending three centre spreads of Geoff Hurst from the magazine to West Ham in the hope that one might be signed. All three came back, signed as requested. Having his letter published, was, he recalls, 'My first brush with glamour.' He continues to be so brushed as a performing poet. 'I never really read the magazine,' John now admits. 'I only bought it for the pictures.'

He was not alone. A common memory of both fans and players from the 1950s and '60s is seeing crowds of young autograph hunters surrounding teams as they emerged from coaches or stadium gates, each holding copies of *Football Monthly*, open on the appropriate page. Some carried whole sets around, to cover all eventualities.

Thus the prey was confronted with multiple images of himself.

But not for much longer, or at least not from *Football Monthly*.

Changing fashions may explain part of the magazine's demise in the early 1970s. For example, in the Programme Exchange columns it is noticeable, as hairstyles lengthened and trousers grew more flared, how more young readers were veering away from programme and autograph swaps in favour of records and pop-related memorabilia. Football itself was entering a period of decline, as the ravages of hooliganism began to take their toll on attendances. Charlie's world was fading rapidly.

But also crucial was the decision by *Football Monthly's* new holding company, Longacre Press, to publish a sister magazine.

Edited in the next door office by a journalist called Alan Hughes, and launched at the Savoy in August 1968 with a predictable bevvy of 'dolly birds', *Goal* was in essence a weekly version of *Football Monthly*. No more, no less. Same format. Same look. Same kind of features. But weekly rather than monthly.

It was an obvious idea, and one that certainly grabbed the attention of this reader, a 13 year old convert from the first issue.

Once *Goal* turned up, old *Football Monthly* started to seem less and less relevant. From being a necessity it was now a dubious luxury. Rather too many of its pages were also being filled with material sent in by readers, and by dull fillers. At one point the magazine even ran the Irish League fixtures. In September 1971 they also dropped Charles Buchan's name from the cover.

It took two years for the tables to be turned; for *Goal* to outsell *Football Monthly*. But worse, a third contender had now materialised in the form of *Shoot*, a brash new weekly, published by IPC.

Shoot and *Goal* each sold over 220,000 copies weekly in 1971, compared with 164,000, and falling, for *Football Monthly*.

In August 1973 the publishers responded by rebranding the title in a smaller format. 'Forward thinking, contentious and alive, *Football Monthly Digest*,' as the magazine was now to be called, 'will fit your pocket in every way.'

But as editor Pat Collins suspected, it was a losing battle, and in August 1974, the title was finally sold to a company based in Baker Street, where it became *Football Magazine*, incorporating *Football Digest* and *Football Pictorial*.

In this new guise the magazine continued until being sold on again in 1995, this time, surprisingly, to Chelsea (whose chairman, Ken Bates had first featured in *Football Monthly* as the brash young owner of Oldham Athletic in 1966.) From Chelsea it was sold to the present owners in 1998, who retain the copyright and maintain the back catalogue as an archive.

And a wonderful archive it is too. Even today, 35 years after the last edition to carry the original name was published in August 1971, there remains tremendous affection towards the very name, *Charles Buchan's Football Monthly*.

They are powerful artefacts, magazines. So strong is their appeal to our memories and emotions, our sense of where we were, and how we were at any particular time, that in revisiting their pages we are also in effect revisiting ourselves.

For this reason, selecting extracts from a total of 240 issues – to provide as representative a sample as possible, as dispassionately as possible – has proved a stiff, and at times agonising challenge. No doubt another editor would have chosen quite differently.

But I did have one guiding principle.

This compilation forms part of the *Played in Britain* series, which seeks to celebrate and preserve these islands' extraordinary sporting heritage.

Heritage is generally thought to reside in historic buildings, in places and landscapes.

What I hope the following pages demonstrate is that there is heritage in ephemera too, and in the shared narrative that make us a nation, and a footballing nation at that.

Simon Inglis
London 2006

CHARLES BUCHAN'S FOOTBALL MONTHLY

1/6

NOVEMBER 1951

The Magazine of Britain's National Game

Edited by
CHARLES BUCHAN
and
JOHN THOMPSON

Cover Picture
JACK MILBURN
Newcastle
& England

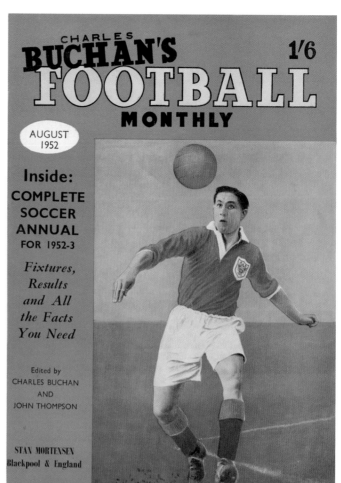

CHARLES BUCHAN'S FOOTBALL MONTHLY

1/6

AUGUST 1952

Inside:
COMPLETE SOCCER ANNUAL FOR 1952-3

Fixtures, Results and All the Facts You Need

Edited by
CHARLES BUCHAN
AND
JOHN THOMPSON

STAN MORTENSEN
Blackpool & England

CHARLES BUCHAN'S FOOTBALL MONTHLY

1/6

FEBRUARY 1952

The Magazine of Britain's National Game

Edited by
CHARLES BUCHAN
and
JOHN THOMPSON

JACK FROGGATT
Portsmouth
& England

CHARLES BUCHAN'S FOOTBALL MONTHLY

1/6

OCTOBER 1952

Inside:
BILLY STEEL
ON
"WHAT'S WRONG WITH SOCCER"
EXCLUSIVE

Full Page Pictures:
SONNY WALTERS
SAMMY COX
GEO. HANNAH
REG LEWIS
JOHN DOWNIE
BILL TONER
JOHN KING

Edited by
CHARLES BUCHAN
and
JOHN THOMPSON

DEREK DOOLEY
Sheffield Wednesday

CHARLES BUCHAN'S FOOTBALL MONTHLY (April 1953)

Inside:

MY STORY BY JESSE PYE

Full-Colour picture of Redfern Froggatt

BERT TANN ON BRISTOL ROVERS

Stories of Great England v Scotland clashes and many other grand articles and vivid photographs

THE WORLD'S GREATEST SOCCER MAGAZINE

NAT LOFTHOUSE Bolton Wanderers and England

1/6

CHARLES BUCHAN'S FOOTBALL MONTHLY (June, 1953)

TED DITCHBURN
Tottenham Hotspur and England

1/6

1951-53

As the Festival of Britain winds up on London's South Bank and British troops remain bogged down in Korea, the first copies of *Charles Buchan's Football Monthly* hit the newstands. 'In this commercial world of ours,' writes Manchester United manager Matt Busby in Issue 2, footballers have never enjoyed such financial inducements. 'The game is attracting the manual worker as well as the cultured youth.'

Eric Wright calls it the scientific age. 'The blackboard brains of today… are strangling every drop of the rich, red blood of personality out of our beloved game.' Today's 'automatons' are in stark contrast to those pre-war footballers who were 'brilliant, tough and sometimes wayward individualists, but who, by golly! were MEN.'

To improve his 'speech-making ability', Wolves and England captain Billy Wright, the son of a Shropshire iron-worker, is reading Dickens and Conrad, though his favourite author is Edgar Wallace. Marriage, he thinks, would be a distraction from his footballing career.

Amateur football correspondent Norman Ackland lambasts the FA for ruling that players who turn professional may never return to the amateur game. A cricketer may switch as many times as he pleases.

'One of these days one of the foreign teams will come here and rub our noses in our own mud, as the Austrians did to the Scots,' predicts Roland Allen, adding this suggestion to readers:'If you want better football – boo!' He decries the 'weedy-looking youths I see, Saturday after Saturday, outside the big soccer grounds, with cigarettes hanging from their lips, and stooping shoulders… "Look how they lap it up," a club manager said to me after we had sat together and watched one of many drab and dreary exhibitions which pass for show football nowadays. "What have we to worry about?"'

Charles Buchan urges the FA to send the England team to Commonwealth countries, not to Argentina, where spectators riot and 'Latin blood' is easily roused. Four months later, after Argentina defeat an England XI 3-1 in Buenos Aires, Buchan writes, 'They were the artists, England the solid workmen, using the wrong tools.'

The banner touting minority who attend Old Firm matches in Glasgow are 'the biggest blot on Scottish football,' reckons Alastair Graham. 'No-one knows how to deal drastically with it, and everyone is afraid that one day something dreadful will happen.'

The government's Entertainment Tax is putting a real strain on club finances, writes John Thompson in March 1953. 'I would like to see the tax burden carried more heavily by American films – and by television. Compared with football both these amusements are unhealthy influences on youth; television because it coops up youngsters in stuffy dark rooms, the films because of their frequent pre-occupation with crime.'

Sheffield Wednesday's bustling centre forward Derek Dooley – Charles Buchan's Player of the Year for 1951-52 – contracts gangrene after breaking a leg at Preston in February 1953. The leg is then amputated. 'In forty years of football I have never known such a spontaneous demonstration of sympathy,' writes Buchan. A fan who had just won the Pools reportedly sends Dooley £3,000.

The 1952-53 season ends with Arsenal as Champions for a record seventh time, followed 24 hours later by 38 year old Stanley Matthews finally winning an FA Cup medal. Matthews orchestrated Blackpool's last gasp 4-3 victory over Bolton at Wembley.

CHARLES BUCHAN says

New Youngsters And New Tactics Will Make This The Best Season

THERE are signs that the 1951-52 football season is likely to be the best since the war. In the five previous years there has been a scarcity of young talent, mainly due to the ravages of the war years. This is being overcome.

Boys of seventeen today have had six years of Soccer since 1945. They have also had the benefit of coaching and kindred schemes. They are making the grade rapidly.

Last season saw the introduction into the League teams of stars in the making like Cliff Birkett and Brian Birch (Manchester United forwards), Bobby Smith (Chelsea centre-forward), and Brian Jackson (Leyton Orient outside-right). They held their own in top class.

There were also youngsters like Ivor Allchurch (Swansea Town inside-left), and Bill Holden (Burnley centre-forward). They burst into the limelight and stayed there.

Allchurch won a place in the Welsh international team and was described by manager Matt Busby as "one of the most promising inside-forwards I have ever seen". Holden, a thrustful leader with craft in his boots, was in the running for an England cap.

Every manager I spoke to last season talked of the many grand young players he had under his control. Some of them will make their mark during the next few months.

Typical of the confidence which managers have in the future is Billy Walker, former Aston Villa and England inside-left, now Nottingham Forest manager. His young second team, most of them fresh from junior ranks, won the Midland League championship. His Colts, made up of "teen-agers", carried off the local League championship. He is banking on young talent.

Unfortunately, the League Management Committee did not have enough time during the close season to devise a system to control transfers of players through a central office. Reluctantly, they had to postpone this desirable reform.

There will be a new team in the League, Workington. Three retiring clubs in the Third Division—Watford and Crystal Palace, in the Southern Section, and Accrington Stanley in the Northern—were re-elected, but New Brighton, much to their surprise, were out-voted by the North-Eastern League club.

There can be little hope of League status for other teams like Chelmsford, Hereford United, South Liverpool and the others who applied for admission. The League is almost a closed shop to them.

They could greatly improve their prospects by forming their own League. A competition run on League lines with Northern and Southern Sections would, I am sure, prove a paying proposition. They could form their own "Football Alliance".

Tactics are going to play an important part in the coming season. New moves were introduced by the visitors in Festival of Britain internationals last May. I know they impressed many managers.

The Argentinian defence at Wembley was noted. There, the right-back took over the "stopper" role of the centre-half and enabled him to roam in midfield in support of the attack. The Austrians, who beat Scotland twice, employed the same methods. I think they are much more effective than ours.

Some years ago, I tried to introduce similar methods into a League team. They were based on the headline "Why not a fly-half in Soccer?" A trial game was played on a London ground but, though the manager agreed they

BILLY WALKER

▲ September 1951

were likely to be successful, he could not take the risk in League games.

I still believe they will come into force. After all, the "stopper" centre-half system is twenty-six years old, brought into the game when the off-side law was changed in 1925. As an Arsenal player I was there at its birth.

It was meant to be a temporary measure, yet it is slavishly followed today. And most of the teams have not the players to carry it out successfully.

Teams like Manchester United, with their forward switches, and Tottenham Hotspur, with their "push the ball and run" style have brought variations with remarkable results. But the basic principle remains. It is time it was changed.

Now I want to see some determined manager go for an all-out attacking policy. The crowds love to see goals scored and a 5-4 result would appeal to them more than 1-0.

There is one way to get goals—by outnumbering the defenders. An attacking centre-half up among the five forwards would give the side a numerical advantage in front of goal.

About eighteen months ago, Mr. Arthur Drewry, Football League President, said he hoped that one day a premium would be placed on goals. I think it would be to the benefit of the game, and the Football League, if it were.

One of the aims of this magazine is to put forward any suggestions that may prove useful either to those whose job it is to run the game or to those actually taking part. We should welcome your ideas!

How many of the millions who watch football weekly understand the thousand-and-one functions of the Football Association and the Football League? We hope to give the views of prominent legislative officials and clear up points that cause controversy.

Soccer is a main topic of discussion up and down the country. We trust that this journal will be a medium for settling many of your arguments.

Of all the debatable points, the one that brings the most heated arguments is the transfer system. Why should a club pay £34,500 for a player—as Sheffield Wednesday did to Notts County for inside-right Jackie Sewell?

We shall give the answer from every side; from the club, the player and the Players' Union.

We shall also take you behind the scenes at the head-

ALLCHURCH

HOLDEN

BIRCH

quarters of a League club. Managers and officials will explain why they need gates of at least £1,000 at every home game to keep the wheels turning smoothly.

Professional football, though, is really a small part of the game as a whole. There are less than 7,000 paid players compared with the hundreds of thousands of keen young men who turn out each week for the love of a good clean game and healthy recreation.

We shall try to keep them informed of what is going on in amateur circles through the agency of the best-known amateur writers.

Young and old alike will be given something to whet their appetites. The quarter-of-a-million schoolboys will have a corner all to themselves with hints by famous coaches. The old-timer will be given glimpses of the "good old days", of men and incidents that are still talked about to this day.

Will This Christmas Dream Come True?

As I sat by the fireside, wondering what Christmas presents to buy, I fell asleep. It was not long before I was in the land of dreams.

I was going to a football match between Aston Villa and Hibernian. As I neared the ground, I read the posters saying this was the National League game of the century.

These teams, I discovered from the gaily-decorated programme with a date line, December 1971, were first and second in the National League, which consisted of twelve clubs from the big cities of Great Britain. The match would decide the winners of the championship.

Later, my next-door neighbour in the tip-up, plush seat, told me that the champions would take part in the World Cup. They had been drawn against New York City in the first round. The Cup, he said, embraced the champion teams in almost every country in the world. It was on knock-out lines similar to the F.A. Cup.

Villa Park looked different, too. It was covered-in on all sides, with an electrically-operated roof and looked to be capable of holding 80,000 people, all comfortably seated.

I had just settled myself down when I awoke. I missed the game of the century. I was in 1951 not 1971.

But the dream had set me wondering what Soccer would be like twenty years on. What changes will the years bring in playing methods and facilities for spectators? What are YOUR views?   C.B.

▲ January 1952

LET'S THROW SOME LIGHT ON EVENING FOOTBALL

by JOHN CAREY
MANCHESTER UTD. AND IRELAND

SINCE my trips to America I have become a "flood-lit Soccer" fanatic. And I am pretty sure that, once you have seen this wonderful spectacle, you will be converted too.

Let me give you an illustration of what I mean. It was in New York, one May evening in 1950, at the Polo Grounds, the home of the famous baseball team, New York Giants.

Two top-line soccer matches were billed to take place. The first, Besitkas (Turkey) v. New York All Stars ; the second, Jonkoepping (Sweden) v. Manchester United, my own team.

As the United players travelled in private cars through Harlem to the Polo grounds, they were filled with an air of expectancy. When they got there, they were thrilled with the wonderful sight.

The vast stadium was an incandescent arena, lit by 640 lamps. Seated around the field were thousands of on-lookers, husbands with their wives and children and their mothers, too. Whole families came as a party to enjoy the fun. They gave the whole affair a homely aspect.

When we arrived, the first game was in progress. As we watched from a veranda outside the players' entrance we were impressed, not only by the colourful scene, but by the play itself. It seemed faster, much faster, than in broad daylight.

When our turn came, we enjoyed the whole 90 minutes. It was not the novelty of the thing that appealed, because we were almost accustomed to it by that time. Nearly all our games in America and Canada were played by artificial light.

Two - Day match?

IT was the atmosphere, the friendliness and the spec-tacular nature of the game that got hold of the United players. But I must make an exception, here, of our winger.

Just as he was about to take a corner-kick during the closing stages of our game—the time was then five minutes past midnight—he was heard to mutter some-thing about games that start on a certain day should at least finish on the same day.

It may have been rather late—or should I say very early—for football but there is no doubt the customers were delighted. They left for home happy, having spent an entertaining evening with their families and friends.

That is the scene I should like to see on English grounds. I can only liken it to a "play" staged in an open-air theatre compared with one indoors.

But I look forward to the day, which I feel sure is bound to come, when it will be a common practice for families to watch our matches in conditions that will bear some relation to those at the cinema or theatre.

If floodlit football is accepted in Britain, what endless possibilities it opens up. Instead of having first-class foot-ball on one day of the week, an ardent fan could see a match every week-day evening.

As it is now he has to be content with his Saturday afternoon game. And there are a million or so who pass through the turnstiles every Saturday just like him. They are Soccer starved.

We are not giving the fan enough opportunities of fol-lowing his favourite pastime. We are certainly not giving many chances to shopkeepers and assistants during the week. They are lucky to watch more than half-a-dozen games each season.

Soccer by floodlight would undoubtedly cure all this. Take in Lancashire for example. There are at least six first-class clubs who could, between them, stage a great exhibition every night of the week.

Manchester United on Monday, Burnley on Tuesday, Oldham Athletic on Wednesday, Bolton Wanderers on Thursday, Bury on Friday and Manchester City on Satur-day. That will give you some idea of what could be done for the followers within easy reach of Manchester.

The same could happen in the North-East, the Mid-lands, and London, etc. In fact, it could be so arranged that, wherever a football fan was in England, he could be within easy reach of a first-class game every evening of the week.

Sunday football, of course, is another matter. So I shall make no comments about it except that if we get Soccer every week-night, the Sabbath should be a day of rest.

Of course, I realise that the real supporter will watch his own team come what may. I don't expect him to travel to watch other sides. But there are hundreds of thousands of "floating" fans who would welcome the opportunity of going to these first-class games.

It should be our business to provide them with all possible opportunities.

▲ November 1951

There are two points that arise here. First, the cost of installing the lights and second, would the public be surfeited with so much football?

With regard to the first, some of the clubs would find the initial outlay financially embarrassing. But the revenue from the increased number of games, would more than repay the cost. I feel it would bring handsome dividends in the long run.

As to the second point, I am certain it would soon find its own level. Instead of saying "Let's go to the pictures," a lot of good folk would say occasionally "Let's go to a match."

Clubs would soon gather a big band of regular supporters, without competition from other big clubs nearby. They would also have the "floating" fans as well.

I must emphasise, though, that everything possible would have to be done for their comfort. And a variety of entertainment provided like a band,

"WELL, FINISHED COUGHING?"

League games, w h i c h would do away with the necessity for the practice affairs, would impose no extra strain.

Some readjustment of the present season would, of course, be necessary. As there would be something like 60 games all told, instead of the present 42 (46 in the Third Division), I think the season could be split up into two parts.

I suggest a period of 15 weeks from the start of the season until the week before Christmas. Then a second period of 15 weeks beginning in February and ending in May.

A n e w competition could be started for the second period. This would afford extra incentive to players and give them something to fight for.

In my opinion, the present League season is too long drawn out. Many clubs at the turn of the year are in the impossible position of having nothing to win or lose. The season drags out with diminishing interest and attendances.

novelty sporting items, variety turns and gymnastic displays.

Most important of all, there must be facilities for getting refreshments. Not as it is now, when only a few can struggle to the bars provided, but real places where the fans can get a proper meal. A visit to a Soccer game must become a real night out.

I am certain the players would not object to the additional matches. You know, professionals are not exhausted at the end of a season by the number of matches played. It is the training, preparing for the games, that takes toll of the stamina both physically and mentally.

As we all take part in a full hard practice match on every Tuesday or Wednesday, I submit that mid-week

Competition is the life-blood of any game, and a new tournament, half-way through the season, would restore vitality to soccer.

Well, there you have the reasons why I am a "floodlit" fanatic. Football under arc-lights is certainly not a new idea and, though it would mean a big change in our well-loved game, I am sure it would prove worth while.

In other countries, the decision whether or not to play a game depends mainly upon the conditions being suitable for the spectators. Here our only concern is whether or not the ground is "playable." We must find a happy medium.

And that medium is football by floodlight, with covered accommodation for the onlookers.

This picture of the World Cup Stadium in Rio de Janeiro shows the perfection reached by floodlighting—better than Manchester on many a Saturday afternoon. Notice the complete absence of shadow.

SHORT STORY

By Ray Sonin

SHE lived just opposite the main gates of the United ground—a lonely, elderly widow who earned a precarious living by sewing and dressmaking. But, however hard her gnarled fingers stitched throughout the day, she would always find time in the evenings to attend to the pile of blue-and-white jerseys and stockings sent over to her from the club, mending and darning them with a tender deftness and industry.

She refused to accept any payment; when it was offered, she would shake her head and smile—her only means of expressing her feelings, for she was dumb.

Her name was Mrs. Lily Matheson, and the players and officials had given her an affectionate nickname— "Jersey Lily."

Older fans remembered how she lost her speech. It happened many years ago when the United were playing the Rovers in a local "derby," and Brookie Matheson—one of the greatest-hearted players who ever wore the blue-and-white—was at centre-forward for the United.

In the wing stand, sitting with the other players' wives, Lily Matheson was watching her husband with a thrilling feeling of pride. He was at the peak of his form.

He had already scored one goal— an opportunist effort—to equalise a snap goal by the Rovers early in the game, and, ten minutes from the end, the score was still 1-1, with both sides straining to get the winner and the crowd pulling out all the stops of excitement.

Then Brookie went through, working his way down the field at bewildering speed. He corkscrewed his way with feints and body-swerves and bored his way into the penalty area. A phalanx of defenders ran back to cut him off and, as they converged on him, he stumbled off-balance, shooting as he fell.

The ball hurtled into the net past the leaping goalkeeper and, in the fraction of a second before the crowd roared its appreciation, two sounds echoed with grim clarity round the ground.

One was Lily Matheson's anguished scream—" Look out!"—and the other was the thud of Brookie's head crashing into the goalpost.

Without regaining consciousness, he died from a fractured skull on the way to hospital. His wife was struck dumb by the shock. Her screamed words as her husband crashed to his death were the last she uttered.

The club was good to her after the tragedy, financially and in every other way. She was sent to the finest specialists, but they could do nothing for her and she took up the threads of her quiet life, bravely overcoming her handicap, and showing her feelings towards the club by making herself entirely responsible for the care of the jerseys and stockings.

But she would never attend a football-match, even though the club put her old seat at her disposal. She had been an ardent fan but, for many years, though she freely helped the club, she would set foot in the ground only as far as the dressing rooms . . . no farther. . . .

Until the day of the Cup-tie with the Rovers.

The congested fixture-list arising from the United's Cup run meant that games were coming along on top of one another, and " Jersey Lily " was kept busy.

On the day of the great match, she was still hard at work, darning and mending, as the crowds began to line up at the turnstiles.

When the jerseys were ready, it was only because the police on duty knew her and made a path for her that she was able to get through to the dressing-rooms and deliver her precious cargo.

But getting out again was a different proposition, for the record crowd surging into the ground swept her away with them until she found herself hemmed in on the terraces.

She could not cry out and her feeble struggles were fruitless against the crush. She stood in the rain, unable to move, tired and exasperated.

She hardly dared look at the playing pitch, but it seemed to draw her eyes in fearful fascination and, as the game started, she could not take her gaze away.

This was the pitch . . . that was the goalpost where it had all happened. She had not seen it for so many years, but it was so familiar.

At first she could not concentrate on the play, for the overwhelming thought that filled her mind, then the magic of the game gripped her. She forgot the past, she forgot the rain; she merged into the crowd, carried away by the excitement.

Suddenly, the United centre-forward broke away and made for the Rovers' penalty area. The backs converged on him. He swerved, slipped on the treacherous turf and took a tremendous kick as he fell sprawling.

The ball went straight for the corner of the net but the forward, slithering in the mud, went straight for the goalpost, his head about to crack on the wood. He put out an arm to save himself. There was a rending sound.

A shrill feminine voice cut through the clamour— " Look out!" screamed " Jersey Lily."

The St. John's Ambulance men revived her after she fainted at the shock of regaining her speech, and the secretary-manager of the United was bending over her as she came to.

He was as excited as she was, and he let her babble tearfully in her overwhelming joy.

" The forward. . ." she asked anxiously. " The one who was going into the goalpost . . . What happened to him?"

" He's all right," the manager said. " He was lucky."

" Lucky?" she repeated. " But what was that tearing sound I heard as I fainted?"

" Oh, that! Well, he caught his arm on the woodwork and made a pretty bad gash. He's gone to hospital. . . ."

She smiled. " Oh, it was his arm? Thank goodness for that! I thought it was his jersey. . ."

Proudly wearing the Sheffield Wednesday colours, young Brian Clifford has a privileged seat in front of the railings. What are his dreams? Your guess may tally with ours.

TRIBUTE TO A SPORTSMAN

By SIR STANLEY ROUS, C.B.E., *Secretary of the Football Association*

IT is with an overpowering sense of personal grief that I am writing these words of remembrance on behalf of The Football Association. I know I have the support of every administrator and player of amateur and professional football in saying that we think of his late Majesty first and foremost as a great sportsman.

Our recent bereavement has been felt by the whole nation as a bitter personal loss, for the King had indeed met many of us in person, and the rest also felt that they knew him as a friend.

Already the sports writers have rightly portrayed the King as an amateur sportsman, capable of holding his own with the leading exponents of many games, and have recalled his qualities as an " all-rounder." ≥

In some sports he excelled, being a distinguished shot and a doughty tennis player, appearing even on the hallowed turf of Wimbledon. So perhaps I may be excused if I call to mind a few personal reminiscences of His Majesty as we of The Football Association knew him.

The King, in his early days a keen player, always took a lively personal interest in soccer, and at Wembley his presence became a familiar part of the traditional scene, which was in every sense a Royal occasion ; he was present among us not only as the King, but also as a sportsman in his own right.

From the year of his coronation when, with the Queen and the two young Princesses, he attended the Festival of Youth organised by the British Sports and Games Association in aid of King George's Jubilee Trust, he became a regular visitor to Wembley.

In fact, the sequence was interrupted only by the early war years—years in which were laid the seeds of the ill health which was to end his life.

Each year some small incident stands out in the memory of those privileged to be close to the King on Wembley occasions.

I well remember last year how, when I handed the Cup to His Majesty, for presentation to Joe Harvey, of Newcastle United, he asked : " Rous, is that the right Cup ? "

I answered : " I hope so, Your Majesty ! "

" So do I," came the reply. " The one I presented three years ago fell to pieces."

I remember, too, the occasion when the late Mr. Gliksten, of Charlton Athletic, was watching his team put up a stiff struggle and was urging them on with his feet.

The King who was sitting next to him turned and said :

" If your players were kicking the ball as hard as you are kicking the stands, they would certainly be able to score ! "

Two unimportant incidents perhaps, but indicative of his sense of humour and his quickness to notice details. He had, too, the happy knack of using these characteristics to put people completely at their ease.

The Football Association will miss King George VI as our King and Patron, and as a true friend among sportsmen.

To the Queen Mother we extend our deepest sympathies, and to Queen Elizabeth II we would like to add to our sympathy the hope that, in the difficult task which lies ahead, she, too, will be able to derive pleasure and relaxation from watching her nation at sport.

We trust that a visit to Wembley will provide a pleasant break from the ardours and duties of statesmanship.

◀ Bert Williams, Wolverhampton Wanderers, October 1951 | April 1952 ▲

Keep These "Reforming" Meddlers out of Football

WHITHER are we going ? That phrase is my constant companion, and the more I read and discuss football with divers people, the more I am certain the answer is not forthcoming.

One bright and sunny day someone will awaken and discover that football is a game and go into sackcloth and ashes over the loss of reams of paper, gallons of ink and years in hours which have been utterly wasted on the bilge written about the sport.

For nearly thirty-two years football has been my bread and butter—or was it margarine when I was playing ?

On reflection, the thought is encouraged that, with certain reservations, I am qualified to say a few words on the game.

When I think of the twenty seasons downstairs the words of Isaac Watts come readily to my mind :—
            " I have been there and still would go,
            'Tis like a little heaven below."
So all ye aspirants to the sanctum with " Boss " on the door, take heed !

It is natural that, when one has been wrapped up in football for so long, one should take a very keen interest in its welfare.

To me, football is in a parlous state through no fault of its own, but through the machinations of a certain set with misguided conceptions of the game—men who refuse to leave well alone.

The biggest crime against the game was committed in 1925 when the off-side rule was altered and the punishment was made to fit the crime—the stopper centre-half for life.

From then we have had the reformers roaming at large with their novel ideas—two referees, goal-line judges, extending the penalty line, etc.

And those of us who love the game find solace in the fact that the path of a reformer is a thorny one, and that none of those " reforms " came to pass.

The off-side rule, however, *was* altered, to assist the brainless forwards who could not obey the fundamental principle of keeping behind the ball.

Now the latest stunt is to prevent the full-back passing the ball back to his goalkeeper.

The full-back who takes a risk, I admit, makes for more spectacular and entertaining football but, unlike forwards who are remembered for their successes, he is remembered for his mistakes, so his maxim should be—" take no risks."

In my opinion, stopping a full-back passing back is tantamount to asking him to disregard another principle of good football—that of playing the way you are looking.

Throughout the years we have had memorable games in the epic category. If the game was not good enough, as it was, then those epics could not have taken place—so to those who don't like the game I say, " Please stop messing it about."

Fundamentally, the game is the same to-day as it was sixty years ago. For that we owe eternal thanks to the far-seeing legislators who framed the rules and regulations when the League was formed.

Yet while, basically, the game is the same, there is a difference. There is more finesse. It is more streamlined —as befits the modern trend.

Gone is the good old-fashioned shoulder charge, for which I personally mourn—the fun, the excitement of pitting one's physical strength against another has to be experienced to be believed.

It made one feel good to be alive, yes, and believe it or not players earned the healthy respect of each other.

There is not enough football played just for the fun of it, the type of football which produced the natural player, not the robot who is the product of an over-coaching system, in which players are lectured to satiation point on tactics until they are " blinded by their own science."

I say : Give them a respite from the carefully-ordered, made-to-plan football and give the natural player a chance to develop.

What produced the Buchans, Mordues, Penningtons, Seeds, Jacks and Jameses and their contemporaries ?

Certainly it was not the lecture room. No, they graduated through the school of experience.

Charles Buchan in an earlier issue of this magazine, tells the story of how Montgomery, of Notts County.

(Continued)

▲ April 1952

WHERE ARE TO-DAY'S DAVID JACKS?

(Continued)

taught him in one sharp lesson not to try to beat an opponent twice-running with the same trick. Please note—*one* lesson.

In the school of experience there is no gown and mortar-board ; the Queen's English may be conspicuous by its absence, but nevertheless, this school turned out more " Honours " pupils than any modern school.

Don't misunderstand me, I am not against coaching altogether, but this coaching, from the primary school age to the provident scheme age, will produce only quantity—not quality.

Are we trying to be too clever in turning football into a science, with all this streamlining and finesse ?

From finesse it is but a short step to largess which brings us to the most controversial point in football.

I should say there is more bilge said and written on soccer finance than on any other football matter by people who ought to have more sense.

It would be all so simple if everyone realised that football is a game, not a business . . .

If it was business, then tradition, sentiment, and all the things that make football what it is would have to go overboard. But we are not prepared to make that sacrifice (which I think is to our credit), so a happy medium must be found.

Football is unique in many respects—none more so than when money matters are introduced. It does not bear comparison with an ordinary business.

And that is where so many fall down. They attempt to apply ordinary business methods, which don't work.

I have discussed the financial angle with responsible officials, Press and players and I have the feeling the latter are being led unwittingly up the garden-path.

Too often, gross figures are quoted. Too often it is forgotten that no individual makes a profit out of a game, that any profit a club makes belongs to the club.

The share capital of most clubs is ridiculously small, with the interest limited to $7\frac{1}{2}$ per cent.

The clubs who have a healthy bank balance can use that money only for the benefit of the club, not for any individual or set of individuals.

The rich clubs are invariably quoted in support of the players' claims for an increase of wages, but the claims ignore the fact that the rules are framed not for the rich clubs alone, but for *all* clubs.

It is possible for a player to receive the maximum in a poor club just as in a rich club.

The wages are decided every year and so long as the rules are framed on the game as a whole the rich clubs cannot pay more than the rules permit.

I will always agree with, and defend the right of, every player to get as much as he can out of the game, if circumstances support him, but every player should realise he can take out only what he puts in.

Every player who signs a contract does so of his own free will. No one compels him. He should realise that a player's life is a precarious one, that he can do a humpty-dumpty act any day.

Through no fault of his own, illness, injury, loss of form can overtake him. But, if he does not take cognisance of these facts he will have a perpetual grouse against the conditions of the game.

No one will deny there is a lot of money in football, but it is not sufficient for a tithe of the grandiose schemes I have heard mooted.

I do, however, sincerely believe that there is more than enough to satisfy a reasonable wage increase and a fund for the support of seriously injured players and those stricken with illness.

I don't profess to be a Solomon, but what I would like to see is the inauguration of a small body of men with professional football in their veins, men born and brought up in the game, with no club connections and no axe to grind.

They should be given a job of solving our problems and keeping the game on an even keel.

They would be employed and paid through the game and it would be money well spent.

I certainly feel that asking clubs to make decisions of paramount importance, within an hour or two, at an annual meeting is asking too much.

JENKINS   Consulting the Linesman

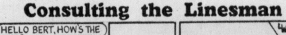

Bolton's Cup Heroes and . . .

The camera has no qualms for Bolton left-back George Higgins—he's used to it—but to his two-year-old son, John, it's something to run to mummy about—while baby sister Sylvia gives him a scornful glance.

Any minute now and Willie Moir (left) and Nat Lofthouse will be lapping the track. Here they don soft shoes for a Bolton training session.

Bobby Langton with his daughter Christine at the Bolton ground. Here Christine is handed over to a friend before Langton does his training.

Favourite pastime of Harold Hassall—apart from playing football for Bolton—is Canasta. Here he is, at home, with his wife, Irene.

WITH —
the gallant Everton lads they beat

Tune for two, played by Cyril Lello, Everton left-half, with the encouragement of his wife, Elsie.

Waiting for the starting signal is "racing motorist" Anthony Eglington, age 20 months. Father, Tommy Eglington, Everton outside-left, and Mrs. Eglington, are ready to put the brakes on.

All smiles as they watch the "dicky bird" are Everton skipper Peter Farrell, eight-month-old daughter, Betty, and Mrs. Farrell.

Everton goalkeeper, Jimmy O'Neill (left), looks as though he's just stopped a good move by centre-forward colleague, Dave Hickson. And he seems to have Hickson worried.

Eglington lends his back as a desk for autograph signing by full-back Lindsay. The others are Jones, Fielding, Parker and Hickson.

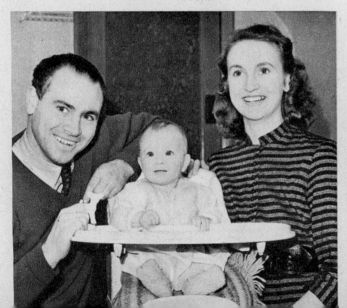

Schoolboy footballers work in the cause of Peace

AS most of you know it is our belief that only good can come from friendship between Soccer-loving boys of every nation.

I have been thinking about that point a lot lately because of a remark I came across in the London Schools F.A. report on the excellent work they have done both in touring the Continent and in giving hospitality to young footballers from abroad.

The Secretary, Mr. S. E. Tye, writes : " It is difficult to believe that intelligent people who desire to live in peace cannot see that the association of the young people of the world is the surest way of eliminating causes of misunderstanding in the future . . ."

That is very true and I am sure that all our Club members, scattered over the world as they are, will agree with it. Many of you, I know, have already demonstrated your enthusiasm to help by writing to fellow-members in other lands.

Sir Stanley Rous, C.B.E., Secretary of the Football Association, has said that he hopes London Schools can arrange further matches between schoolboys of ALL COUNTRIES. He adds : " The financial and other difficulties are immense but such international contacts at all levels help to turn the abstraction ' peace ' into something more concrete and understood."

Mr. Tye seems to have an excellent idea for getting round the problem. He suggests that, to save expensive hotel bills, the boys from abroad should be put up at boarding schools and training colleges.

Perhaps he is right, although I am rather inclined to think that the happiest solution is for them to stay in the homes of the boys against whom they are playing. This system has worked very well for visits of young swimmers from the Continent. Mothers have even triumphed over rationing problems to make these visits a success !

But whatever method is chosen they can count on our support and good wishes. And in the meantime I know that all members of our Club will continue the grand work they are doing to strengthen the soccer-ties that bind us to our friends in other parts of the world.

Until next month, cheerio and the best of luck.

Sincerely yours, *Charlie Buchan*

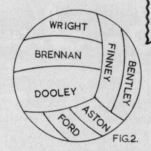

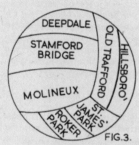

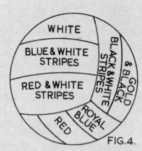

HOW TO WIN A FOOTBALL

HERE is this month's competition. It is in two parts, both parts to be completed. Mark your envelopes Comp. No. 15. Don't forget that neatness counts and you must mention your club number. A football is the prize.

1.—In Fig. 1 (in the illustrations on the left) you will find the names of seven famous football clubs. Pick one of these, for example, Chelsea. Move on to Fig. 2 and find the player who plays for them, in this case Bentley.

In Fig. 3 you will find Stamford Bridge, their home ground, and then in Fig. 4 the colours of their shirts—in Chelsea's case Royal Blue.

Your answer to this section would read : Chelsea, Bentley, Stamford Bridge, Royal Blue. We want you to match up all the seven names and write them down in four neat columns as we have done in our example.

2.—Rearrange the letters in the following phrase to form names of a popular Cup-Tie tonic—REG'S SHY GANDER.

Competition No. 12 Winner

WINNER of Competition No. 12 was Leonard Worley, of " Cragside," Nortoft Road, Chalfont St. Peter, Bucks. Nice work, Leonard, and all of you who did so well.

— GROWN-UPS MOVE ON!

REX MARTIN

▲ October 1951

SOCCER

By LESLIE YATES

"WELL, FANCY THAT"

INJURY often ends a player's career, but the manner in which Jack Smith, Reading's manager, was forced to end his playing days, is surely unique?

Jack, a Chelsea full-back, slipped on a Wolverhampton kerbstone during the war, and an omnibus ran over his foot.

A thick-soled shoe minimised the injury, but the accident ended his playing career.

Jack had previously played for Wolves and he recalls, with amusement, the light of recognition that came into the anxious bus driver's eyes when he dashed from his cabin to help the victim.

"If it's not Jack Smith!" he exclaimed. "And me a Wolves supporter!"

MAPSON'S SPRING-TIME

IT'S always spring-time for Johnny Mapson, Sunderland's long-service goalkeeper.

Mapson combines football with an assignment as salesman in interior springs for mattresses and three-piece suites of furniture.

He covers the north-eastern area for a firm at St. Helen's, in Lancashire, and is able to expand his activity on their behalf during the close season.

Mapson tells me that next season will be his seventeenth as a League professional. That is a record of which the Roker Park star can rightly feel proud.

Everyone there sees Kelly

THE close season is no period of retirement from the public gaze for Hugh Kelly, Blackpool's Scottish left-half.

Hugh is now working at top pressure in the ice-cream parlour run by his wife's family at Gynn Square, on Blackpool's North Shore.

A stream of football fans on holiday make their way into the shop to have a word with Kelly. Added attraction is the fact that he is always ready to oblige with his autograph.

Holiday Pay

SEVERAL Millwall players are feeling the benefit of last season's bonus money.

The New Cross players have the option of drawing the extra cash when due, or allowing it to accumulate until the season's end.

The latter course has proved popular at the Den, and Johnny Johnson, Millwall's outside-right, tells me his lump sum from points gained last season has paid for his holiday with the family at Cliftonville.

He must like it!

Paddy Blatchford, Leyton Orient winger, is the footballer who never gets a holiday.

Blatchford combines football with his work as a civil servant in the trade marks department of the Patents Office.

He is allowed 28 days' leave per year, but finds that the entire period is used up in keeping away engagements with the Orient club.

'date'-minded

WALTER TAYLOR, assistant-manager to Birmingham City, and one of the shrewdest talent-spotters in the game, often yearns for the old days.

Walter recalls the time when the offer of a trial brought a flush of excitement to a young player's face.

"But times have changed," he says. "Some of the youngsters of to-day seem more concerned about keeping an after-match date than making good as a footballer."

ANIMAL-LOVER

Johnny Ingham, Gateshead's centre-forward, is a great animal-lover.

Friends and neighbours know that their pets are in good hands if left with Johnny; he is always willing to look after them when their owners are away from home.

Ingham, who also breeds pigs, has been a Gateshead player since 1942. Before turning professional, he was employed as a shipyard electrician.

Selected from 1951-53

SIDESHOW

BY THE RIGHT—SIGN !

FOOTBALLERS are signed on in the strangest places. Albert Whiteley, Leyton Orient outside-left, was serving in the R.E.M.E., at Honiton, Devon, when Sid Hobbins, chief scout to the London club, arrived with a registration form.

Sid's arrival coincided with the parade of the regimental sergeant-major—and bystanders were unwanted.

Hobbins was hustled into the guard room with Whiteley, and the form was signed against the wall of a military detention cell !

The Levellers

FOR some years there has been a troublesome dip in the turf just outside the penalty area at the wharf end of Fulham's ground.

The defect has been given special attention in the close season, and no longer will the ball play freakish tricks on that particular patch.

The job of levelling has been carried out by Harry Freeman and Bob Thomas, Fulham players who are also respected at Craven Cottage for their green-keeping knowledge.

Trams stop

THE old tramcars that served Plymouth Argyle as miniature stands for directors and officials after all accommodation on the Home Park ground had been destroyed during the war, are still in use.

Steady progress is being made at Plymouth in the rebuilding of the ground on modern lines. But the trams, located between the new stand and the dressing rooms, remain as colourful relics of Argyle's grimmest days.

One is used as headquarters by the Supporters' Club, and another serves the ground staff as a drying room.

Tippett Is A Bright Spark

TOMMY TIPPETT, Bournemouth's outside-left, will spend the summer recess in sensible fashion.

A relative of Tippett's runs an electrical business, and the Bournemouth winger has decided to give him a hand during the off-season months.

It's a trade Tippett knows plenty about. Before turning to football for his living, he was employed at the Ilford Electricity Works.

Perhaps that accounts for the sparkle he has shown on Bournemouth's left flank !

JIMMY LOGIE
Arsenal

▲ November 1951

CHARLIE TULLY
Glasgow Celtic
and Ireland

▲ May 1953

SID GERRIE
Hull City

▲ March 1953

TOMMY LAWTON
Brentford and England

▲ September 1953

June 1952 ▶

CHARLES BUCHAN says

Attendances fall — but clubs can't blame B.B.C.

FOOTBALL League clubs, at their annual general meeting in the summer, will, it is certain, have to revise their opinions on the effects of broadcasting on attendances at League games.

Though the matches to be put over the air have been kept secret, it has had no effect on broadcasting. I understand from good authority that listening figures for the commentaries have been maintained and, in some cases, improved.

Attendances on the other hand have slumped considerably. The reason for this cannot be attributed to the broadcasts, nor to the weather, which, on the whole, has been reasonably good.

It will, I think, be a wise move if the clubs agree at their meeting to lift the ban on advertised radio. No good has come from the present policy. The more publicity football gets from radio, the better it will be for the game.

The one sure way to stop the decline in attendances is to serve up a better brand of play. The present negative methods are out-dated and a more spectacular style must be introduced.

Progressive Arsenal recently tried the "roaming centre forward" plan with dashing Peter Goring acting as schemer-in-chief in midfield. Though it may not be the answer to the "stopper" centre half, it is, at least, a step in the right direction towards brightening up the game.

We can do with a lot more young players like Tommy Harmer of the Spurs, the little wizard who bids fair to make an international reputation. People will pay to see him juggle with the ball even if the side does not happen to be winning.

They will turn up in thousands to watch newcomers like the dynamic Derek Dooley of Sheffield Wednesday, who has set the soccer world alight with his scoring feats. There are other Harmers and Dooleys around.

It seems to me clubs are paying too much attention to winning points. The quality of the play does not matter. And here, I think, is the main reason for the falling attendances.

Teams like Spurs, Manchester United, Portsmouth, Wednesday, Arsenal, Newcastle and Preston, who are serving up attractive football have no attendance worries. Even clubs at the bottom of the League will attract support provided they play good football.

The effects of relegation from the First to the Second Division have been exaggerated beyond all proportion.

There is little difference, nowadays, in the support accorded to the leading clubs in the Second Division from that of the senior teams. I have never yet heard of a club that was reduced to bankruptcy through dropping to the Second Division.

Very soon now we shall be approaching the dead-line for the transfers of players eligible to take part in the various League struggles for promotion and relegation. The last day is March 16. So it is very disturbing to hear of so many players asking to be placed on the transfer list.

In my playing days it was almost unknown for such a thing to happen. I would not have dared to approach the Sunderland manager, Bob Kyle, and ask for a transfer. He would have told me he was the man to decide that.

Ivor Broadis

Control seems to be much more lax now than it used to be. A player dropped from the first team immediately seeks a transfer instead of being more determined than ever to win his place back.

After all, a player signs a contract for a year and should be prepared to carry it out. The time to ask for a transfer is when the contract has expired. I am convinced that if managers insisted on this, the trouble would almost disappear.

There are exceptions, of course, such as when a player is being "barracked" by the crowd, or on the question of ill-health. Then a move may be better for both sides.

▲ March 1952

THE CUP THAT CHEERED WALTHAMSTOW

In the last minute of extra time DENNIS HALL scored to win the Amateur Cup for Walthamstow Avenue—for the first time in their history—against Leyton, at Wembley. Above, Avenue captain, DEREK SAUNDERS (with the trophy), is "chaired" by his team mates. Avenue won 2—I, JIM LEWIS scoring their other goal. ERIC SKIPP scored for Leyton.

ARSENAL, Champions of the Football League. Back row: Daniel, Milton, Goring, Kelsey, Forbes, Roper. Front row: Wade, Logie, Mercer, Smith, Lishman. Insets: Swindin, Holton, Shaw.

SHEFFIELD UNITED, Second Division Champions. Back row: Hutchinson, Brook, Furness, Burgin, Latham, Shaw (G.), Shaw (J.), Jackson (trainer). Front row: Ringstead, Hagan, Browning, McNab, Hawksworth.

▲ June 1952 | August 1953 | August 1953

HONOURS 1951-53

1951-52
Division 1 Manchester United
Division 2 Sheffield Wednesday
Division 3S Plymouth Argyle
Division 3N Lincoln City

Scottish A Hibernian
Scottish B Clyde

FA Cup Newcastle United
Scottish Cup Motherwell
Amateur Cup Walthamstow Avenue (*top*)

Charles Buchan's Best XI Gil Merrick (B'ham), Johnny Carey (Man Utd), Lionel Smith (Arsenal), Billy Wright (Wolves), Harry Clarke (Spurs), Jimmy Dickinson (Portsmouth), Tom Finney (Preston), Johnny Morris (Derby), Derek Dooley (Sheff Wed), Ivor Allchurch (Swansea), Bobby Mitchell (Newcastle)
Manager Billy Walker (Nottm Forest)

1952-53
Division 1 Arsenal (*centre*)
Division 2 Sheffield United (*bottom*)
Division 3S Bristol Rovers
Division 3N Oldham Athletic

Scottish A Rangers
Scottish B Stirling Albion

FA Cup Blackpool
Scottish Cup Rangers
Amateur Cup Pegasus

Charles Buchan's Best XI Sam Bartram (Charlton), George Young (Rangers), Alf Sherwood (Cardiff), Alex Forbes (Arsenal), Harry Johnston (Blackpool), Bill Dickson (Chelsea), Tom Finney (Preston), Ivor Broadis (Man City), Nat Lofthouse (Bolton), Allan Brown (Blackpool), Vic Metcalfe (Huddersfield)
Manager Joe Smith (Blackpool)

SEPTEMBER, 1954

Charles Buchan's
FOOTBALL
MONTHLY

TOM FINNEY
AND HIS SON

1'6

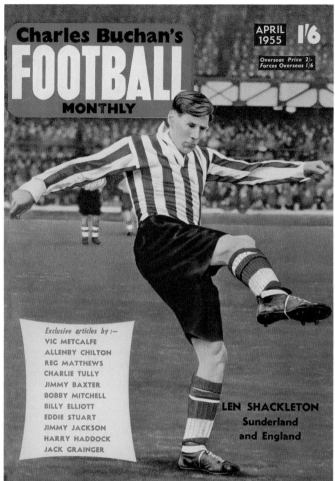

Charles Buchan's
FOOTBALL
MONTHLY

APRIL
1955

1'6

Overseas Price 2/-
Forces Overseas 1/6

Exclusive articles by :—
VIC METCALFE
ALLENBY CHILTON
REG MATTHEWS
CHARLIE TULLY
JIMMY BAXTER
BOBBY MITCHELL
BILLY ELLIOTT
EDDIE STUART
JIMMY JACKSON
HARRY HADDOCK
JACK GRAINGER

LEN SHACKLETON
Sunderland
and England

1'6

Charles Buchan's
FOOTBALL
MONTHLY

DECEMBER
1954

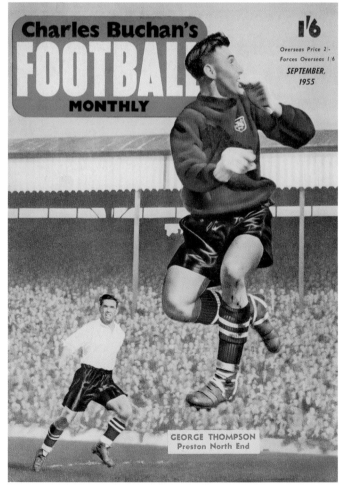

Charles Buchan's
FOOTBALL
MONTHLY

1'6

Overseas Price 2/-
Forces Overseas 1/6

SEPTEMBER,
1955

GEORGE THOMPSON
Preston North End

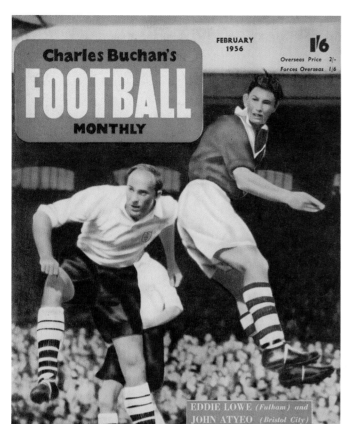

EDDIE LOWE (Fulham) and
JOHN ATYEO (Bristol City)

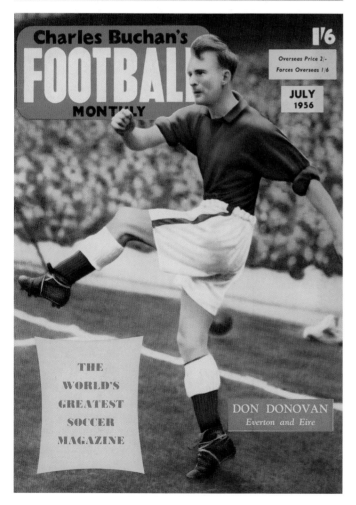

THE
WORLD'S
GREATEST
SOCCER
MAGAZINE

DON DONOVAN
Everton and Eire

1953-56

FEBRUARY 1956 1/6
Overseas Price 2/-
Forces Overseas 1/6

JULY 1956
Overseas Price 2/-
Forces Overseas 1/6

A Union Jack flies proudly on the summit of Everest as 20 million British people seek out all available television sets to watch Queen Elizabeth's Coronation. Reporter Brian Glanville, then aged 22, warns readers that Hungary, due to visit Wembley in November 1953, are deeply impressive. 'Constant playing together enables the Hungarians to give the impression that they could find each other with their eyes shut.' England are duly humbled 6-3, forcing Charles Buchan to lament that 'only the most optimistic would give us the slightest chance, with our present set-up, of putting up even a passable show' at the forthcoming 1954 World Cup in Switzerland.

Dundee's players will travel to Switzerland in a bus, camp out at night and take turns to make the morning tea. They see Scotland trounced 7-0 by Uruguay, who then eliminate England. 'Scotland will not play in the World Cup again. Of that I am very sure,' writes Alastair Graham. Charles Buchan is glad England were knocked out. 'The World Cup has developed into a "win at any price" adventure. It is no longer a game, but political propaganda.'

Before Wolves beat Moscow Spartak 4-0 in a floodlit friendly at Molineux, John Thompson spots a local fan give the clenched fist salute of Communism. He then sings God Save the Queen with gusto. 'I wondered if any other land but this blessed realm of ours could produce such sweet contradiction...'

Roger Bannister breaks the four minute mile. England win the Ashes under their first professional captain, Len Hutton. The emergence of 'Edwardians', or Teddy Boys, raises concerns about Rock and Roll.

Celtic's preference for white balls leads to complaints from opponents, while Doncaster's goalkeeper Ken Hardwick reckons the new orange balls swerve unpredictably and 'must be banned'.

Len Shackleton, the self-styled Clown Prince of Soccer, causes a stir with a chapter in his autobiography entitled 'The Average Director's Knowledge of Football' followed, 'in accordance with the author's wishes', by a blank space.

Deploring graphic scenes of crowd violence in South America (where a referee is photographed carrying a pistol), Charles Buchan insists that 'such terrible scenes could not occur in our land'.

Yet gates at home are falling alarmingly. Buchan describes the raising of minimum admission prices to 1s 9d, in 1952, as the biggest mistake in post-war football. 'I can get a seat at my local cinema for 1s 9d, and enjoy a three hour show.' In August 1955 the minimum rises to 2s.

Also in 1955 Buchan hosts a sponsored broadcast on Radio Luxembourg, featuring conversations with Bolton's Nat Lofthouse and Don Revie, 'a modest young man' famed for his new role as a deep lying centre forward for Manchester City. Buchan has also watched three games on television. 'How anyone can judge just what is happening throughout the game I cannot imagine. But I must say it is lively entertainment.' He does not, however, approve of reporters who refer to players using their Christian names. It adds an unnecessary 'touch of effeminacy'.

Len Boyd of Birmingham City asks why cricketers receive enormous benefits tax free while footballers are taxed on their five yearly benefits 'of a mere £750?' But he supports the maximum wage, then set at £15 a week. 'Football is a team game. The stars can't twinkle without the aid of their team-mates. The day that football favours individuals will be the day when I'll walk out.'

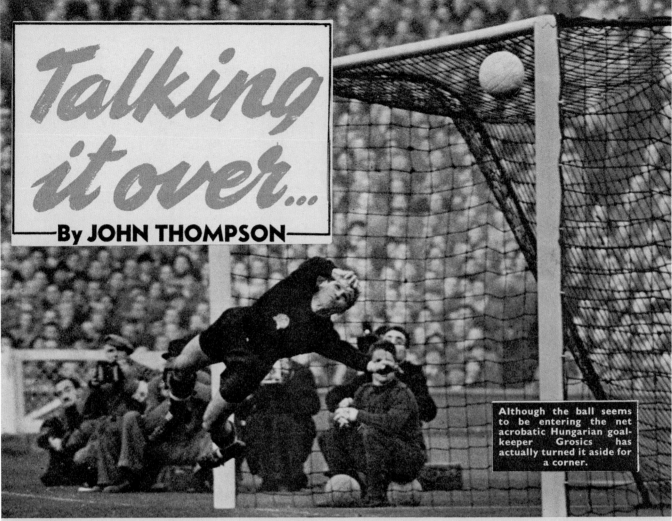

Talking it over...

By JOHN THOMPSON

Although the ball seems to be entering the net acrobatic Hungarian goalkeeper Grosics has actually turned it aside for a corner.

HUNGARY'S calm conquest of England at Wembley Stadium did not surprise me. It was as inevitable as sunset that a country which does not take the game seriously should eventually be routed by one that does.

In England the national team is regarded as an irrelevant appendage to the serious business of League and Cup competitions. There is no sense of urgency in the preparation of the chosen players. There is a smug refusal to learn from the methods adopted by foreigners.

The outlook is dark. There is at present no reason for hoping that England will soon regain her post-war supremacy.

The fiasco of the last World Cup apparently taught us nothing and it is probably too late now to do anything to improve our chances in the next World tournament in Switzerland in June.

Yet the fault does not lie entirely with those at the top. It stretches throughout a game which is suffering from complacency.

In the first issue of this magazine Football League president Arthur Drewry described the manner in which South American and Continental clubs make their grounds into social and sporting centres for local youth.

He added : "In my estimation those far-sighted enough to embark on such schemes would reap a rich reward."

There is no doubt at all of the truth of this. To-day thousands of boys lose interest in football when they leave school.

But how magnificently that enthusiasm would be maintained if more of our great League clubs took a more active interest in the care and happiness of boys who live in the neighbourhood of their grounds.

Lack of accommodation is a poor excuse. With imagination it can be overcome—even if it meant hiring a hall once a week

Mr. Drewry's wise words were published in "Football Monthly" in September, 1951. Yet few clubs have done anything about it. Too few have had the sense to see that by such schemes they would not only increase the number of potential stars but also add to their revenue in future gates.

I charge them with lack of ambition and of lethargy in carrying on in the same old way.

I charge them with being self-satisfied, with failing in their duty to young players in their neighbourhood.

I condemn them for spending ridiculous sums on transfers instead of spending it on the talent that exists on their own doorsteps.

Do not blame those outclassed English

players for the Wembley defeat. For them there was no disgrace in being dazzled by such brilliance.

And let us not take away any credit from the Hungarians. They proved, each one of them, that they were masters of their craft in all its skills.

They proved, too, that in team-spirit and in sportsmanship they had learned well from us—both in technique and in spirit.

England's bid to hold them was made gallantly and with courage. Yet it was as pathetic to watch as Canute must have been when he tried to stay the tide.

The English players too often made wild passes. The Hungarians found their man nine times out of ten. The English made two moves to bring the ball under control to every one made by their opponents.

Yet out of the gloom spectators could grasp the memory of ten flaming minutes of English glory.

The spell preceding the interval was inspiring to all of us because of English skill and perseverance. For those few moments there were dreams of what-might-have-been, visions of a wonder that never materialised.

Once again the English were fighting against impossible odds. Once again they were refusing to acknowledge hopelessness.

But with the fading light so did our hopes fade. After the interval was over the Hungarians hit back, ruthless in their mastery, calm and superbly confident.

Perhaps England's most glaring fault was the team's lack of understanding. When Hungarian players passed the ball they seemed to know instinctively where to put it.

The English in contrast were doubtful

▲ January 1954

of their colleagues' whereabouts and wasted precious seconds looking around them.

It was only natural that this should be so. The Hungarians had played together repeatedly and the English players had met each other only a few days before the game.

The players I most admired in the English team were Stanley Matthews, who kept three Hungarians busy for long periods, Stanley Mortensen, who proved again the size of his invincible heart, and Harry Johnston, who towered splendidly above the other English defenders.

But for Johnston the Hungarian score might have reached double figures.

Our wing-halves, Billy Wright and Jimmy Dickinson, can rarely have been so severely tested as they were by the incalculable Hungarian inside-forwards, Kocsis and Puskas. Both took a delight in doing the unexpected.

Player I felt most sympathy for in the English attack was George Robb. He rarely received the type of quick through-pass suited to his style and was often kept in idleness.

Jackie Sewell and Ernie Taylor were far below their normal form and compared unfavourably with their counterparts in the Hungarian side.

Star of the Hungarian forward line was centre - forward Hidegkuti whose hat-trick demonstrated that shooting ability is no longer a lost art on the Continent.

Hungary's other goals were scored by Puskas who back-flicked one into the net and hit the other by diverting a free-kick. The incomparable right-half, Bozsik, scored the sixth.

Sewell, Mortensen and Ramsey (from a penalty-kick) scored for England.

Afterwards there could be a wry kind of pride in the thought that England had first taught Hungary how our game should be played.

There could be a determination that, in humility, we should begin all over again,

And there could be the hope that, with English pluck, the faded glory might one day shine again. . . .

As the Hungarian players left the field the spectators applauded them. Smiling, they waved at the crowd. Then they ran down the tunnel leading to the dressing-rooms, into sporting history. . . .

" I thought since thousands are seeing my back all afternoon, I'd let the space for advertising!"

OPINION

A chat between Buchan (right) and Puskas, the Hungarian captain and inside-left. In the centre is Mr. Zebes, Hungarian Soccer and Sports Chief.

By
Charles
Buchan

The truth about England

ONCE again the Hungary national team showed, by the 7—1 thrashing they gave the England side in Budapest on May 23, how low is the standard of British Soccer at the present time.

It is no use blinking at facts. The plain truth is that we are many years behind Hungary, and other Continental teams, in all the essential points, speed, ball control, distribution and teamwork.

We persist in methods that were very effective when introduced by Arsenal immediately after the change in the offside law was made in 1925.

Except for occasional teams like Tottenham Hotspur, Manchester United, Wolves and Portsmouth, we have plodded along in the same old way, preening ourselves that we were the best in the world.

We took little heed of the amazing progress made by Continental and South American teams. We complacently said : " Yes, they play pretty midfield football but it does not bring goals."

Well, now, the pretty football *is* bringing goals. The Hungarians have scored 13 against us in the games at Wembley and Budapest.

Something must be done about it pretty soon, *before we are written off as a second-class Soccer nation.*

There is nothing supernatural about the Hungarians' play. They are just quick-thinking, fast-moving and clever players working together for the interests of the side.

The methods that beat England so decisively were simple and carried through by wonderfully fit and receptive players. The ball was cleared by a Hungarian defender to an inside-forward positioned intelligently in midfield clear of the opposition, just like Alex James in his palmy Arsenal days.

Forwards quickly moved into position to receive the ball. A few passes interchanged between the inside-forwards lured England's defenders upfield. Once that had been done, a well-placed through pass gave their even-time wing-forwards, Toth and Czibor, a clear path to goal.

The only variation to this method was the quick, low pass on the " blind " side of the full-back, made as he was moving forward to tackle. The Hungarians had the speed off the mark to take full advantage of this very effective

Continued

Continued

move, one rarely seen nowadays in our League games.

Of course, the Hungarians had one big advantage. They have played together and trained together, as a team, for several seasons. On the other hand, the England players rarely meet except on special occasions like the May Continental trip.

That, of course, is one excuse for our downfall. But not a reason. After all, we can do the same if we really mean to set about the business. We can have a National team built on similar lines to the Continental countries.

There are snags in building a National side with our present League system ruling the roost. But none that could not be overcome by determined men set upon putting England back where she rightfully belongs in the Soccer world.

Our national reputation should come before the winning of League championships. So let the F.A. start now on the task of building an England team.

I should prefer a Great Britain team myself but I know that is wishing for the moon. England must stand on her own feet. There is nothing to stop her standing firmly.

Tom Finney, England outside-right, said to me after the rout in Budapest : " We must get together between 20 and 30 players before the start of a season and train them together on the lines of a League club. Then we could meet Continental opposition like the Hungarians on equal terms."

That is a sound argument. I can only hope that the F.A. will take some such action, no matter what the consequences.

There can be no doubt that a recognised England team, not a collection thrown together for each game, would

The England team lining up before the start of the game against Hungary. They are (left to right) : Byrne, Broadis, Finney, Owen, Jezzard, Harris, Dickinson, Sewell, Staniforth, Merrick and Wright.

bring some immediate improvement. But the root of the trouble is far deeper.

Our coaching methods must be completely revised. The modern youngster must not only be thoroughly groomed in the various skills of the game but have instilled into him the arts of positioning, covering and general team-work.

He must also be speeded up in all his movements. And taught to think about the game, not just to kick a ball about.

We have not enough brainy players in the game today, mainly because youngsters have not been taught the right way. They play more or less instinctively, doing the first thing that comes into their heads. They learn only from experience the essential factor of

looking ahead and anticipating the run of the game.

Most of the players do not think for themselves until they reach the late twenties. Then it is too late in many cases.

I must confess, too, that our crowds do not help the younger players today. It seems to me that the majority go to see their favourite teams win, irrespective of the quality of the football displayed.

When a player holds on to the ball, the cry goes up : " Get rid of it." If another holds off a tackle, hoping to delay his opponent long enough for his colleagues to get into position, there are howls of : " Get stuck in."

Huge kicks that relieve danger to their goals are greeted with hearty cheers. The short pass that starts an attack from well over the half-way line brings groans and : " Hit the ball."

Only the established stars like Stanley Matthews, Tom Finney, Len Shackleton and Alf Ramsey can express their personality and get the cheers. Yet it is the youngster who needs encouragement. More often than not he gets his spirit broken by jeers.

It is an old saying : " The onlooker sees most of the game." But he does not have to play. He should do all in his power to help those who do.

So let the spectators help in the revival of English Soccer by appreciating the finer points and spurring their teams to higher standards. I am certain the players will respond.

THRILLS FROM THE HUNGARY GAME

Cold up there ! Yes, and safe, too . . . safe in the capable hands of Hungary's goalkeeper, Grosics, who rose to dizzy heights against the despairing England forwards.

▲ July 1954

ALF WOOD
Northampton Town

▲ February 1954

ERNIE SHEPHERD
Queen's Park Rangers

▲ March 1954

BILL PATERSON
Doncaster Rovers

▲ April 1954

SAM McCRORY
Plymouth Argyle

▲ January 1954

ALBERT QUIXALL, Sheffield Wednesday and England, says

I'm not big-headed —just determined

THEY call me "big-head." Well, if having confidence in myself is big-headedness I plead guilty to the charge.

From the moment I first kicked a football—not so long ago—I determined, if possible, to carve a career for myself. **If determination is taken for a swollen head, there is nothing I can do about it.**

From my schooldays, I was obsessed with one ambition —to play for my favourite team.

Need I say it was Sheffield Wednesday? Immediately that ambition was realised, I thought I would set myself another goal—to play for my country.

Now I have played for England three times, I have yet another height to scale.

If at all possible, I want to become an automatic choice for England.

I know what a difficult task that is because one has to maintain a very high standard of play all the time. But if I do not succeed, it will not be for want of trying.

You see, I think it is very important for every youngster starting his career to fix himself a "goal." To hit the target, he must be keen to improve his play as much as he possibly can.

Keenness means practice and practice brings a higher standard.

Whenever I can, I talk about the game with older and more experienced players. They can be very helpful. My advice to all is to listen, study and even copy them if you think it will help.

Reap the benefit from their experience.

I owe a lot to the cheery words of Wednesday inside-right Jackie Sewell, to our right half Eddie Gannon, and to other club colleagues. They have been more than eager to help me along.

Often I have been told that I have been "cocky" on the field. Again, I can only put this down to confidence and to my everlasting habit of wanting to improve my game.

Perhaps people get the impression I am "cocky" because

▲ May 1954

Jackie Sewell (arrowed) heads a goal in the Sixth Round Cup Replay between Sheffield Wednesday and Bolton Wanderers.

I seem to be the only player in England to wear abbreviated shorts, and because I like to do a few tricks with the ball before the start of the game.

My reasons for these seem to me to be perfectly good.

I get more freedom of movement in the legs, the higher my shorts are, and as for the ball-juggling act, I think this form of practice helps me to get my " eye " in and establish my " touch " with the ball.

Even though I am young, I have definite ideas about the game. One of them is that each player of a team must be master of the ball.

The more practice I can get with a ball, the better I like it.

On a Saturday morning before a game at Hillsborough, I practise with a small ball on the back porch of our home, with my younger brother, George.

It is surprising what fun I get from these " kick-abouts," and how it helps during the actual play.

After all, did not the Hungarians prove they were masters of the ball, and did not everybody rave about their wonderful exhibition ?

Every man in that Hungarian team appeared to be able to do almost anything he liked with the ball. One or two of them did a few physical exercises, too.

They were not called " big-heads."
They simply oozed confidence. As soon as a player received the ball, he knew what he was going to do with it—mainly because his colleagues had moved into position ready for the pass.

They played as a team, from goalkeeper to outside-left. They had the spirit which confidence gives.

They did not care if the left-back was in the outside-left position so long as he made things easier for a colleague and his side had possession of the ball.

They knew that possession meant they were on the attack.

These fundamentals are always at the back of my mind whether I am playing for Wednesday, the Army, or in a minor game with my Army unit.

I like to think that one day I shall be able to follow in the footsteps of the Middlesbrough maestro, Wilf Mannion, a man of my own size and build, and an expert in positional play.

At times, too, I have watched with delight the wizardry of Stanley Matthews, that great outside-right. I wonder whether one day I shall equal his footwork.

JACKIE SEWELL . . . whose cheery words have often helped Quixall.

I may not be able to, but at any rate I shall try my best.
Is that " cockiness " ?
At twenty years of age, I am one of the " modern youngsters " who are compared with those of yester-year. Some of the comparisons are not very favourable.

The one I do not like is that all the moderns play football just for what they can get out of it.

Speaking for myself, I must say that that cap does not fit. I can honestly state that I play for the love of the game.

I simply cannot resist kicking a ball about, any time, anywhere.

It was this love of the game that made me give up my job as an apprentice joiner so that I could devote my whole time to football.

Frankly, I do not think that a player should work at another job which demands the concentration and energy that should be put into his efforts if he wishes to get to the top of the football tree.

Giving up my job meant that I had to start my period of National Service. I have never regretted the step.

My biggest thrill so far came when I was first selected to play for England. I cannot explain my feelings in words, but I felt like crying.

I made up my mind to give all I had in the game.

I hoped that the ball would run kindly and was determined to do all in my power to put up a good show.

It is surprising how much I have learned during my England games, from the example of great players like Tom Finney, Nat Lofthouse, Billy Wright and Jimmy Dickinson.

They strengthened my impression that, despite what happened in the game with Hungary at Wembley, England still has the best players in the world.

It is my firm belief that if England could only select about eighteen of her best players and train them together for at least a month, we could beat any other team in the world.

In fact, I'll make a prophecy. If the England players have a substantial period of training together before going to Switzerland in June they will win the World Cup.

Already I am beginning to go through the " ups and downs " of a professional's life. After the elation of my first cap, there came recently the misery of an F.A. Cup semi-final defeat.

Wednesday were beaten by Preston North End—and Tom Finney—at Maine Road. I felt as if the bottom had dropped out of my world for the time being.

But it has only increased my determination to improve my game. There are not enough years ahead to learn all there is to know.

Always at the back of my mind is the knowledge that if I fail there is always somebody ready to step into my place. I don't want that to happen.

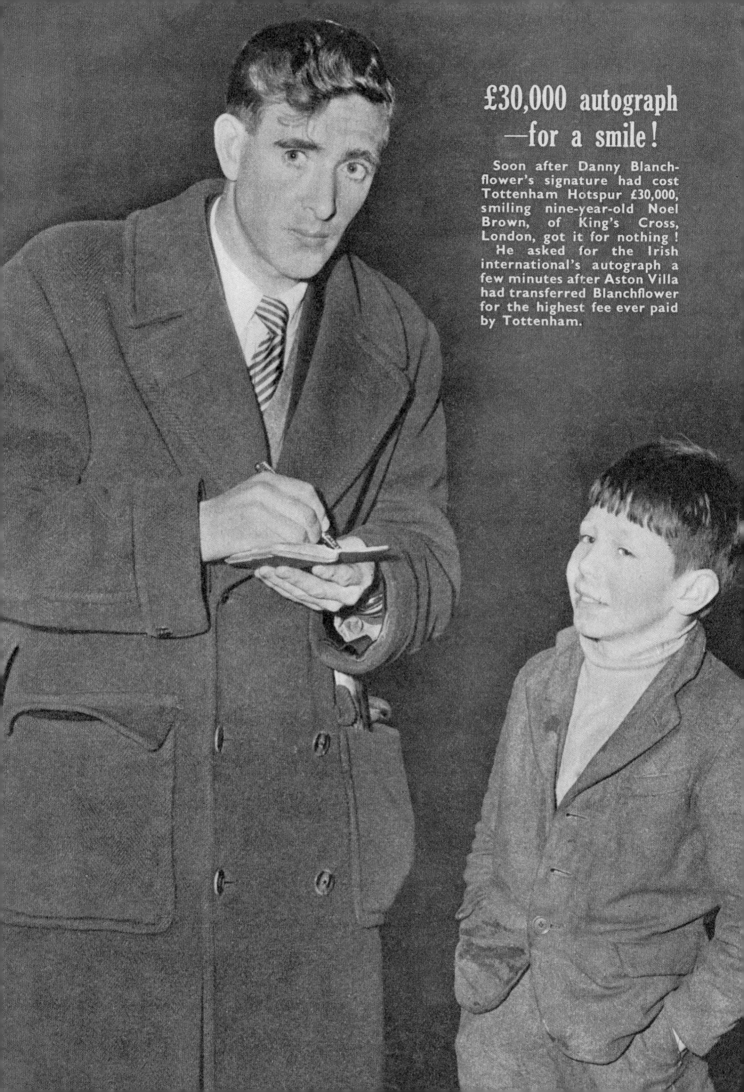

£30,000 autograph
—for a smile!

Soon after Danny Blanch-flower's signature had cost Tottenham Hotspur £30,000, smiling nine-year-old Noel Brown, of King's Cross, London, got it for nothing! He asked for the Irish international's autograph a few minutes after Aston Villa had transferred Blanchflower for the highest fee ever paid by Tottenham.

by
CON MARTIN
Aston Villa and Eire

Happy and in form again, Con Martin leads out the Villa team.

My climb from the Pit of Despair

PERHAPS you have experienced the sort of feeling I am going to tell you about; the feeling of climbing from the dark pit of depression into a bright new world full of laughter.

Such was the happy change which came my way in season 1954/5. I started the season a miserable player, thinking half-seriously of asking Villa to release me.

There was nothing wrong with the club; everyone at Villa Park was helpful. But I just could not find the form I knew I should be showing.

It seemed that I was at the turn of my career, the slide back into obscurity, the fade-out from top-class Soccer.

Not a happy thought and all the more ironic because I knew in my heart that it should not be so.

Fortunately, I never quite got to the point of asking the club to let me return to Dublin.

"Have another try . . . just one more," I continually told myself. But I knew it could not go on indefinitely.

My food was tasteless; I feared internal trouble.

And, though I spent many sleepless nights imagining I was playing great games for Villa, I could not produce that dream form on the field.

Then came a fortunate meeting with former England skipper, Joe Mercer.

I was in London, with Villa one week-end, and, worried, I sought his advice.

"How old are you?" he asked me. "Thirty-one," I replied. "Well, you should have years of football in you yet. Why don't you see a doctor?" he said.

I decided to have a complete examination. The specialist found no internal trouble, but discovered the reason for my tummy upset.

"You have a cracked bone in your nose," he said. "Can you recall getting a bang?"

I thought over the past and suddenly remembered when the accident had happened.

Five years previously, I had collided with Blackpool full-back Tommy Garrett. His head had smacked my nose.

For those five years I had unknowingly played with the injury. It had affected me so badly that when I went to bed I breathed through my mouth, never used my nose.

This was quickly put right and I began to feel fine, polishing off food with relish. But still I did not strike form.

I got back at centre-half in the first team, but was still mainly bashing the ball.

Then Danny Blanchflower came on the scene. Coming back from an away match he asked: "What on earth is wrong, Con? This isn't the real you."

"I've seen you play heaps better than this," he added, "and there is only one reason why you are not doing so now. You've lost confidence in yourself. Hold the ball and stop kicking it wildly."

Was this the answer? Did I lack confidence? If so, could I regain it? These thoughts flashed through my mind.

I accepted the challenge and forced myself to try to be constructive. But it wasn't so easy to turn the idea into fact on the field.

Then came a stroke of luck. We had been going through a poor spell when we visited Bolton and pulled off a fine 3—3 draw.

All the lads seemed to have the same idea of passing the ball to a colleague and I quickly found myself doing so.

In no time I had the confidence to take my time, pick my spot when clearing, then send the ball there with a placed clearance.

As the season progressed I found it easier to do this; no longer did I worry about form. I looked forward to each match, keen to get into action and prove myself.

My worries were whisked away; I began to be settled and happy again, and this mental uplift was translated into much improved form.

The happy story continued. Before the season ended I had not only won a permanent first-team place, but been made skipper of the side.

Later, I regained my international place and earned the award which goes to an Eire player who wins 25 caps.

WILLIE BAULD

Hearts and Scotland

Our first trophy in nearly half a century

Hearts' much-discussed centre-forward who was capped against England in 1952, tells of his close-season trip to South Africa, which, he believes, stimulated Hearts to win the League Cup this season—their first trophy since 1906

FOR years Hearts have supplied newspapers with a pre-season speculation—" Will this be Hearts' year ? " For years the answer was " No."

Always we were on the verge of great things, but, when the last whistle had shrilled, we had no silver ware on the sideboard. We were finalists and semi-finalists in the Scottish Cup, and runners-up in the League, but seldom winners.

The record book had a monotonous look. We seemed doomed to be in the top-class but seldom to get the trophies associated with that class.

At least, that was the position until this season, when we won the League Cup. It's too early to predict further successes, and I'm not going to do so.

As everyone knows, form and luck are impossible to forecast.

I think our close-season tour of South Africa was beneficial to us.

The trip to that sunny land refreshed and invigorated us, and gave us a new confidence.

It was part of manager Tommy Walker's shrewd encouragement.

He told us, last season, that he had arranged the tour in the summer and that selection would depend on the form and eagerness we showed till the end of the season.

Of course, we strove to finish at the top of the League table. We failed. Again we were runners-up; this time to Celtic.

It was a trip to remember. We had an exhausting 36-hour flight, with stops at Rome, Cairo, Khartoum and Livingstone, before we touched down at Jo'burg.

We snatched sleep between stops, for unlike Ava Gardner, we did not ask B.O.A.C. to install sleeperettes. From Jo'burg it was a footballers' paradise.

At every stop we met exiles who were glad to hear our Scots accents, and anxious to know what was going on at home.

In the second Test against the South Africans, at Durban, we were beaten by the odd goal in three.

It was the last but one of ten games and I played with two stitches in a head injury I had received three days earlier against Transvaal at The Rand Stadium.

In the same game Alfie Conn was injured, and we were without him in the Test.

The games I remember best were against Western Province, at Cape Town, and Southern Transvaal, in Jo'burg.

When we played against Western Province we were against a team undergoing a strenuous three-month coaching session from Reggie Smith, who went out for the close-season.

Against Southern Transvaal I played for the first time under floodlighting. It was a pleasant experience.

When we trotted out for the kick-off it was unusual not to see a wall of faces from the opposite terracing.

We got a shattering ovation from the spectators, and that added to the oddness.

It was rather like listening to a hidden loudspeaker.

And, when the crowd was silent—not often—I felt as if I was playing without spectators.

There was also difficulty when the ball was kicked high into the air. It was almost impossible to judge the arc of flight, and it was comical to see the ball drop behind a player who was waiting expectantly but had misjudged the flight.

After six weeks of air-hopping (we didn't travel by rail during the tour) we enjoyed the leisurely sea journey from Cape Town to Southampton, and, at the end of July, were back in light training at Tynecastle.

What a contrast between the light, springy turf of South Africa, and the heavy, gluey grounds on which we so often play at home !

Miss Ava Gardner, the popular film star mentioned by Willie Bauld, meets two stars of Soccer at a Variety Club luncheon. That's Roy Bentley of Chelsea on the left with smiling Alf Ramsey of Tottenham on the right.

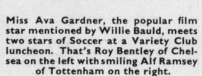
▲ March 1955

SAM BARTRAM
Charlton Athletic

▲ August 1954

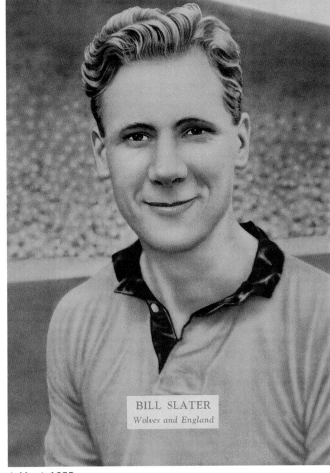

BILL SLATER
Wolves and England

▲ March 1955

SID OWEN
Luton Town and
England

▲ September 1955

BILLY LIDDELL
Liverpool and Scotland

▲ June 1956

A BALL ARTIST HITS OUT

::

"How can any of our coaching ideas possibly succeed if the chaps doing the coaching are not 100% masters of ball control?"

Make England coaches pass MY test

says LEN SHACKLETON, Sunderland and England

THERE are big things wrong with big football in England, and when Charles Buchan invited me to air my views in " Football Monthly " on this highly topical subject I was, quite frankly, delighted.

Our international teams have been severely criticised for the poor results obtained from recent games, and as an active participant in big-time Soccer it is perhaps only natural that I should take up my pen on behalf of that much-maligned character, the player.

I have in mind those two games last May, against Yugoslavia and Hungary.

Now, to be quite fair, it must be remembered that our lads had just completed a season, most of them having figured in 40 or 50 League and Cup games. And, from experience, I can tell you that by the time a player has operated throughout such a full programme he has had sufficient football for a month or so and is ready for a rest.

Granted, once upon a time our League clubs could go abroad after a hard season at home, play against Continental clubs and even international teams, and win quite easily. But times have changed.

The Continentals are just learning the game, compared to the time it has been an organised business with us. They have proved apt pupils, and we now have to face the grim fact that, whereas they play the game *properly*, we don't.

Look at the Hungarians. Their players have the ability to control a ball perfectly. They can " kill " it stone-dead in an instant or, if the needs be, pass it very accurately first time to a team-mate.

Every man throughout the team is master of the ball. Which is more than you can ever say of any current England team. And that, I am firmly convinced, is where England's international headache begins.

Quite candidly I have little faith in our coaching system.

We have developed a big coaching scheme, quite a costly business (provided largely, may I add, by professional football). Therefore, to criticise the system is quite a serious matter. But there you are; I am pulling no punches.

In the first place I will ask a very simple question. How can any of our coaching ideas possibly succeed if the chaps doing the coaching are not 100 per cent. masters of ball control?

No man has the right to be coaching young boys (our future internationals) if he is not master of the subject which he is called upon to impart. And that, believe me, is the state we are in at present.

Mastery of the ball is the be-all and end-all of football. It is useless to drag out the blackboard with all sorts of phoney ideas on the game if you haven't first of all mastered the centre of attraction—the ball.

Maybe it's an easy thing to claim " I'd tell you what I would do." But give me control of this coaching

LEN SHACKLETON . . . is here almost submerged by a surge of boyish admirers.

system of ours and one of the first things I'd do would be to make all the so-called qualified F.A. coaches take a test in ball control. Those who failed to pass the test would come straight off the list.

Believe you me, if we are to regain our rightful place as the premier Soccer nation we must do this.

Unfortunately, to quote the greatest coach of them all, Jimmy Hogan (he taught the Hungarians), our Soccer is becoming the wrong type of " B's."

Jimmy says football is, above all, both " B's "—Brains and Ball Control, and not Bash and Boot.

The more I consider it, the more I realise that our Sunderland boss, Bill Murray, isn't talking through his hat, as so many people imagine, when he says our only salvation is to suspend the " bashing " for points in our League programme for at least one season and concentrate on letting our younger players learn to play the game the proper way—the Hungarian way, if you like.

This instead of throwing them into the fray as incomplete masters of their trade.

By this drastic action we could make up the ground we have lost to the Continentals. And, so far as I can see, it is the only chance we have.

The Continentals served their apprenticeship without the distraction —nay, wear and tear—of League and Cup hurly-burly such as ours. That, believe me, is how they have to-day become our masters.

The future alone will, of course, tell whether they eventually suffer our own experience and go in for the big business of league " warfare " and find themselves unable to replace star players by fully trained youngsters.

But we are not concerned with the future of the Continentals. It's England's future that matters, and we must not forget that it is the present that takes care of the future.

YORK CITY'S GIANT-KILLERS

On the left : Billy Fenton at home with his wife and 6-year-old son Stephen. Above : Centre-forward Norman Wilkinson.

ARTHUR BOTTOM prolific goalscorer (left)

The team. Standing—Jones, Whiteside, Forgan, Phillips, Slatter, Howe, Granger, Charlesworth, Tom Lockie (Trainer).
Sitting—Hughes, Bottom, Spence, Stewart.

George Howe enjoys a kick-about (left) with his 3-year-old son Geoffrey, behind their Wakefield home.
Above, inside-left Sid Storey.

Talking it over...

by John Thompson

THERE are fifteen thousand members of the Buchan's Boys Club, and I have been wondering about the brave new world of sport which they will help to build. . . .

Many of the members will be watching football in A.D. 2000. That is a curious thought—and an intriguing one. And, of course, the Soccer they will see then will be the type of game which they, and the millions like them, have caused to be played.

Its faults and its improvements will be their responsibility—as the present state of British football, with all its good points and its bad, is the responsibility of older generations.

Long ago old William Pickford, Football Association president, looked ahead into a Jules Verne world of aeroplanes and giant stadiums. His vision must have seemed utterly impossible. Yet it came to pass.

Who knows what fantastic developments A.D. 2000 will reveal?

Latest to make a bid to emulate Mr. Pickford as a prophet is Don Featherstone, the distinguished physiotherapist, who looks after the aches and injuries of Southampton footballers. He and a friend have made an imaginary visit to a Saints' match of the future. Let us join them. . . .

Our trip begins with the arrival of Mr. Featherstone and his pal Brian at Southampton station.

Mr. Featherstone, lifted unexpectedly from the world of to-day, is perturbed at the thought of the buses being crowded. . . .

★

"BRIAN looked disgusted and said that you didn't need buses if you supported the Saints, because they had one of the latest auto-pavements installed."

Sure enough, when they got outside the station there was the moving pavement, steadily cruising along at fast walking pace as it wound up the hill to the stadium.

"We were soon carried into the large undercover forecourt that lay in front of the stadium, past the tennis courts and the swimming pool and the sports cinema."

At this stage Brian, a citizen of the new world, explained to the bewildered Mr. Featherstone that these refinements were added in 1964 because the authorities had then decided to take a percentage of the fortunes made out of football pools.

This had enabled the Saints to imitate the foreign idea of opening the club as a general sports centre, admitting local members for a small fee.

They ran twelve football teams, an athletics side, and teams which excelled in boxing, wrestling and swimming.

Nearly every local boy belonged, and you never found kids lounging at street corners because they were always enjoying themselves at the club in their leisure time. . . .

"As Brian was a full member he signed me in and we entered the well-appointed foyer. Brightly-lit corridors led to dressing-rooms, a gymnasium, lounges, cafeterias, and a restaurant, overlooking the pitch, where it was possible to sit and have a good meal while you watched the match."

The gymnasium had a non-slip glass floor and concealed lighting. Neatly placed in labelled alcoves were the training items used by the players.

Carefully stacked, too, was the radio headgear worn during practice matches when the coaches gave verbal instruction to each player. . . .

"Just as we were leaving the gym the place was invaded by track-suited Saints' players, beginning their pre-match warming-up period. This lasted half-an-hour. Brian pointed out that the track suits were artificially heated with electric elements running inside the fabric.

"Every now and then a player would be called by one of the medical staff so that his pulse rate and temperature could be taken. Thus it was ensured that every man was at his personal best temperature and pulse rate before he was permitted to ease down his warming-up work."

Don and Brian were then taken to their seats on the fourth level of the new stands. As it was a little damp outside—*at least the climate hadn't changed*—the sliding roof over the stadium had not yet been withdrawn, and clouds of tobacco smoke were swirling around under its vast dome.

On the cycle track last year's British sprint champion was competing with the Russian champion, while on the running track the last lap of a slowish mile was taking place, the winner easing up as he came home in 3 minutes 27.4 seconds.

The false floor was still over the actual playing pitch and a junior side was playing ice-hockey against a team that had flown from Brazil that morning. . . .

Brian remarked: "I sometimes think the club gives us *too* much these days."

A disturbance on the terraces broke out. . . .

"Those South American spectators got so excited that I wondered if it was a fight, although I was comforted by the thought that they had been disarmed of their atom pistols on the way in."

With these reflections comfortingly dismissed—and the ice hockey match over—Brian and Don watched the floor over the pitch being slowly rolled back into its slots behind the goals—which had emerged like fast-growing trees from the turf.

A Master of Ceremonies, dressed in a scarlet hunting coat, came on to the field and boomed details of the match, the heights and weights of each player, and the bonuses which the teams would receive.

The field was then artificially darkened and two spotlights were turned on to the dressing-room tunnels as the teams emerged.

The referee silently flashed across

the pitch on a little cable car suspended twenty feet above the ground, and the game began.

Huge clocks at each corner of the ground flashed into action. They were operated so that the full ninety minutes football could be played, stopping when the ball was out of play.

Mr. Featherstone pointed out there was little to comment on the game except that both teams played nine men in attack and that the score was 6—6 at half-time.

During the twenty-minute interval, the Harlem Globetrotters played Southampton Giants at basket-ball, and a nine-heat speedway match took place on the outer track.

Ignoring these attractions Brian and his friend took a walk backstage, visiting the medical room, with its staff of five physiotherapists, its gleaming equipment all surrounded in a germ-proof transparent plastic envelope.

The players were having an oxygen bath and an automatic massage so that they would continue the game completely fresh.

They saw, too, the tactical room from which coaches could flash the number of the particular "tactic" that they wished to be put into operation.

The number, in code of course, was flashed on to a section of the stand so that the goalkeeper could see it and pass on the message to his colleagues.

"The Saints did not use this method very much. They preferred the 'thought-suggestion system' in which the team were given short rest periods each day during which whispering voices told them the tactics they were to utilise in their next game.

"These instructions were repeated so many times that each man automatically knew his part. He was then released from his semi-hypnotic sleep."

At the end of the match the 120,000 crowd, many of whom had come from South America for the day to cheer their team against the Saints, were dispersed from the stadium in less than ten minutes.

Some left by the auto-pavements and others by the huge corporation-owned helicopters. . . .

And so back to this day and age . . . perhaps with a sigh of relief for the old and established way of life, the rattle of trams and the long patient queues, the stamping of feet on cold terraces, the grumbling and the smell of wet rain-coats, Chelsea as unpredictable as ever and the sturdy British distrust of any change even if it is for the better!

▲ January 1955

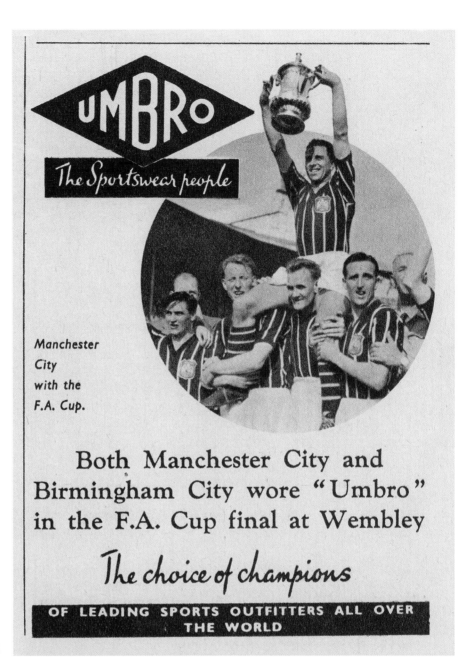

▲ October 1956 | September 1956

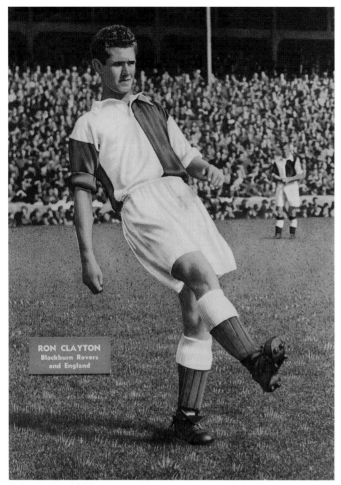

▲ September 1956

▲ June 1954

▲ August 1956

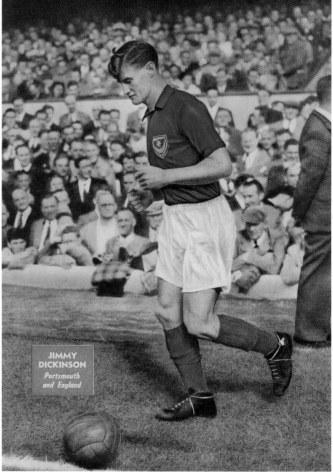

▲ February 1956

FOOTBALL IS A
Family Business
WITH THE MILBURNS

says

STAN MILBURN

Leicester

(he has

brothers,

cousins,

nephews

all over

the place)

My father knew director Stan Seymour well—the family tell me I was named after him—so to St. James' Park I went.

Another teenager at the club at the time was cousin Jackie Milburn—another relative.

I moved on to Ashington, mixing Soccer with pit work. By now, George had left Leeds for Chesterfield and he came to see me with his manager, Mr. Bob Brocklebank.

Soon I was on my way to the Derbyshire town where, after a few months, I made my League debut as George's partner.

Oh! how he used to "go on" at me. There were times when tears came in my eyes.

But mingled with his strong words was some practical advice which sprang from many years of League experience.

He did not cuss for the sake of cussing, but to make sure I understood.

Honours soon came my way. An England "B" game against Holland, at Newcastle, with dozens of relations watching; two outings for the Football League; then the F.A. tour of Canada and America.

I never expected to make such a trip. We travelled thousands of miles, saw wonderful sights, played most extraordinary games.

In Vancouver I met many North East exiles. I did not know any of them, but they all remembered my family and its football tradition.

We played one game on a ground which had previously been used for a rodeo, then a car park.

But despite the terrible conditions I learned a lot by playing behind those great wing-halves Tim Ward and Harry Johnston.

On such a lengthy trip we needed men with a strong sense of humour.

Nobody possessed this better than Jimmy Hagan, and Nat Lofthouse—who, incidentally, never lived down the time we lent him to a local club . . . then beat them 19—1.

The season after that trip, Chesterfield were relegated.

Now playing in the Third Division is not my cup of tea.

It is difficult to play good football, one has to tackle hard and there is little atmosphere because of the small crowds.

In the higher grades it is easier to play football of quality.

In Division One you have to be well equipped technically, and must be able to anticipate quickly.

Consequently, there is less need for hard tackling because the ball is moved more quickly and colleagues run into position better.

So, when an offer came to join Leicester, in 1951/2, I was glad to return to "big time" play. And in my third year we won promotion.

It was a tremendous season for us. We also reached the sixth round of the Cup.

Not until the final matches, however, were we sure of the championship.

Unfortunately our stay in Division I didn't last long.

A season later we were back in Division II, having been relegated after a long run of injuries and bad luck.

THE name of the Milburns is well-known in football which, for us, is a family business. Brothers . . . cousins . . . nephews . . . my relations have been on the scene for years.

And the future is provided for by a couple of youngsters who promise to have as bright a career as any of us.

The Milburns of Leeds used to be famous defenders. Strong, hardy players, who fought for every second of each game, they were respected by everyone.

George . . . Jack . . . Jim. Perhaps you remember them.

The first two were partners at Elland Road for a time when brother-in-law Jim Potts was in goal.

Later, George went to Chesterfield and Jim stepped into his place.

Football was the main topic in our house. My father had been a professional, so had my grandfather.

Even my sisters played!

Quite often, the three girls kicked a ball, very capably, with the Ashington youths at the pit top.

So, to me, football was something I just had to follow for a living. I felt that I must succeed—or let the family down.

I was encouraged in this ambition by my sister, Mrs. Elizabeth Charlton.

It was to her I went when my mother died. She brought me up, and also reared two youngsters, of whom you will hear a lot about in the future.

John and Bobby Charlton are my nephews—two football stars of the future.

Both are fine, strapping youngsters. Centre-half John followed tradition by going to Leeds, while Bobby, a forward,

got the chance he always wanted—that of joining Manchester United.

Take my tip—watch their progress.

But back to me. When my three brothers came home to Ashington during the summer months they had many tales to tell of Leeds. I used to listen, enthralled, and wanted to follow in their footsteps.

Instead, I was signed by Newcastle.

WILLIE SANG OPERA

WILLIE FAGAN, player-manager of Weymouth, the Southern League Club, is the footballer who failed to achieve an ambition in another sphere.

Fagan, who played inside-left in Liverpool's Cup Final team of 1950, started out in life with the hope of becoming an opera singer.

It didn't work out that way for Willie, but he has not lost his enthusiasm for singing.

His other interests, apart from football, are golf, swimming, gardening and photography.

By LESLIE YATES

" It's difficult to tell if he's really hurt, doctor — he's a Soccer star ! "

He's a brick

LIVERPOOL'S decision to appoint Bob Paisley as assistant-trainer after placing him on the transfer list, came as a relief to his club-mates who live in the same district of Merseyside.

Before turning to football for his livelihood, Paisley worked as a builder, and he has gladly carried out countless odd jobs at the homes of his Anfield friends. It is a comfort to them to know that, if anything goes wrong, Bob is on hand to advise or put things right.

Paisley, who served Liverpool well at left-half, turned professional for the club immediately after winning an Amateur Cup medal with Bishop Auckland in 1939.

BOB PAISLEY . . . club-mates sighed with relief when he was appointed assistant trainer.

Just too late

BOBBY ROBSON, the former Fulham inside-right, who recently moved to West Bromwich Albion, has many admirers. One of the keenest is Bill Anderson, the Lincoln City manager.

Mr. Anderson recalls the time when he travelled north to sign Robson, then playing in minor football in the north-east.

He knew that big clubs were after Robson, but was still hopeful when he reached the Robson homestead at Langley Park, Co. Durham.

Imagine his feelings when he was invited in—and found Bill Dodgin, Brentford manager—who was then in charge of Fulham—chatting with the Robson family. Robson had just agreed to sign for Fulham.

Songster

THE talents of Andy Donaldson, Exeter City's centre-forward, are not confined to the football field.

The former Middlesbrough and Newcastle United player is also a singer of popular songs, a number of which he has had recorded.

A gramophone recital of Donaldson's records is a popular diversion for Exeter's players.

The humorists among them are, of course, quick to remind Andy that a spot of record-breaking would not be out of place !

Likes roses

BILL LEWIS, Norwich City's left-back, is having a busy time this summer. Shortly before last season ended, he bought a bungalow in Thunder-lane, Norwich, and in quick time has prepared an attractive garden.

Lewis is no novice at the gardener's art—some of his blooms would take prizes at flower shows.

Roses make a colourful splash in the Lewis garden. His speciality is the McGredy's Wonder, a bedding rose of coppery orange.

The salesman

BEFORE Ted Purdon, Sunderland's fair-haired centre-forward, was persuaded to try his luck in English football with Birmingham City in 1950, he was a salesman at the O.K. Bazaar, in Johannesburg.

He was doing well, but the success of Bill Perry, a fellow-townsman, who had left for Blackpool a year earlier, encouraged him to follow the Soccer trail to England.

Smith, B.E.M.

ALBERT SMITH, wing-half of Ashford Town, the Kent League club, is among the professional footballers who have a military decoration.

Albert, who spent his playing prime with Queen's Park Rangers, was awarded the British Empire Medal while serving with the Royal Artillery during the war.

In addition to playing for Ashford, he now runs a fish bar, in partnership with Arthur Jefferson, the Aldershot left-back, in Melina-road, Shepherd's Bush.

FUNNY MAN

STAR off-field entertainer among Fulham's players is Jimmy Hill, the right-half, who joined the Craven Cottage club from Brentford.

Hill's impersonations of stage and radio personalities are up to professional standard, and his act is always in demand when the team is on its travels.

Jimmy's star turn is an impersonation of Tommy Cooper, the television and stage comedian.

He wears a "Cooper" fez, and copies Cooper's high-pitched laugh and mannerisms with amazing accuracy.

Selected from 1953-56

SIDESHOW

Shoe-shine boy

JOHN SELLARS, the Stoke City right-half, has had a busy summer.

Sellars combines professional football with his job as a designer of ladies' shoes.

At the end of last season he left England for the United States, and spent most of the close-season studying American styles and patterns on behalf of a large firm of shoe manufacturers.

John, who has spent all his football career with Stoke, is a son of Harry Sellars, who played at left-half for the Potteries club before the war.

JOHN SELLARS . . . when not playing football he designs ladies' shoes.

Sexton comes 'home'

DAVE SEXTON, West Ham United's inside-right, was introduced to League football by Luton Town.

As a youngster, with a Chingford youth club, he was recommended to West Ham by Norman Corbett, then a star wing-half at Upton Park.

Sexton, then 15, played two trial matches for West Ham, but their suggestion that he should be placed with a junior club at Benfleet for development, did not appeal to him.

West Ham showed fresh interest in Sexton some years later, but were thwarted by Chelmsford City, whose firm offer of professional terms was more acceptable to him.

Sportsman of the Year

MANY celebrities saw Gordon Pirie receive the "Sportsman of the Year" trophy and replica at the Savoy Hotel, London. This presentation followed the national ballot organised annually by Sporting Record, in which Pirie topped the poll for 1953.

The "Sportswoman of the Year" trophy was presented to Pat Smythe, Britain's famous show jumper, who polled the highest number of votes of any sportswoman.

The presentations were made by Lord Aberdare, who was introduced by Mr. H. C. Drayton, Chairman of Sporting Record.

Famous sporting personalities present included Geoff Duke, O.B.E., Chris Chataway, Sam Bartram, Freddie Mills, Alec and Eric Bedser, Sydney Allard, Roger Bannister, John Disley, Sir Jack Hobbs, Patsy Hendren and Tommy Lawton.

The lecturer

TO Pat Welton, the Leyton Orient goalkeeper, "team spirit" is no idle term.

Welton is a member of the panel of lecturers who visit youth and boys' clubs for the Economic League, a non-party organisation; team spirit is the subject of his addresses.

He usually treats his audience to a few glimpses behind the scenes in big football, and finds that this part of his talk always goes down well.

Welton comes from Chislehurst, in Kent, and has been with Orient since season 1949-50.

EARLY RISER

LEN WHITE, Newcastle United outside-right, is one of football's early risers. He works three days each week at a pit at Burradon, six miles from Newcastle-upon-Tyne, and his starting time is 7.30 in the morning.

White, who joined Newcastle from Rotherham United, is not at the coal face. He is engaged on haulage, and works a routine shift that ends at 4.30.

Mining has exempted White from military service, but he is compelled to carry on with his present work for another three years.

"I think I'll get myself sent off I'm dying for a smoke!"

The bricklayers

A LOT of the brickwork at Southend United's new ground is the work of Kevin Baron, the club's stylish inside-forward.

The former Liverpool player spent most of the close season working on the new ground as a bricklayer. Assisting him was Jackie Bridge, Southend's local-born utility forward.

The walls that enclose the dressing-room tunnel were built by Baron and Bridge.

Water bright

A BIG reputation as the stalwart centre-half of Lincoln City is not Tony Emery's only distinction.

A non-smoker and teetotaler, Tony drinks nothing but cold water!

Emery, who runs a smallholding in his spare time, is a local Lincoln product. Fred Emery, the Carlisle United and former Bradford manager, is his uncle.

A few seasons ago, Newcastle United and Wolves were keen to secure his transfer, but Lincoln preferred to keep Tony at Sincil Bank.

TONY EMERY . . . keeps a small-holding and drinks nothing but water.

Good for Harry

ALDERSHOT made a profit of approximately £1,100 last year.

That's quite an achievement for the struggling Hampshire club, who played to an average home League gate of only 5,572 last season.

Chief credit goes to Harry Evans, who saved the club £1,000 in wages in his first season as secretary-manager.

It shows what can be done with astute control.

ROLAND ALLEN has something to say about those Football Revolution plans . . .

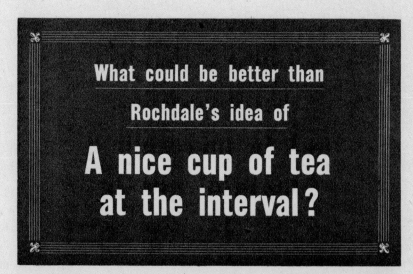

ONE of the most commendable of British characteristics is that we do nothing about almost everything until it is too late. Then, realising that there is no point in doing it, anyhow, we are saved the trouble.

We get terribly worked up about it, of course, when, as an example, we discover that our football, the game we thought of first, has suddenly deteriorated.

We hold a meeting or appoint a committee. Everybody knows the answers —all different. Plans and suggestions come thick and fast.

These are dramatic, revolutionary, drastic, and even fantastic, because we know, really, that there is not the slightest intention of putting any of them into force.

Is not that a fair summing up of what has happened during the last year or so ?

As it is getting a bit late now, the idea seems to be to put off the revolution until next year.

After all, that worked reasonably well last year, didn't it ? Then there were the Cup-ties, and the snow, and all those games to be played off, and the sudden rush of foreign teams under British floodlights, and that bright idea that if only the Pools people would fork out a fortune a year for nothing everything in the garden would be fine.

I suppose the philosophy is that if we do nothing about anything for long enough it will put itself right.

England's victory over Germany, the world champions, and the wonderful Wolves, in their treatment of Spartak and Honved, might be held to support that philosophy—rather than to prove that new methods, which might have been introduced at international, or club, level, suddenly put England back on top of the world.

It does not take much to persuade the football people that the patient has recovered.

The question seems to be not whether we are in the middle of a revolution, but whether, in the opinion of the people who can do something about it, we have had it.

We can almost hear some of them thanking goodness it is over, as they settle themselves more comfortably into the rut, to wait for something else to turn up.

That Pools money, now. Well, they have a chance there—about as much as you and I have of winning £75,000.

Perhaps it is not quite fair, from their point of view, to say nothing has been done. Yet those England practice games, and a few tactical and training changes, are like drops in the ocean against the background of the whole problem.

None is new, and we shall not achieve much by reverting to old-fashioned ideas, even if they are sound in principle.

Some people have said to me that the craze for playing foreigners has got out of hand with the clubs and the Associations.

★

When the novelty has worn off, they say, and more foreign clubs have proved to be much below the standard of their advance publicity, we shall realise that we really have a wonderful set-up here, and that whatever is wrong will right itself.

That is, more or less, what has happened. And I will say this—I found last season more entertaining than many in the past.

I saw more matches I shall remember. I believe the players, as a body, were more fit. I think the football people have seen the amber light, and that is something.

They seem to be a little shamed, slightly scared, and a trifle bewildered.

Things have got a bit complicated. They are scared of— and puzzled by—television, floodlighting, the fall in attendances and the competition they have to face from speedways, grey-hounds, and other entertainment.

The entertainment tax is a serious problem.

They will not solve all these perplexing problems by doing nothing and hoping for the best. Nor will they be put right by a revolution.

I remember reading about the Rochdale club, who had opened a new stand, seating 300 at 5s. a time, *with a cup of tea at the interval.*

Now, there is the right idea. Why not try to make the small, struggling clubs into the social centres of the place ? Look after the customers' comfort. Let them know what is going on. There are all sorts of ways of getting people interested.

That would, indeed, be a revolution worth having.

▲ July 1955

BRISTOL CITY, Champions of Division III (S.). Standing—Wilf Copping (Trainer), Milton, Guy, Anderson, Atyeo, Williams, Thresher. Sitting — Peacock, Rogers, White, Burden, Boxley.

WOLVERHAMPTON WANDERERS

Back row—Slater, Stuart, Swinbourne, Williams, Shorthouse, Clamp. Front row—Hancocks, Broadbent, Wright, Wilshaw, Smith. Inset—Flowers.

WEST BROMWICH ALBION:

Back row—Millard, Williams, Dudley, Barlow, Sanders, Brookes, Kennedy. Front row—Griffin, Carter, Allen, Nicholls, Lee and mascot John Tremans.

▲ July 1955 | November 1955 | March 1956

HONOURS 1953-56

1953-54
Division 1 Wolverhampton Wanderers *(centre)*
Division 2 Leicester City
Division 3S Ipswich Town
Division 3N Port Vale

Scottish A Celtic
Scottish B Motherwell

FA Cup West Bromwich Albion *(bottom)*
Scottish Cup Celtic
Amateur Cup Crook Town

Charles Buchan's Best XI John Anderson (Leicester), Stan Rickaby (WBA), Roger Byrne (Man United), Danny Blanchflower (Aston Villa), Jimmy Dugdale (WBA), Ray Barlow (WBA), Peter Broadbent (Wolves), Johnny Haynes (Fulham), Tom Finney (Preston), John Charles (Leeds), Bill Perry (Blackpool)
Manager Freddie Steele (Port Vale)
World Cup West Germany

1954-55
Division 1 Chelsea
Division 2 Birmingham City
Division 3S Bristol City *(top)*
Division 3N Barnsley

Scottish A Aberdeen
Scottish B Airdrieonians

FA Cup Newcastle United
Scottish Cup Clyde
Amateur Cup Bishop Auckland

Charles Buchan's Best XI Reg Matthews (Coventry), Jeff Hall (Birmingham), Peter Sillett (Chelsea), Ron Flowers (Wolves), John Charles (Leeds), Duncan Edwards (Man United), Derek Tapscott (Arsenal), Dennis Wilshaw (Wolves), Stanley Matthews (Blackpool), Don Revie (Man City), Frank Blunstone (Chelsea)
Manager Stanley Cullis (Wolves)

1955-56
Division 1 Manchester United
Division 2 Sheffield Wednesday
Division 3S Leyton Orient
Division 3N Grimsby Town

Scottish A Rangers
Scottish B Queen's Park

FA Cup Manchester City
Scottish Cup Heart of Midlothian
Amateur Cup Bishop Auckland

Charles Buchan's Best XI Bert Trautmann (Man City), Maurice Norman (Tottenham), Jack Mansell (Portsmouth), Ronnie Clayton (Blackburn), John Charles (Leeds), Roy Paul (Man City), Bobby Johnstone (Man City), Jimmy Gauld (Charlton), Johnny Berry (Man United), Tommy Taylor (Man United), Colin Grainger (Sheffield Utd)
Manager Les McDowell (Man City)

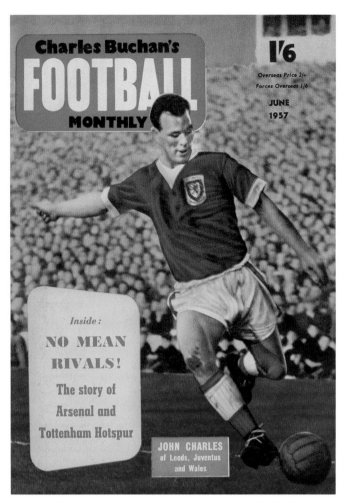

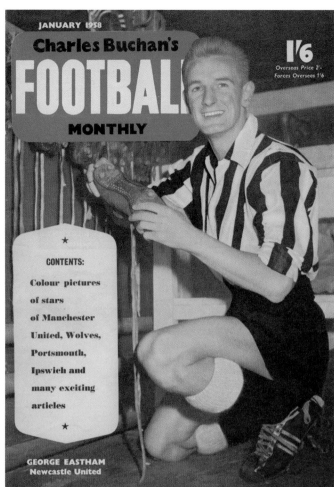

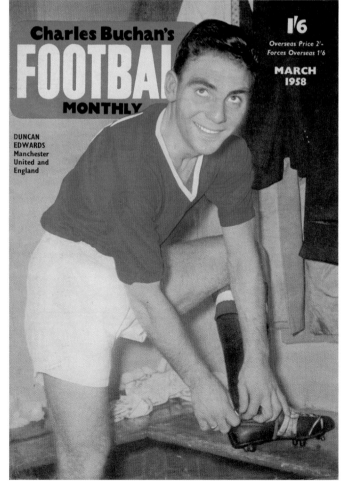

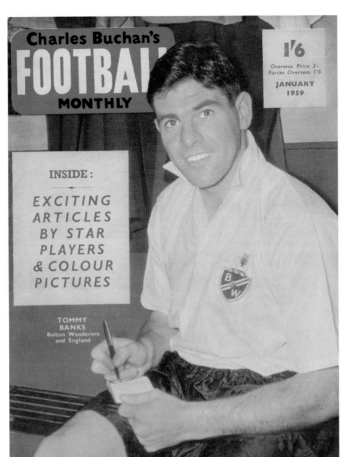

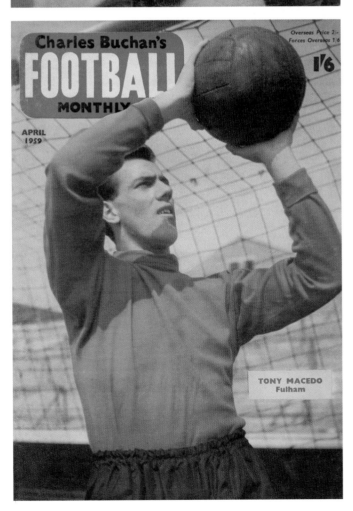

1956-59

The release of Bill Haley's film *Rock Around the Clock* sparks off teenage riots in British cinemas. In Budapest, Soviet tanks crush Hungarian dissidents. British troops are sent into action to seize the Suez Canal. Distance runner Chris Brasher and boxer Terry Spinks capture Golds at the 1956 Olympics in Melbourne.

The sudden death of 58 year old Arsenal manager Tom Whittaker in October 1956 highlights the growing pressures of modern football. Charlton boss Jimmy Seed tells John Thompson of his 'worry and sleepless nights.'

John Macadam observes in December 1956 that football crowds are changing. The 'old-style muffler-boys with their raucous friendly wit' are being superceded by county beret types. Some wear duffle coats. But this could be good news, as the 'new social brigade' are unlikely to be content with 'a lump of pallid dough and a cracked cupful of lukewarm tea'. Their presence might also lead to improved manners on the pitch.

Stanley Matthews is awarded a CBE. Charles Buchan wishes it had been a knighthood so that Mrs Matthews might share in the honour. 'Happiness at home means that he is free to concentrate on his play.' On the vital role played by wives, Buchan adds, 'if the home atmosphere is happy – and, I must mention, the cooking is good – then the player has every chance to keep up a high standard.'

Clifford Webb goes further. 'Any club that chooses to ignore the women's angle these days is throwing away a potential fortune.' The National Federation of Supporters Clubs' new contest to find Britain's Most Beautiful Soccer Supporter – the Football Queen of 1959 – is therefore 'obviously a step in the right direction,' says Webb.

The March 1958 edition of *Charles Buchan's Football Monthly*, featuring Duncan Edwards on its cover, goes on sale only hours before the player dies from injuries sustained in the Munich air disaster.

The Juventus forward line, valued at £400,000, includes Hamrin (Sweden), Charles (Wales) and Sivori (Argentina). 'Some countries wouldn't stand for such strong foreign flavouring,' comments Bill Croft. Soon after, Italy fail to qualify for the 1958 World Cup in Sweden. Uniquely, England, Scotland, Wales and Northern Ireland all qualify, the latter pair reaching the quarter finals. England and Scotland fail at the group stage. 'We are now rather backward pupils in a craft that is mastered only by foreigners,' laments John Thompson.

For his contribution to Brazil's triumph in Sweden, midfielder Didi is rewarded by a new house, armchair, telephone, TV set, bicycle, gold watch, life insurance and a lucrative transfer to Real Madrid, who have also reportedly offered £100,000 for Didi's team-mate, the teenage sensation Pelé.

England's returning players have the consolation of a rise in the maximum wage, from £18 to £20 a week. Outspoken Welsh striker Trevor Ford is unimpressed. 'I do not believe that the star player is paid his worth. I feel ashamed that I had to secure my future and make my family comfortable by under-the-counter methods...'

The regional Third Divisions North and South are replaced by national Divisions Three and Four. Peter Morris predicts financial ruin. 'How much is going to cost Torquay United to travel up to Crewe?' Or is the move a deliberate ploy to trim the number of professional clubs? For too long, admits Morris, the League has been 'cluttered with clubs who find it hard even to live from hand-to-mouth.'

CHARLES BUCHAN'S FOOTBALL MONTHLY

Edited by — CHARLES BUCHAN
and JOHN THOMPSON

Associate Editor — J. M. SARL

NOVEMBER, 1958 - - No. 87

CONTENTS

Published by Charles Buchan's Publications Ltd., Hulton House, Fleet Street, London, E.C.4. Printed in Great Britain by Eric Bemrose Ltd., Liverpool and London. Distributed by Hulton Press Ltd., Hulton House, Fleet Street, London, E.C.4. World Copyright strictly reserved by the Publishers.

OPINION BY CHARLES BUCHAN

Soccer must learn to live and let live

NEW ideas are always welcome in Soccer, but I wonder if the latest development will have a good reception. It is the playing of League games on Friday and Saturday evenings.

The games at Accrington and Wolverhampton were undoubted successes and many clubs will want to follow their example. But now the League Management Committee have sanctioned Friday and Saturday evening games, where can they draw the line between the new and the old?

There can be little doubt this is the thin end of the wedge. I wonder how long it will be before we have regular Friday and Saturday evening games throughout the season?

I may be considered old-fashioned, but I hope it will be a very long time indeed before there is any big change in the present system of Saturday afternoon League football.

I know there are many points in favour of evening football. For instance, if more games were played during the week, Saturdays would be free for matches with opponents from the Continent or America.

The clubs could, quite naturally, expect a bigger yearly income.

And week-end evening games would possibly tap a new source of customers, such as shop assistants, Saturday afternoon workers and many thousands of amateur players who rarely get the chance to watch the professionals in action.

But I believe these advantages would be heavily outweighed by the many disadvantages. Firstly, by the weather, especially in mid-winter. There will be little pleasure watching a game on a bitterly cold, and possibly foggy, evening.

Then there would be the problem of transport to and from the grounds. There might not be the facilities laid on as there are for most Saturday games. I cannot visualise many people supporting the visiting team and struggling back to their homes in the early hours of the following morning.

Another point against is that such matches would lose a lot of publicity from the Press. And, however much they carp and grumble, club officials recognise they owe a lot to the newspapers.

Worst of all, from my point of view, is that evening games would poach on other people's preserves. They would compete with the cinema, greyhounds and all local sources of entertainment.

Cricket has already suffered much from the lengthening of the Soccer season during recent years. SOCCER CLUBS SHOULD REMEMBER THE OLD TAG: 'LIVE AND LET LIVE'.

There are occasions, such as replayed Cup-ties, postponed League games and 'friendlies' with star clubs from abroad, when evening games could be a blessing.

But I sincerely hope they will be confined to such occasions and that Saturday afternoon will stay as it is now; a Soccer institution giving pleasure to millions.

What do you think? Please write and let me know.

★ ★ ★

▲ November 1958

TALKING IT OVER . . .

by
JOHN THOMPSON

IT is a little disturbing for this proud Sassenach to linger on the thought that a Scot has done more for the prestige of English Soccer than anyone else in recent years.

The triumphs of Manchester United, so ably guided by Matt Busby, the most soft-spoken immigrant of them all, have done much to make foreigners forget England's dismal failures in two World Cups since the war.

They might even one day erase recollections of our humiliating defeat by the United States of America.

The reason for Mr. Busby's success is probably more subtle than his assessors have imagined. Thousands of words have been spilled in attempts to analyse his methods.

I am reminded of the racing tipster who said : " If I knew just one ' certainty ' in a year I would not be working for a living as a racing tipster."

In the same way, if I knew Mr. Busby's secret, I presume I would be drawing his substantial salary at Old Trafford.

It may be that the secret lies somewhere between his acute knowledge of the game and his quietly composed personality.

It is certain that his players respect him for both these qualities and that their respect is increased by the fact that Matt Busby was himself a great footballer.

I was reminded of this point when I heard players of another club discussing their manager.

" He doesn't seem to know what he's talking about," they said.

It was embarrassing to listen to them. Be sure that such talk would not be heard at Manchester United.

★

ALTHOUGH I have no local loyalty for the celebrated Lancashire club I have never been so excited by any broadcast as I was by Alan Clarke's excellent description of United's conquest of Bilbao at Maine Road.

I listened to the broadcast in a lonely farmhouse. With his remarkable skill in conveying excitement without becoming hysterical, Mr. Clarke made me let out such a cheer at the finish that they must have heard it in the village a mile away.

Perhaps many other listeners-in felt as I did, that Manchester United were not playing for the grey capital of the North but for all England.

And England doubtless shared my pride that we could still produce players of such skill and spirit.

★

I SUPPOSE the next danger for Manchester United is that they will become as disliked as Arsenal were at the height of their glory.

There are peculiar specimens among our fellow-countrymen who are irritated by success and snipe spitefully at those who gain it.

Manchester United are unlikely to be put out by these mean and jealous little men.

They are big enough to shrug them aside . . . and to carry on enjoying every game as they so obviously do.

Long may they flourish ! They have brought a glint to our tarnished reputation.

★

WHEN one talks of men who have brought Soccer prestige to this country it is, of course, a stupid error to omit Stanley Matthews.

He is idolised wherever Soccer is played, and yet even from the England selectors he has not always received the credit due to his unique mastery.

Looking back through some cuttings that tell the story of this season, I read again an extract from a most pertinent and cutting column in the " Sunday Graphic," by Scotty Hall.

After Matthews had bewildered the Yugoslavs, Mr. Hall wrote :

You can spot them by their beetroot blush every time Stanley Matthews speaks for Soccer England.

I spotted them at Wembley after Stan had shown the Yugoslavs how to raise mere Soccer to the level of a Greek Olympiad.

THE GUILTY FACES OF THE GUILTY MEN WHO TRIED TO VETO STAN AS AN ENGLAND PLAYER.

They are the world's most embarrassed Soccer - men— the England team-choosers

who tried to write Stan off three seasons ago as an England proposition.

Every time Stan plays another blinder they flush with guilt.

Every time somebody like the Yugoslav team manager, Mosa Marjonovic, tells them—" Matthews ? He is the Chopin, the Schubert, the Beethoven of soccer "—their blushing embarrassment tinges from deep beetroot to deep purple.

I know who they are.

I trust you have approximately as much pity for their embarrassment as I have. NIL !

Mr. Hall's remarks reminded me of a day in the seething stadium at Belo Horizonte when a collection of American lads humbled our World Cup side.

On a bench behind me sat, in idleness, Stanley Matthews, the man who could have thrown those raw Yankee lads into complete panic.

MATT BUSBY . . . soft-spoken Scottish immigrant, who has done so much for English prestige.

Who'll get there first? An interesting picture from the England v. Scotland International, as nine players study the flight of the ball. (Left to right): Edwards, Fernie, Hodgkinson, Kevan, Mudie (with hands on ground), Wright, Clayton, Reilly and Byrne.

Here comes the England equaliser (above) scored by Kevan (left), watched by Docherty, Thompson, Hewie, Finney and Young. (Below): The Scotland goal, scored by Ring (dark shirt). Others in the foreground are Byrne, Clayton and Wright.

▲ October 1957

▲ November 1957

◀ June 1957 | January 1957 ▲

▲ March 1957

JACK OVERFIELD

ERIC KERFOOT

WILBUR CUSH

JIM DUNN

JOHN CHARLTON

GRENVILLE HAIR

▲ December 1958

THE CAMERA CALLS ON BIRMINGHAM

JEFF HALL

DICK NEAL

JOHN WATTS

GIL MERRICK

BUNNY LARKIN

EDDY BROWN

HARRY HOOPER

▲ February 1959

THE DOCTOR DIAGNOSED
RHEUMATIC FEVER. NO
MORE GAMES FOR YOU, HE
ORDERED, BUT FOOTBALL
IS IN MY BLOOD . . .

TEAM spirit is something you just cannot buy with money. It's a priceless asset which makes a quite ordinary side play great football because every man is pulling for his mates.

Rotherham have always had outstanding team spirit. There was one time when they possessed a spirit which had to be sampled to be understood.

It was in my early days with the club—I joined them in 1944. Most of the side had been built from players found playing among works teams within a radius of about ten miles.

Eight of us were miners—Jack Edwards, Horace Williams, Danny Williams, Jack Shaw and George Warnes among them. We had so much in common off the field as well as on that a super team spirit was created which no club in the game could ever surpass and very few equal.

. . . and I couldn't keep away from Millmoor

Yet, had I heeded medical advice, I most certainly would never have joined in the fun and frolics of those days.

Within a few months of signing professional I fell ill with rheumatic fever. For twenty-six weeks I was in bed, and though I'm far from being a gloomy person, I didn't look on the future too happily.

You see, the doctors made it pretty clear they thought my footballing days were over. When I was up and out of bed, their instructions were to get a light job.

The next football season came round and I decided to accept the doctors' advice to walk and cycle. After a time I was riding fifty or sixty miles without feeling any effect.

And as I rode my lonely way round Yorkshire, what more natural than that I should get to thinking about football and the happy band of players at Millmoor? It was an easy step to tell myself that if I could ride so strenuously I could play again.

Soon I was checking in at the club once more, and quickly played myself into the first team . . . and a spot of trouble.

Before the end of the season, we went to play at Doncaster, which is not far from my home. The game over, I was sitting on the dressing-room bench when who should walk in but my doctor.

He was also honorary doctor to the Doncaster club, and had been staggered to see me out on the field when I was not supposed to be doing anything strenuous. He fairly tore a strip off me.

But I got a little of my own back later. From time to time I had a check-up and no ill effects were found. Recently I went along once again . . . and the doctor told me that round the heart I was in better condition than the majority of people.

Yes, football has been in my blood for a long time.

One other point which illustrates our club spirit is that never, since I have been with Rotherham, has training been supervised unless the officials had something special to show us.

My biggest disappointment was when we so narrowly failed to make the First Division in 1955. It would have been a

wonderful thing for a small club like ours to win a way among the wealthy and famous.

With a couple of games to go we were fairly confident of doing it. Three points from the last two games would have clinched it, and we were due to face Port Vale, away, and Liverpool at home.

Vale were not playing specially well at the time and a point from them seemed likely. But they managed to pip us, and there were some unhappy faces among our younger players.

But the older, more experienced men cheered them a little and said, "Never mind, take it out of Liverpool on Monday."

We did just that . . . 6-0. Then we had to wait a couple of days until our rivals, Birmingham, played Doncaster. They had to win to beat us on goal average, and, quite honestly, I always thought they would do it.

Doncaster did give them a first-half fright, but were finally well beaten. We heard of their success while playing in a charity match at Darlington, and though more or less expecting the news, naturally felt miserable.

Three seasons earlier we had won our way to Division Two after many near misses. We got off to a bad start in the new grade, losing at home to Nottingham Forest. Next game was against classy Cardiff, and we didn't expect to do well.

But we turned in one of the finest games I can ever remember a Rotherham team play, to win 4-2 at Ninian Park. Arriving at the big ground, we had rather felt like poor relations begging to come in . . . we left feeling mighty different.

My biggest thrill in football? Well, I get one whenever I score a goal, and I usually manage that about once a season. I think an unorthodox upfield dash by a defender is a good thing on occasions because it unsettles opponents to find someone with a No. 2 or 3 on his back galloping into their penalty area.

WIGAN PREPARES TO JOIN THE LEAGUE

— 23rd TIME LUCKY?

FOUR years ago, Wigan Athletic were riding the crest of the wave —a gallant Cup failure against First Division side Newcastle behind them, and ahead the bright promise of admission to the Football League.

But things did not work out that way. At the annual meeting of the Football League, Wigan's application was rejected, and now those prosperous days of what will always be known as 'The Newcastle Era' are just a proud memory.

Since then, when Wigan could justly claim to be the prince of non-League sides, the crown has slipped a little, but the directors of this Lancashire Combination club claim that a new era is about to begin.

After four years of only moderate success, the Board has completely changed its policy on team-building. Whereas, up to this season, the wage bill has usually exceeded £150, it is now less than half, primarily because most of Wigan's playing staff is composed of young amateurs — the pick of local junior teams.

In fact, only seventeen of Wigan's seventy-seven players are part-timers — there are no full-time professionals—and this accounts for some of the disappointing results last season.

If and when the League clubs do recognise their claims, Wigan are prepared to spend, if necessary, thousands to strengthen their team.

They believe that this year is **their** year. They base this opinion on the assumption that struggling clubs at present in the Fourth Division might throw in the towel, beaten by the increased travelling expenses.

Even if that does not happen, Wigan argue that the League's policy on re-organisation seems to point to some alteration which will provide a loophole for prominent non-Leaguers.

THEY ARE CONVINCED THAT THIS, WIGAN'S TWENTY-THIRD APPLICATION, WILL BE SUCCESSFUL.

The question everyone is asking is— what happened to Wigan? What has gone on during the last four years to turn a once thriving club into the struggling organisation it now is? Let the club's vice-chairman, Cllr. Walter Walsh, answer those questions:

"We have been the victims of circumstances," says Cllr. Walsh, who is also Chairman of Bolton Corporation's Transport Committee. "When the players we had four years ago went over the hill, we brought other experienced men to fill the gaps, but unfortunately we seldom seem to have hit upon the right players.

"On our books now we have many promising young players who need only the benefit of experienced colleagues to bring out the best in them.

"Of course, if we did obtain election to the League," said fifty-year-old Cllr. Walsh, "we would improve our ground."

Since Ted Goodier left Wigan four years ago, the club has had ten managers. It is now managed by a former player, Jimmy Shirley, and the first and second team trainers, Sammy Lynn and Ken Banks, are also former players.

At the time the club was beginning its climb to fame in the early 1950s, a new member joined the Board — Mr. Sidney Littler, a wealthy businessman,

by ALLAN RIMMER

who is now Chairman of Wigan Athletic and the club's main shareholder.

It was mainly through Mr. Littler's financial assistance that the club recovered from the stunning blow of April, 1953, when the main stand was burned down.

He was largely responsible for the building of the fine new Phoenix Stand, which cost £22,000 to erect, seats 1,800 and covers a further 1,400.

This boosted the club's assets to their present figure of £30,000 and increased the ground's capacity to well over 35,000.

Wigan have won the Lancashire Combination Championship four times, the Combination Cup twice, the Lancashire Junior Cup three times, the Cheshire League Championship three times, and the Liverpool non-League Cup twice.

On Wigan's books at the time of writing, are only three players with League experience—Jimmy Prescott, 26, inside-left who has played with Southport and York City; left-winger Derek Leaver, 27, former Blackburn Rovers outside-left; and Bill Baird, a full-back who has played Scottish League football.

The rest are youngsters, teenagers like right - half Eddie Birchall, full - backs Gerry Baker and Joe Murphy, and left-half Derek Houghton.

And finally, from this Lancashire town, come these facts: Within a radius of seven miles of Springfield Park live 310,000 people; the town is on the main rail and road routes north; it has ample accommodation for visiting teams; it has a fine ground.

PROUD WIGAN : Standing—Baker, Barrass, Houghton, Kirwen, Shepherd, Ryan. Sitting—Holt, Prescott, Smith, Birchall, Banks. Note: Barrass, Kirwen, Holt and Smith have left the club.

JIMMY BURKITT
Nottingham Forest

'SOME ITALIAN TACTICS WOULD BORE YOU!'

says JOHN CHARLES

Juventus and Wales

John Charles and Gigi Peronace

FOR some time now, people in England have been wondering if I will come back to Britain and quit the fantastic Italian Soccer set-up which, although paying me far more money than I could ever earn in the Football League, does not measure up to the football I know and love at home.

Well, I am going to make no bones about it . . . I AM homesick for English Soccer. And I don't care who knows it.

This is not to say I am unhappy with Juventus. Far from it, for this famous Italian club have treated my wife and I splendidly and, after all—I did agree to join them thanks to the persuasive powers of agent Gigi Peronace.

But after 18 months in Italian Soccer, I miss playing in England. The fact is that Italian League football, despite all its so-called glamour, big money and fanatical hero-worshipping crowds, is not all it is cracked up to be.

For one thing, the atmosphere is entirely different and the tactics adopted by most teams would, I feel, bore English crowds to tears if they had to watch this kind of slow motion football week after week.

The majority of Italian First Division clubs base their whole style on defensive Soccer. Why? Because they cannot bear to lose too many goals.

This applies particularly in away matches. Many teams against whom I have played have marshalled eight men in defence against Juventus who, as you know, have a very clever and forceful attack, packed with expensive signings like Enrico Sivori and Hermes Muccinelli, not to mention our captain Boniperti and myself.

The Italians are faithful adherents of what we call the "bolt" defence system in which defenders funnel back into their goalmouth at the first sign of danger.

It then becomes a battle of wits, with the forwards trying to lure a defender out of position to create a shooting opening, and the defenders playing so close that you are smothered.

Sometimes I have found myself with two centre-halves to beat when playing at centre-forward for Juventus.

But I have managed to score 35 goals so far for Juventus and last season, of course, we won the Italian League championship.

But, believe me, it has been hard work at times and I sometimes long for the quick, exciting open play which is so characteristic of English League Soccer.

Boniperti is our schemer-in-chief at Juventus and although he has a powerful shot, he often lies right back behind his own wing-halves.

In England, almost every good side has a different style of play. Not so in Italy. Most clubs play exactly the same type of football week after week. In fact, I often think if you have seen one team play then you have seen the lot.

Much has been said and written about the huge signing fees and bonus payments in Italy, but it is my belief that this has done a lot of harm to Italian football, particularly at international level.

Too many players play for themselves and to the gallery—hoping that their crowd-drawing appeal alone, will ensure them an even heftier "inducement" to sign on again for the following season.

There is seldom any team work, as I knew it with Leeds United, for instance —although probably Juventus have as good a club spirit as any in Italy.

Last November we went to Highbury for a prestige game with Arsenal and were well beaten by a side that fielded several reserves and two players who had already appeared earlier in the day in the England v. Wales international in Birmingham.

☆   ☆   ☆

I think that game, more than anything, showed up the basic differences between Italian and English League Soccer.

Arsenal were quick and enthusiastic, had terrific staying power and were always eager to shoot. We started well enough, but they tell me we looked tired, slow and dispirited in the second-half.

Now a word about those fabulous payments in Italy. Well, it will surprise a good many of you when I tell you that the basic wage is only the same as the maximum allowed in England—£20 per week.

But the difference is marked when it comes to bonus payments for wins and draws. For instance, if we draw away from home, we at Juventus get a bonus of £12 to £13 per man. If we win—it's stepped up to £30.

A win on our own ground brings in a bonus of £15 per player. Compare these payments with the £4 for a win and £2 for a draw, home OR away, which English players receive.

How are Italian clubs able to pay this kind of money? It is because their average admission prices to matches are far higher than ours. In fact, at the Juventus stadium, the cheapest place on the terracing costs between nine and ten shillings!

I have found that Italian crowds are quite fair minded despite the Latin temperament which, in places like Naples, can lead to bottle and stone-throwing, and fireworks, too, if the visiting side happens to be winning, or the referee gives a "bad" decision.

There's nothing like the off-field social life between players as there often is in England—or so I've found.

As you know, we play our League games on Sundays in Italy. We usually have a tactical talk on a Sunday morning before a home game—round about 10-30. Then we remain at the club, playing cards until just before the kick-off.

Juventus have a practice ground in Turin where we do our training, sometimes in the mornings and sometimes in the afternoons. Usually we train for about two hours.

In other words, the schedule is pretty much the same as that adopted by English clubs.

The Juventus stadium is owned not by the club, but by the Turin Municipality. As a result, we are allowed to train on our home ground only about three times a year.

Our training sessions are often watched by as many as two or three thousand of our fans—each of whom pays an admission charge of 100 lira (about 1s. 2d.).

Of course, there are plenty of brilliant individual stars in Italian football—but most of them are foreigners.

Now, no club can field more than one foreigner in its team. Italian football chiefs feel that not until their League clubs are composed mainly of Italian-born players will Italy recover her lost world Soccer prestige.

Our season lasts from September to June.

This year my contract will come up for renewal. Whether I shall sign on for another season remains to be seen.

Quite honestly, I sometimes feel that I would come back to England to play again in League Soccer just for the £10 signing on fee and the maximum £20 a week—if given half the chance.

English Soccer may be 'written off' in many parts of the world, but for me it's the best there is.

▲ February 1959

SLEEP!

He has 15 hours

By BILL CROFT

a day to stay on top

MANY foreign trainers use an expression meaning "recharging your batteries," and emphasise that the best "re-charger" is sleep.

I've often heard of foreign players sleeping 12 hours a day, and haven't always believed it. I've taken it to mean 12 hours in the horizontal position.

I'm now told that the combined sleep and 'horizontal relaxation' ration of French forward, Just Fontaine, top scorer —13 goals in six games—in the World Cup in June, *is 15 hours a day.*

Normally, he goes to bed at 10, and his wife wakes him at nine, so that he can get to training on time. After lunch he sleeps, or 'rests horizontally', for four hours.

He admits that many players get along nicely on fewer than 15 hours of sleep, or just lying down, but says that as relaxation is one of the secrets of success in sport, professional footballers should develop the gentle art of slumbering.

★ ★ ★

FONTAINE, whose club is Rheims, is 25, likes music and films, and, after the World Cup, was sought by several Spanish clubs.

As his mother was Spanish before her marriage, he wouldn't count as a foreigner if he played in Spain. His knowledge of the language would also help him.

He turned down the Spanish offers when Rheims promised him £2,500 to remain, at any rate, one more season with them. If he is transferred to a foreign club next season, he'll get a percentage of the fee if it reaches a certain sum.

What that sum is, and just what Fontaine's share would be, are secrets.

Of the publicity his World Cup scoring feats gave him, he says *"It increased my cash value — and the amount and vigour of the attention I get from opposing players."*

★ ★ ★

SPAIN has captured some notable foreign players this season, but none more news-making than Brazil's World Cup-winning centre-forward, Vava—real name, Edvaldo Izidio Neto.

He was signed by Atletico of Madrid for a figure which I have seen given as anything from £50,000 to £80,000.

Some of these foreign deals, and arrangements for paying the players, are so complicated that you can't see who gets exactly how much.

Anyway, Atletico at once started to get some of their money back, for a practice match at which Vava was chief attraction, drew a crowd of 100,000.

I asked a Spanish reporter if any big clubs in the Peninsula had eyes on British stars.

"I don't think so," he said. "You have some grand craftsmen, but the Spanish prefer artistes, of which you have only a dozen or so. It's also exceptional for British professionals to be happy abroad."

★ ★ ★

YOU may remember I predicted that, by 1980, the United States may be as proud a Soccer country as Brazil is today.

A sidelight on the game's growing appeal to Americans is thrown by M. Pierre Delaunay, French Federation Secretary, who had a call from an American who had seen the World Cup games in Sweden.

This American made two extraordinary proposals to M. Delaunay.

One was that an 'Atlantic League' should be formed of teams from cities on the Atlantic coasts of European countries and of America.

The other was that the United States should have one or two teams in the French League!

The American thinks his country would field teams of sufficient ability once they were admitted to the circle of those that draw big crowds.

Jet planes would, of course, play a big part in a League comprising teams from the Old World and the New.

But feeling on the European Continent is that, although international games and competitions will continue to increase, the ideas advanced by this American would, for some years, be quite impracticable.

★ ★ ★

MANY teams abroad have been trying the 'four backs, two halves, four forwards' formation often used by the triumphant Brazilians. Very few have succeeded.

Instead of giving dynamism and speed, the formation has slowed down some of them. It has even 'half paralysed' a few of the imitators.

Says a critic: "The Brazilians were great attackers and great defenders. Most of their imitators find their attacks are weakened. Some are even weaker in defence. It's not a method in itself, but how you perform it, that counts. *What's good for the Brazilians may not necessarily be good for others."*

▲ January 1959

▲ February 1958

▲ May 1959

▲ October 1958

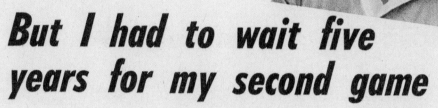

FIVE years between League début and next appearance in the first team is a long time. A worrying, waiting period wondering if luck will ever turn and bring promotion. A time when you wonder if you are ever going to win a way to the top.

Sometimes disappointment creeps in and you begin to doubt that football is such a fine life after all. But if you love the game as much as I do you stick it out even when determination

I'D HAD MY FIRST TEAM DEBUT
AND WAS FULL OF DREAMS OF
A GOLDEN FUTURE . . . .

But I had to wait five years for my second game

weakens a bit. How do I know? Because it has all happened to me.

I started my junior footballing days in Upton, near Doncaster, and, following a season with the local colliery side, moved to Leeds as an amateur player.

Eighteen years old, I got the soccer stardust in my eyes and dreamed of great things. Leeds were willing to retain me as an amateur.

I wanted to be a professional, however, and deciding Elland Road held no future for me, moved back to Upton.

Here it was that Doncaster chief scout Cliff Duffin spotted me and offered a trial. I had a couple of games with the Midland League side and was taken on as a part-time professional.

It was tough working by day then travelling to the club for evening training. I was only 19 and had to compete with more experienced players who also had the benefit of full-time training.

The following season, 1949/50, Peter Doherty joined the club as player-manager. I went into the newly-formed Yorkshire League side, got occasional reserve outings, and made my first team début in the last match of the season.

Trainer Jack Martin had told me to report at the ground on the Wednesday night. Arriving in the dressing-room I was told: " Get stripped, you are playing." That outing, against Tranmere Rovers, made me feel I was on the way up, especially as Doncaster were going into Division II.

I played left-half and in front of me was the greatest inside-forward I have ever seen—Peter Doherty. What an inspiration he was.

Some stars are not too kind to youngsters making their way, but our present manager provided the confidence I needed.

A cheery word, an encouraging shout. I felt I must play my heart out for such a man.

Since taking over solely as manager Mr. Doherty has continued to cement the team spirit he first brought into being on the field. There is never any argument in our dressing-room because " The Boss " always stresses it is not necessary.

In addition he tells us there is no need for bad language.

Having ended the 1949/50 season on such a high note I hoped to be in the side when we began in Division II. I wasn't, and was upset.

After doing well in my début I felt discouraged. Looking back I realise experienced players had to be given preference while the side consolidated its position in the higher grade.

So for two or three seasons I became a utility player. Half-back, forward, full-back, everywhere but in goal.

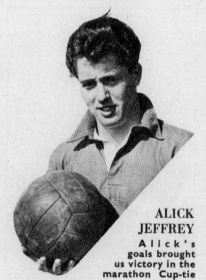

ALICK JEFFREY
Alick's goals brought us victory in the marathon Cup-tie

Late in 1955 Bill Paterson, the first choice centre-half, was transferred to Newcastle. This meant little to me at the time because Jim Lawlor took his place.

But soon I was called to the office and Mr. Doherty said : " You are selected at centre-half against Plymouth tomorrow."

I was taken by surprise because I had been playing wing-half, but once on the field I restrained my desire to move out of position and chase the ball and I settled down.

Two weeks after getting back in the team, at the end of January, came the most remarkable Cup series I ever expect to sample. It started with a fourth round tie against Aston Villa.

That resulted in a 0-0 draw, and a broken nose for opposing centre-half Con Martin. The following Wednesday we went to Villa Park with a lot of determination, but not much hope.

At the end of extra time it was 2-2.

On we moved to Manchester where I played the best game of my career in a 1-1 tie.

We wondered whether a decision would ever be reached and very tired legs took us to Sheffield. After 90 minutes another 0-0 result; extra time could not be played because of darkness.

West Bromwich provided our fifth meeting in 17 days and we had to thank sixteen-year-old Alick Jeffrey for two of our three goals.

Three days later we met Birmingham in the fifth round. All the extra games did not appear to have blunted our play, but we went down unluckily 2-1.

Before finishing I must pay tribute to the Doncaster crowd. Always they have been kind and provided encouragement.

This has been especially so since I have won a regular first team place. And just as the fans have given me support so will I always endeavour to do my best for them.

Discovered ON

RALPH BRAND
Glasgow Rangers

THEY say that television is making folk more sport conscious. Well . . . I've a lot for which to thank it. It was the TV film of a schoolboy international at Wembley Stadium which gave me my big chance in Soccer.

In April, 1952, I was picked to play inside-left for the Scottish Boys against England, at Wembley. We lost by the only goal—but, watching the televised game back home in Scotland was the late Mr. Willie Struth, famous manager of Glasgow Rangers.

As far as I know, he had never previously seen me play, but it seems he was impressed with my showing on the TV screen. As a result, Rangers invited me to Ibrox Park for an interview.

I am not a Glasgow boy—I hail from Edinburgh—but the chance of joining fabulous Rangers was too good for any Scottish youngster to turn down.

I did not become a Rangers player right away—I was too young. I was "farmed" out to an Edinburgh Juvenile club, Slateford Athletic. But the Ibrox club had an option on me and soon I got a few games with their junior team.

In 1954 I was called back to Ibrox to sign as a professional and, at 17, made my League debut against Kilmarnock. I was lucky. Willie Waddell was hurt and the club were short of a right-winger.

It was hard on Waddell, but it gave me a chance and I celebrated by scoring twice in our 3—1 win. In goal for Kilmarnock that day was Jimmy Brown who had helped to coach me as a schoolboy.

I kept my place for three games, and then I became ill. When I returned I had to be content with a reserve place.

But half-way through last season, just when Rangers were having a sticky time, I won a regular first-team place again. Manager Scot Symon had decided to "blood" a few youngsters—and the experiment proved successful.

We started to play well, finished the season in second place to League champions Hearts. We also reached the semi-final of the Scottish Cup, after a replay with Hibs.

That was a disappointing game. Ten minutes from time we were 1—2 down, but pressing hard. I went up for a ball with Lawrie Leslie, the Hibs goalkeeper.

He lost the ball and Max Murray swept it into the net for what we thought was the equaliser. The referee pointed to the centre spot, but then spotted a linesman waving his flag.

I was alleged to have handled the ball and the goal was disallowed. Believe me, I did NOT handle that ball!

But Soccer is like that. You have to take the rough with the smooth.

My red letter day was my wedding day. I was married in the early afternoon, dashed to Ibrox from the reception and played against Third Lanark—and celebrated with a hat-trick

I was playing at outside-right that day, but I prefer inside-forward. I seem to have settled down in that position this season.

But Rangers are still looking for the ideal blend, so I might find myself switched again. There are a lot of people who tell me I am a better winger than an inside-man.

Apart from my three schoolboy caps, I've won only one representative honour so far. That is for the Under-23 team against England, at Goodison Park, last season.

The pitch was very muddy after heavy rain, it was so wet that we did not expect the game to go on. But for me it was a grand experience.

In the Scottish side with me were those fine young players Bobbie Beattie, the Celtic goalkeeper, Alec Parker, now with Everton, Davie MacKay, Hearts and Scottish skipper, Alex Young, of Hearts, and Eddie O'Hara, who, like his Falkirk clubmate Parker, also went to Everton.

The schools match at Wembley will always stand out for me, of course. It was the first time I'd been to London and I remember that when England scored, the ear-splitting cheer from thousands of schoolboy throats nearly deafened me.

They talk of the Hampden Roar!

I am 22, and have only just begun my career. I have still a lot to learn but I feel I am with a fine club in Rangers.

They have certainly given me a good run. I have now appeared in every forward position except centre-forward for them.

▲ March 1959

"They'll soon be playing
soccer all the year round"
"I know. They only stop for
about $3\frac{1}{2}$ MONTHS as it is"
"Yes - just long enough for

UNITED STEEL STRUCTURAL CO.

to design, fabricate & erect this
GRANDSTAND FOR
SCUNTHORPE UNITED F.C.
to seat 2,350 people"

Steel for Speed

"On the ball"

▲ December 1958

▲ December 1957

▲ October 1957

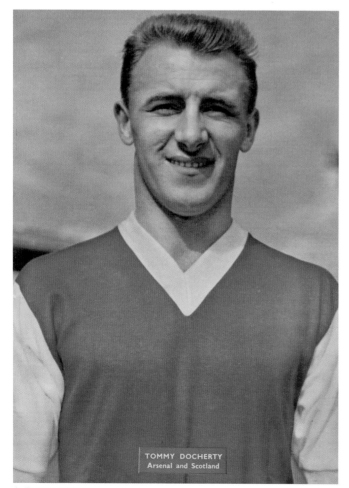

▲ February 1959

▲ March 1957

PEP-TALKS—PHOOEY!

says

John

Macadam

YOU have heard some of these dramatic stories, and, I dare say, read some of them : the kind of stories that tell of how Manager This or Director That went into the dressing-room of a losing team at half-time and delivered a Pep Talk.

These Pep Talks come in several colours, but the most popular one is simply this: " Boys . . . I know the ball isn't running for you. I know you're better than this. I'm asking you to go out there in the second half and get a hatful of goals—for me ! "

The upshot of this is that the boys go out in the second half and win 4-3.

Now, if you believe that, you will believe anything. Anybody who was gauche enough to go into a Soccer dressing-room and talk to a licked side like that would be met, at the very best, with a deep, pained silence. At worst, there would be a hollow, ironic groan, or maybe a muttered invitation to the speaker to go take a running jump at himself.

I have been in many dressing-rooms in many varying circumstances, but I have never heard one of these so-called Pep Talks, and I hope I never shall. If these things exist outside American sporting films, I shall be very much surprised. So it was with a start of considerable surprise that I read not so long ago of a club director who had shocked his players by doing it.

He is reported to have formed the habit of going in with his little exhortations, win, lose or draw, and his players, rightly, were reported to have become very embarrassed indeed by the whole thing.

Certainly, there is a type of elder statesman—mercifully, his numbers get fewer and fewer—who feels impelled occasionally to lecture the practising footballers in this way, and it is certain that it is only the innate sympathy of the boys for approaching senility that protects the " pepper-uppers."

The fact is that you don't have to tell a team of pros that they are having a poor day. The players know better than anybody in the directors' box or along the touchline that this is not their day.

It takes, then, a very tried and trusted friend to claim the right to say anything to them at all. Officialdom of any sort, and most particularly the pompous kind, is simply like a red rag to a bull to them.

As for the idea that you can *talk* a player who is having a poor day into having a good one—phooey ! There are times when, with everything else in order —physical condition, mental well-being, weather—the ball will simply not run for a man and the harder he tries the less well will it run.

He knows that, and all he wants when he gets into the dressing-room at half-time is to be left alone. If all of them are in the same boat, they either want to be quiet or, at best, blow off steam with a lot of ribbing.

What they do not want and will not tolerate is a load of pompous nonsense from a potentate who maybe has never kicked a ball in earnest, or if he has, did it so many years ago that it was probably square. I have been told often of one of these dear old gentlemen who probably epitomises the lot of them.

There was some talk around the board-room table about a very promising player with a team in a certain part of the country; before anybody else, including the manager who brought the name up in the first place, could do anything, our Mr. Director, claiming an intimate knowledge of that part of the country in which the player lived, had undertaken the signing.

He got to the village and, knocking on the door of a small house in a humble street of cottages, was invited to enter. A young man was seated at a table, reading, and Mr. Director wasted no time on preliminaries, but produced a form right away.

" I know you'd like to play for so-and-so," he said, " and here are the papers. All you have to do is sign and I'll do the rest."

" But——" said the young man, getting up slowly.

" Never mind the buts, my boy," said Mr. Director. " Just you sign, and leave the rest to me."

So the boy signed and drew his signing-on fee, and then showed the visitor to the door. He did so with some difficulty because he had a club foot. It was his brother that Mr. Director had come for.

None of this, of course, is to denigrate the tremendous part that the great managers play in pressing their sides on to success. The Messrs. Busby, Cullis, Smith and Walker are an integral part of their teams' successes.

But it is done with the quiet (or occasionally cutting) word. It is never done with the Pep Talk.

THERE is an amusing story behind the crew-cut hair style of Maurice Setters, the West Bromwich Albion wing-half. When he was a youngster with Exeter, he was due to play in a youth trial. Now in those days Maurice brushed his hair flat . . . Norman Dodgin, present Oldham Athletic manager, then in charge of Exeter, took Setters on one side.

"Go to the barber for any sort of hair-cut that would make you stand out," he said.

"That's the way to gain the attention of the selectors."

Setters did as he was told—and the hair-style has stuck!

by LESLIE YATES

Weighty subject

JACK KELSEY, Arsenal's Welsh international goalkeeper, is far from idle this summer.

Kelsey is helping to run a weight-training school at a studio in Holborn, Central London.

Weight training was introduced as part of Arsenal's schedule, and Kelsey was so impressed by its benefits that he decided to make a serious study of it.

He will, of course, take time off for family holidays. He plans to visit his old home near Swansea, and also to stay with his wife's family at Kidderminster for a time.

A holiday beside the sea at Bognor Regis is also on the Kelsey agenda.

Likes to laze

TERRY DYSON, Spurs' diminutive winger, believes in taking things easy during the summer.

"I get few chances to visit my Yorkshire home during the playing season," says Dyson, "so I like to make a complete holiday of the summer break."

Dyson's home is at Malton, and his chief off-season recreation is tennis.

He is a member of the Malton Archery Tennis Club, and his skill on the courts has attracted the attention of the Yorkshire County selectors.

Dyson comes from a racing family. His father is "Ginger" Dyson, the well-known jockey.

" If you're coming, for goodness sake put on something sensible ! "

SPEAKS FOUR TONGUES

TONY MACEDO, Fulham goalkeeper, speaks Spanish as fluently as English, and can get along quite well with Italian and Arabic.

Macedo was born in Gibraltar, but for many years has lived at Hackney. His mother was born in Spain, and Spanish is still spoken frequently in the Macedo household.

He is in the R.A.F., but spends a lot of time in the gymnasium, and gets plenty of football practice.

Selected from 1956-59

Learn by film

ANALYSIS of his team's play by means of the cinema screen is a regular part of manager Ted Bates' routine at Southampton.

At each home League match a film is made. The cameraman is advised on which shots to take, sometimes by a player who may be out of action through injury.

Only 200 feet of film is needed, and only important aspects of the team's play are required. For example, the positioning of the players when a corner-kick, free-kick or throw-in is being taken.

"These films have taught us a lot, and the players find it interesting," says manager Bates.

Changed his mind

FIRST impressions are not always best. That's what Eddie Lewis, West Ham United centre-forward, thinks now he has had time to settle with the London club.

When Lewis was with Preston North End, he played in a Cup-tie at West Ham.

On the coach drive from central London to the Upton Park ground he scanned the area, and felt it was not the sort of district he would want to live in.

Lewis did not at that time think the likelihood would ever arise.

When it came, early this season, he did not allow that fleeting impression to hold up his transfer.

He now lives at Upton Park, and is full of praise for the district.

Which just shows how wrong a first impression can be.

Paid to train

WHEN Tesi Balogun, the Nigerian centre-forward, is training with his Queen's Park Rangers club-mates, he must sometimes reflect on the time when he used to pay to train.

Early this season, Balogun, then without a club, was paying sixpence a session to keep himself in trim at the Paddington Recreation Ground.

While having his sixpennyworth, Tesi got into conversation with some Rangers' supporters. Hearing that he had played for Peterborough and Skegness, they suggested he should apply to Rangers for a trial.

Balogun took their advice and Rangers were glad to sign him. He trains in the mornings, and studies at the London School of Printing in the evenings.

SOCCER STREET

THERE is something special about Susan Street in the Ballamacrett district of Belfast.

Three present-day footballers of note were born there. They are Derek Dougan and Sammy Chapman, of Portsmouth, and Jimmy Walker, of Portadown.

SIDESHOW

SCOTS STAY HAME

"THERE was a time when Scotland was packed with junior talent, but nowadays there is as much in England as anywhere."

That is the opinion of Jimmy Trotter, manager of Charlton.

He is not alone in this view. Although most big clubs still employ scouts in Scotland, there is no longer a regular trek of youngsters from north of the border.

The shrinkage keeps pace with the slump in the standard of League Soccer in Scotland.

Part-time professionalism has a lot to do with it. Many of the most famous clubs in Scotland now depend a lot on part-time players.

Playing 'twins'

JOHNNY HAYNES (Fulham) and Frank Blunstone (Chelsea), who have formed a left-wing partnership in England representative teams, were born on the same day.

Haynes and Blunstone, now 22, celebrate their birthday on October 17, and usually exchange greetings cards.

It was Blunstone who discovered this link.

An autograph hunter asked him to sign his name in a diary at the appropriate place for his birthday. The Chelsea outside-left turned to October 17 and found the autograph of Haynes already entered.

Two-job Mann

RON MANN, Aldershot full-back, puts his mid-week afternoons to good use by working as a linotype operator at an Aldershot printing works.

Harry Evans, Aldershot's manager, was responsible for getting Mann this part-time job.

This is Ron's first season with the Hampshire club. He was signed from Notts County last summer.

GOOD SEASON

LAST season was Ray Wilson's best since turning professional for Huddersfield Town in 1952. He held a regular League place at left-back, and experience has added polish to his play.

Wilson, who worked for a year as a railway fireman, was originally an inside-forward. But when he returned to Huddersfield after his Army service he was switched to left-half.

Wilson played an odd game or two at left-back in the reserves, and when injury put both Lawrie Kelly and Brian Gibson out of action, he was pressed into service at full-back in the League team.

Ray did so well, he has stayed there ever since.

HOME FROM HOME

ABOUT three years ago, Accrington Stanley had the idea of running a hostel in the Lancashire town for their young players.

The object was to provide them with good living accommodation, good food and the benefit of each other's company.

The scheme has worked out well.

Twelve young Accrington players are living at the hostel, and officials of the Lancashire club are convinced that the setting up of a community centre has done a lot to combat the feeling of homesickness that assails many youngsters living a long way from their own homes.

"Ironically enough, I'm an inside-forward!"

BALLET LOVERS

WHENEVER a leading ballet company visits the Sheffield area, Cliff Mason, the Sheffield United full-back, and his wife are among the audience.

Mrs. Mason is a great ballet lover. "I'm almost as keen, and I never tire of ballet music," says Cliff. His favourite production is 'Giselle'.

Mason is the former Darlington and Sunderland player. A York man, he left Darlington for the Sheffield club in the summer of 1955.

BESIDE THE SEA

ROY HARTLE and Eddie Hopkinson, Bolton Wanderers' right-back and goalkeeper, will have a seaside holiday together this year.

Roy and Eddie, with their families, will spend the first week of July at Woolacombe, North Devon.

Hartle has made a lot of progress at golf. In the autumn he hopes to compete in the Professional Footballers' Tournament.

BRIGHT(ON) IDEA

BRIGHTON is the place for bright ideas. Bill Lane, the club manager, has found a novel way of keeping the dressing-room floors tidy.

He has had old railway luggage racks fixed around the dressing-room walls. These add to the convenience of the players, and cut out much of the litter that finds its way on to the benches and floor.

The racks were fixed by Joe Wilson, Brighton's trainer, and brother of Glen Wilson, the club's stylish left-half.

NO WORRY NOW

HARRY CATTERICK, Sheffield Wednesday's new team manager, served his apprenticeship the hard way.

His first official position was as player-manager of Crewe Alexandra, where money has never been plentiful. Harry did well on a shoe-string budget.

He moved to Rochdale in 1953, and in five years there was forced to exercise strict economy to keep the club in existence.

With Wednesday, Harry is at last free of financial worries.

Forest capers

AS a variation in training, Leyton Orient have found cross-country running of tremendous benefit in their first season back in the Second Division.

The players go by coach to Epping Forest one day each week, and every fit player takes part in the run.

To add a competitive element, a prize of two golf balls is awarded to the player who comes in first.

We will remember them . . .

BENT   COLMAN

JONES   WHELAN

TAYLOR   PEGG

ROGER BYRNE

DUNCAN EDWARDS

DESPITE the many thousands of words that have been written about the terrible air disaster on February 6 that cut down so many Manchester United players and officials, I find it difficult to realise they will no longer delight us with their skill and courage.

United had become world-famous, even to a greater extent than Arsenal in their palmy years. They owed a great deal to the sportsmanship, the ability and the team spirit of great men like Roger Byrne, Geoffrey Bent, Eddie Colman, Mark Jones, Bill Whelan, Tommy Taylor, David Pegg, and Duncan Edwards.

To the relatives of these lovable young men who lost their lives I extend, on behalf of many "Football Monthly" readers who have asked me to do so, and my staff, our deepest sympathy. May time heal the deep wounds inflicted.

And to those United members severely injured, like Matt Busby and Johnny Berry, I sincerely hope they will soon be restored to complete health; and that before long they will be able to take up life's threads where they were broken.

To me personally, it has been a great shock. I had seen them, at Highbury the previous Saturday, give a wonderful exhibition of Soccer, one of the best for many years. I thought, then, United, blossoming further with more experience, would become the finest Soccer machine of the century.

Adding to the shock was the loss of so many journalistic friends with whom I had travelled to many corners of the earth and spent so many happy hours.

They were able men who wrote about the game and players without fear or favour.

Since the war, Manchester United have been without rival in League, F.A. Cup and European Cup.

It was a team of experts playing for the good of the side as a whole. And now some of those experts have passed away, their parts in the victory plan will not be overlooked or forgotten.

England, too, will sorely miss the artistry and wholehearted work of Byrne, Edwards and Taylor.

I have been in the company of these outstanding players many times. Their modest, unassuming behaviour was a credit to their club and to their country.

Every day that passes, I receive messages of sympathy from all over the world. I pass them on to United officials with a sad heart. With the memorial words of former heroes: *"At the going down of the sun and in the morning, we will remember them."*

CHARLES BUCHAN.

▲ April 1958

Talent worth a fortune in transfer fees: Back row—Whitefoot, Colman, Foulkes, Wood, Byrne, Blanchflower, Edwards. Front row—Berry, Whelan, Taylor, Viollet, Pegg.

IPSWICH TOWN — BACK ROW (left to right): Dai Rees, Elsworthy, Bailey, Phillips, Garneys, Malcolm. FRONT ROW: Pickett, Millward, Carberry, Derek Rees, Leadbetter.

BRIGHTON: Promoted from Div. III (S.): Standing—Billy Lane (manager), Tennant, Bates, Gill, Whitfield, Wilson, J. Wilson (trainer). Sitting—Gordon, Thorne, Sexton, Harburn, Foreman, Howard. Inset—Ellis.

▲ January 1958 | January 1958 | August 1958

HONOURS 1956-59

1956-57
Division 1 Manchester United *(top)*
Division 2 Leicester City
Division 3S Ipswich Town *(centre)*
Division 3N Derby County

Scottish 1 Rangers
Scottish 2 Clyde

FA Cup Aston Villa
Scottish Cup Falkirk
Amateur Cup Bishop Auckland

Charles Buchan's Best XI Harry Gregg (Doncaster), Maurice Norman (Spurs), Roger Byrne (Man Utd), Ron Clayton (Blackburn), Jackie Blanchflower (Man Utd), Duncan Edwards (Man Utd), John Berry (Man Utd), John Atyeo (Bristol City), Brian Clough (Middlesbro), Arthur Rowley (Leicester), Peter McParland (Aston Villa)

European Cup Real Madrid

1957-58
Division 1 Wolverhampton Wanderers
Division 2 West Ham United
Division 3S Brighton and Hove Albion *(bottom)*
Division 3N Scunthorpe United

Scottish 1 Heart of Midlothian
Scottish 2 Stirling Albion

FA Cup Bolton Wanderers
Scottish Cup Clyde
Amateur Cup Woking

Charles Buchan's Best XI Tommy Younger (Liverpool), John Bond (West Ham), Tommy Banks (Bolton), Danny Blanchflower (Spurs), Billy Wright (Wolves), Reg Pearce (Sunderland), Jimmy McIlroy (Burnley), Bobby Charlton (Man Utd), Bryan Douglas (Blackburn), Bobby Smith (Spurs), Derek Hogg (WBA)

Inter Cities Fairs Cup Barcelona
European Cup Real Madrid
World Cup Brazil

1958-59
Division 1 Wolverhampton Wanderers
Division 2 Sheffield Wednesday
Division 3 Plymouth Argyle
Division 4 Port Vale

Scottish 1 Rangers
Scottish 2 Ayr United

FA Cup Nottingham Forest
Scottish Cup St Mirren
Amateur Cup Crook Town

Charles Buchan's Best XI Tony Macedo (Fulham), Jimmy Armfield (Blackpool), Graham Shaw (Sheff Utd), Ron Clayton (Blackburn), Bobby McKinlay (Nottm Forest), Ron Flowers (Wolves), Graham Leggat (Fulham), Peter Broadbent (Wolves), Terry Bly (Norwich), Bobby Charlton (Man Utd), Albert Scanlon (Man Utd)
Manager Archie Macaulay (Norwich)

European Cup Real Madrid

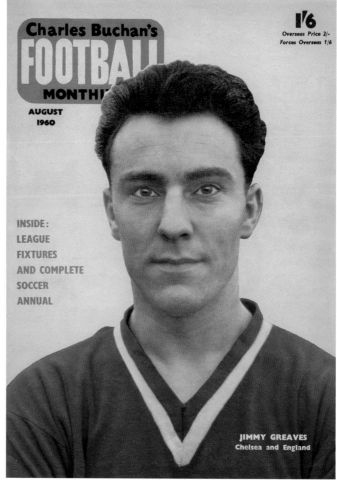

GEORGE SHOWELL
Wolverhampton Wanderers

No.100 SPECIAL BIRTHDAY CELEBRATION ISSUE

JIMMY GREAVES
Chelsea and England

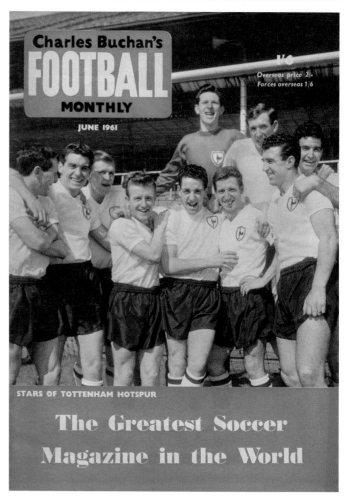

GERRY HITCHENS
Aston Villa

STARS OF TOTTENHAM HOTSPUR

The Greatest Soccer Magazine in the World

1959-62

Thousands of sightseers converge on the newly opened M1 motorway. The British Motoring Corporation launches its latest model, the Mini. Conservative Prime Minister Harold Macmillan tells the electorate, 'You've never had it so good.'

Abandoning their longheld reluctance to deal with gambling interests, both the Football League and Scottish League secure payments from the pools companies of one half per cent of gross stakes, worth perhaps £400,000 a year.

Correspondent Bill Croft notes that 'more than a hundred negros' are active in French football – 'most of the dusky players' are from the Ivory Coast – and also that for a recent match against Real Madrid, Athletic Bilbao suspended their practice of allowing free admittance to boys wearing knickerbockers. Shortly after, in May 1960, Real Madrid win their fifth European Cup in a row, beating Eintracht Frankfurt 7-3 in an epic floodlit final at Glasgow's Hampden Park. The gate is officially stated as 127,621.

A 30,000 crowd at Deepdale sing *Auld Lang Syne* to mark the retirement of Preston winger Tom Finney. After 17 attempts, Peterborough United are elected to the Football League. Gateshead drop out. The following month Charles Buchan dies while on holiday in Monte Carlo. At the Olympics in Rome a young boxer called Cassius Clay catches the eye. National Service, introduced in 1939, ends in December 1960.

Led by dashing chairman Jimmy Hill, the Players Union – now rebranded as the Professional Footballers Association – uses the threat of strike action in January 1961 to force an end to the maximum wage. 'What struck me most forcibly,' comments John Macadam on the protracted and much publicised negotiations,

'was the youthful vigour of Jimmy Hill, and by severe contrast, the advanced age of his opponents.' Bill Slater of Wolves reckons 'it will be only a matter of time before a number of really outstanding clubs emerge and a Premier, or Super League, establishes itself.'

Hill's team-mate Johnny Haynes becomes the first £100 a week player, even though, notes Peter Morris, Fulham are the only top club still without floodlights.

Blackpool's Stanley Matthews turns 46, while four of Britain's hottest young strikers are lured to Italy. Hibernian's Joe Baker and Manchester City's Denis Law move to Torino. Chelsea's Jimmy Greaves – scorer of a hat-trick in England's record 9-3 victory over Scotland – switches to AC Milan. Aston Villa's Gerry Hitchens goes to rivals Inter.

Yuri Gagarin becomes the first man in space. Tottenham become the first team to win the League Cup and Double since 1897. They then pay a record £99,999 to bring an unhappy Greaves back to London.

The Berlin Wall goes up. Accrington Stanley go under. Geoffrey Green asks John Cobbold, chairman of 1962 League Champions Ipswich, what he will do if Town are drawn against Real Madrid in the European Cup. 'I suppose we shall put in a good supply of the best sherry,' replies Cobbold. Explaining Ipswich's success, manager Alf Ramsey says, 'We never ask any player to do more than he can... We aim at doing the simple things at the right time... Some players can elaborate... rather than do the obvious and simple things. Such a player would not fit in here.'

At the World Cup in Chile England's young strikers fail to live up to their billing as Brazil, the eventual tournament winners, knock out Walter Winterbottom's team at the quarter final stage.

We must become Continental to win

CHARLES BUCHAN

ON ENGLAND

SINCE that dismal November day six years ago when Hungary trounced England 6—3, our international reputation has sunk to a low ebb.

But not in home games. On our own soil we defeated most of the foreign opposition during our own season and in our own conditions.

Abroad, however, we suffered the humiliating 7—1 defeat in Hungary — only six months after the Wembley affair —World Cup failures in 1954 and 1958, and various Continental and South American tours that flopped badly. All these emphasize our shortcomings.

There is no doubting the fact that our performances at home compared with those abroad are as different as chalk from cheese. There must be some reason.

When you think back only ten to twelve years ago, and browse over outstanding victories like those over Portugal in Lisbon (10—0) and Italy in Turin (4—0), then the poverty of our recent performances stands out more vividly.

Those were the days when Stanley Matthews and Tom Finney were at their best and we had brilliant inside-forwards like Wilf Mannion, Tom Lawton and Stan Mortensen.

And I think the recent talk of curtailing end-of-the-season tours a sign of defeatism.

We expect Continental and foreign teams to come here and meet our best— for instance we have recently lost to Sweden at Wembley and will face Yugoslavia there in May—so it is only just that we should travel at least once a year to oppose them in their own surroundings.

In fact, the more we play abroad, the better it will be for our players. They would be blooded in the tense atmosphere associated with all foreign internationals.

The next World Cup will take place in Chile in 1962. Our youngsters, who will form the backbone of England's team then, must have some experience of the conditions they will encounter in the South American summer months.

The World Cup is now the real criterion of the Soccer worth of a nation. We have a poor record in this great competition and it is time we showed the world our true value.

What are the real reasons for our poor performances against other nations on their soil? There are several.

A dearth of outstanding personalities like the great players I have already mentioned; lack of direction at the top; continuing with out-dated methods, while foreign teams and players have improved by leaps and bounds, notably in team-work and tactics.

There are plenty of fine young players in Britain. In fact, I think there is a bigger crop now than we have had for years.

Youngsters like Bobby Charlton, Jimmy Greaves, Tony Allen, Tony Kay, Ray Wilson and Dave Burnside rank with budding internationals of past generations.

Yet the selectors cannot hit upon an effective combination that practically chooses itself, as it did in former days.

They have tried many players, all up to international standard when playing for their own teams. But very few of them have carved a permanent place for themselves in the National side.

It is not the fault of the players. They are plunged into internationals in teams lacking a strong personality who could encourage them and give them confidence; and they get little guidance as to the tactics and methods of the team.

A personality like Raich Carter or Stan Cullis could bring a great improvement on the field.

But where is he to be found? And a Matt Busby, as team-manager, could inspire the team and introduce workable plans of campaign.

But what I think is the most impor-tant reason for our failure is our persistence in sticking to the British style, fashioned since the change in the offside law in 1925.

These methods, improved by teams like Manchester United, Spurs—in their championship years, Wolves — against teams like Honved and Spartak, and West Bromwich Albion—in Russia, are now hopeless against Continental opposition.

For example, we know full well the Continental methods of man-to-man marking, obstruction whenever possible, and no charging of goalkeepers.

Yet we still persist in trying to overcome these handicaps in our own way.

We will not accept the facts that long wing-to-wing passes and long kicks upfield by full-backs are useless. And that players trying to run, or dribble, round opponents are doomed to failure.

It is clear to me that our modern England teams lack directive from the top. We need somebody in charge of our National side who can introduce new tactics.

The Brazilians have done it with their 4-2-4 formation. We can do it with a blending of our present style and the more modern 'on-the-ground' passing.

We must find something new, not merely revive ideas from the old days.

You see, the Continentals are coached from a very young age in the arts of team-work and positional play. It will take something original to upset their rhythm and balance.

The new scheme, whatever it is, would have to be fully tested against foreign opposition.

Some Continentals — the Hungarians, for one—have already started their preparations for the 1962 World Cup.

Why should we give them a two-year start? Why not start planning now?

I am certain that, if the matter is tackled with all our strength, England can be the next World champions.

LET US GET ON WITH THE JOB STRAIGHT AWAY.

▲ December 1959

£400,000

...IS VERY NICE...

BUT WHAT ABOUT SOME BETTER FOOTBALL?

WHAT would *you* do if, suddenly, £400,000 were landed in *your* lap?

asks

JOHN MACADAM

It would be a bit of a poser, wouldn't it? I mean, you would be in a bit of a predicament about whether to go straight out and buy that pair of flannels, that motor-cycle, or that wrist-watch for young Joe, or the pipe for grandpa.

There is hardly any doubt that in such circumstances you would not be short of willing advisers. And that is just what has happened to the Football League in the matter of this belated windfall from the Pools people who—bless their great, understanding hearts—would have given them it years ago, anyhow!

The League have not been short of advisers.

Every Tom, Dick and also Harry has been pouring out advice, adjuration and command to such an extent that Joe Richards and Alan Hardaker—the highly intelligent and operational architects of the scheme—**could resign now and leave the matter safely in the hands of every column writer and public bar-rister in the country.**

They could sit back and watch new grounds, with cinema-seated stands, being erected, and a national Soccer Stadium erected within a couple of minutes of Leicester Square with a capacity of 150,000 well-dressed citizens who needn't worry about their well-cut, expensive blue-striped serges.

There would be manicure parlours to which partisans could repair at half-time for—well, manicure. And there would be no pushing and no shoving, and every-

body would have a perfect view of the play—and everybody would have a wonderful time.

Furthermore, the way the advisers have been talking, no football player would have to leave the game at the end of his active career and take up life anew—at the age of thirty-five or thereabouts—as the landlord of a corny old country public house or a city restaurant.

No such indignity! Every footballer who came to the time of hanging up his boots would be automatically on a Pools Money Pension that would assure him and his family of peace and plenty for the rest of his expectation of another thirty-five, or more, years of life.

The way the unpaid advisers of Messrs. Richards and Hardaker have got it all worked out, this Poolspondulick is going to cure every ill that Soccer is heir to.

There will (heaven help us!) be more and more coaching schemes and more (better!) running-tracks on the grounds so that Prince Philip and Sir Stanley Rous, with their National Council for Physical Recreation, can play, too.

There will be everything but a hand-out of oranges and ice-cream as you leave the ground at the end of the game on a Saturday evening.

WHAT A LOT OF NONSENSE IT ALL IS!

To start with, who wants all this gilt - and - gingerbread stuff, anyway? Certainly not the sturdy councillors of Wolverhampton.

The Wolves have a most splendiferous plan for a super-duper ground with seating arrangements for everybody. But the council say they will have none of it.

That, of course, is pie-eyed, but the fact is that there is a vast body of opinion in this land of ours that is against change.

Somehow or other, football has always been associated in the British mind with discomfort . . . pushing and shoving and getting wet. And there is a very strong feeling that it should continue that way.

For me, the comparative comfort of a stand seat every time—my job demands it, anyhow. **But I know plenty of people with a lot more money than I shall ever have, who would never think of going into the stand.**

"Give me the terraces," they say cheerfully. "Give me the crowd and the jostling and the shouting. Out there, it is so much more friendly and intimate. You feel closer to the movement of the game. What if you do get wet and cold? This is Soccer, not ping-pong. And anyhow, there's a whole lot of you getting wet and cold together."

It is a widely-held view, and the planners who want gilded stadia are likely to find themselves firmly confronted with a vast indifference to plans for increased amenities.

When it comes to handing out doles of that Pools dough, Messrs. Richards and Hardaker will have other things to think about.

My feeling is that the poorer clubs are going to get a big disappointment if they think their grounds are to be transformed overnight into something that looks like the local cinema.

This is not to say that football grounds are not, in the main, dirty and uncomfortable and lacking in the ordinary amenities. But the fact is that if general conditions were ten times as bad, we would still go along—**if the football were attractive enough.**

All the comforts of Babylon will not get people to see much of the stuff that is being served up nowadays. **Therefore, it is in the provision of better football that the money will be best spent.**

The players will howl for their cut, but I think they will be unwise to do so. They are pretty well off as it is, and paying a moderate performer half as much again is not going to make him anything more than he is—a moderate performer.

A more effective course would be to remove that bugbear, the maximum wage, which condemns players like Stanley Matthews and Mel Charles to the same rate of payment as the team-mate who is really only there to make up the eleven.

If players were able to negotiate their own terms according to their proved worth, there would be greater incentive all round—and better football.

But if the League really want to give the game a much-needed shot in the arm, why not buy Real Madrid?

As Real Londres, they might do quite well in the Fourth Division!

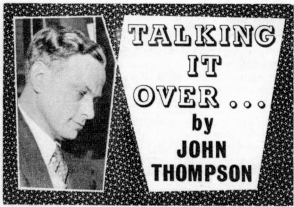

TALKING IT OVER ... by JOHN THOMPSON

THE TOWN THAT SHOULD BE ASHAMED

A FIRST Division club would probably go out of business if it was not helped by people like the milkman who comes to my village.

The town in which the club plays is for the most part so disloyal that it should be ashamed of itself, and the club prospers only because of the shrewd husbandry of the directors and the affection of folk who make long treks from faraway districts to support the team—*people like my milkman*.

The club is Luton Town. And it is to my mind a disgrace that the people who live in this bustling, prosperous community should take so little interest in a team which reached the F.A. Cup Final last season . . . a team which seldom fails to provide attractive football, even in periods of defeat.

The most exciting game I have watched this season was the tussle at Kenilworth-road between Luton and Newcastle United.

It was eventful and packed with skill and enthusiasm. After it, Mr. Stan Seymour, the shrewd Newcastle director, turned to me in utter perplexity to ask:

"Why on earth are Luton at the bottom of the table? They've no right to be there at all on this form."

And the attendance for this memorable encounter? A meagre 14,524!

Producing football of quality at Luton must be like preparing a lavish meal and waiting for guests who never arrive.

*   *   *

LAST season's Luton League gates averaged only 19,893. At the time of writing this season's attendances average around 17,000.

Why is support so inadequate? Officials feel there are several reasons.

"Transport is the main bugbear," says chairman Percy Mitchell. "Most clubs, particularly in the North, have special football buses laid on by the local transport body, but we cannot obtain this advantage."

"Lack of parking facilities is another headache. People from the outlying parts of the town are chary of coming by car owing to this difficulty. In some cases the only alternative is to walk."

Careful examination of the situation locally has proved my contention that a substantial percentage of the support given to Luton Town comes from outlying districts.

The club is well aware of the loyalty of folk in such districts as Hitchin, Hemel Hempstead, Bletchley, Aylesbury, Leighton Buzzard . . . and even my milkman's little Barkway.

If the loyalty of the townspeople equalled the loyalty of supporters from these areas gates would be increased tremendously. Why then is support from townsfolk so meagre?

In addition to the transport and parking problems there is the fact that Luton is one of the most cosmopolitan towns in the country. In size, it has trebled in thirty years, drawing on people from all parts of the country.

To them the local team is of scant interest.

Another excuse I have heard is that overtime at local factories cuts gates. Still another is that it is so easy to get to London to watch Arsenal or Tottenham Hotspur.

I am not entirely convinced by any of these excuses and agree with manager Syd Owen when he says:

"I feel that we deserve better support than we are getting. After this season's match with Spurs I received dozens of letters saying that the football produced was the best seen for a long time.

"We can carry on without trouble but it would be encouraging if more of the townspeople came to support us."

One of the oddest points about this problem is that Luton is an enterprising club. This season they have brought over attractive foreign teams like Banik Ostrava, of Czechoslovakia, and F.C. Austria, of Vienna.

The attendances? They averaged just over 6,000 for each game!

*   *   *

IN spite of pathetic support, Luton do not skimp their players. There are top wages for all first-team men, first-class travel and the best hotels.

The enterprise they show, made possible by the careful husbandry which brought a £22,000 profit in the season before last and probably a bigger one last season, has led Luton to hopes of a new stadium.

Designed on modern lines and situated midway between Dunstable and Luton it would cost in the region of £250,000.

Capacity will, in the first place, be 50,000.

Will the townsfolk of Luton rally round and help to fill the new stadium? *Or will they leave it to people like my milkman . . . ?*

Bill McCullough and Jim Standen of Arsenal —in play against Manchester United—are the central characters in this picture by C. Thomas, of the Evening Chronicle, Manchester. Mr. Thomas won First Award in the Sports Category of the British Press Pictures of the Year competition, organised by Encyclopædia Brittanica.

A tussle between Tony Hateley, Notts County centre-forward, and Harris and Jones of Yeovil.

A combination of a Rugby hand-off and a ballet leap here, by West Bromwich Albion centre-forward Keith Smith as Villa goalkeeper Geoff Sidebottom punches clear from him.

YOU CAN'T MAKE A FORTUNE OUT OF FOOTBALL ---says--- CLIFFORD WEBB

WILL the take-over procedure, which has been so marked a feature in industry this year, ever spread to professional football clubs?

Will any of the gigantic industrial concerns, with seemingly endless financial resources for speculation, make an all-out bid for control of one or other of the leading teams—Arsenal, Aston Villa, or Manchester United, for instance?

Would it pay one of the vast business organisations to attempt to gain control of a club, spend thousands of pounds on rebuilding grandstands, offices and dressing-rooms, on super-stadium lines in the hope of reaping big profits later on?

These are questions I have been asked many times. Frankly, they are questions not easy to answer without going into intricate detail.

On the face of it, there would seem to be quite a case for the take-over in football.

Everybody agrees there is ample scope for improved accommodation for players and spectators. There is room for social clubs, restaurants and other amenities, which would make Soccer-going so much more a pleasure and so much less an ordeal.

So, you may ask, why don't the big shots of commerce move in on Soccer?

Well, to begin with, the rules are so framed as to prevent anybody making much personal profit out of the game.

No directors' fees are allowed—and in big business, directors' fees are often quite substantial.

Dividends in football are limited to seven-and-a-half per cent., which, after tax deduction doesn't amount to very much.

Practically all the Football League clubs are under-valued from the point of view of shares available. And any shares that are available are never quoted on the Stock Exchange because the clubs are private companies.

Before you start writing to me, how-ever, let me point out that a notable exception is the Glasgow Rangers Club, whose shares do, in fact, have a daily quotation in Scotland. But Rangers are unique.

As an example, take Tottenham Hotspur, reputedly one of the wealthiest clubs in the country with assets of more than a quarter of a million pounds.

To pay all their shareholders seven and a half per cent. costs Spurs less than £300 a year, so that if my arithmetic is correct the total capital of Tottenham Hotspur F.C. Ltd. is not more than £4,500.

No further issue of shares can be made without permission from the Football Association. No bonus shares may be given.

It is, obviously, extremely difficult under existing regulations for personal fortunes to be made out of professional football in this country.

It is, of course, possible for a bidder offering a really high price per share to get hold of enough to gain a controlling interest in a club.

Possible, but highly unlikely. Most football club shares are held by families and handed down from one generation to another.

They carry such privileges as cheap season tickets, first chance of Cup Final tickets and other items which enable the holders to resist the temptation to sell, even at a high figure.

Directorship of a successful club also carries a tremendous amount of local prestige — and it would be difficult to deny that many business men find it helps trade to become a football club director.

Nevertheless, there still **seems** to remain one way to a football fortune.

Suppose that by a really substantial offer to shareholders and some other means of persuasion, a financier did manage to gain control of a club.

What is there to prevent him from pulling out of the League, selling all the players, closing down the club and disposing of the ground to speculative building interests? The answer is that regulations take care of this, also.

On the winding up of a club company, no shareholder is allowed to take out more than he originally put into the club.

Any surplus (says the relevant F.A. regulation) . . . 'Shall be given to the Football Association Benevolent Fund, or to some other club, or institution in the city (or county) having objects similar to those contained in the Memorandum of Association, or to any local charity, or charitable, or benevolent institution situate within the said city (or county) . . .''

See how neatly everything has been tied up. Professional Soccer is about as wide open to the financial speculator as a reluctant oyster.

Every financial aspect of the game is controlled — except, strangely enough, transfer fees. These have been allowed to soar to unlimited heights, the argument being, presumably, that the money goes around inside the game and that no individual gains any benefit.

Sports administrators in many other countries are baffled—but sometimes a little envious—by the spectacle of directors devoting much of their time to the running of football clubs without prospect of personal profit.

American baseball, for instance, thrives on take-over activities. Big firms like Wrigley's, the chewing-gum manufacturers, can buy and sell baseball clubs at will, enormous sums being involved.

Most of our grounds are woefully out-of-date. If the restriction on dividends was removed and financiers allowed to take unrestricted profits from earnings, as in other businesses, there might be a rush of new money, with keen competition to modernise grounds and attract more customers.

But even here there's a snag.

No matter how much money is poured into a club, playing success cannot be assured. British football history is full of examples which bear this out.

Tribute to Real Madrid

Real Madrid have gone into the record books as one of the greatest teams in the history of Soccer. This star-encrusted side of all the bewildering European and Latin-American talents won the European Cup for the first five years of its existence. They bowed only to Barcelona, last season, and Benfica are the new champions. "Football Monthly" is proud to publish this picture, which shows:

Back row: Vincente, Marquitos, Santamaria, Casado, Vidal, Pachin.

Front row: Canario, Del Sol, Di Stefano, Puskas, Gento.

A NEW LEASE OF LIFE

BOBBY ROBSON, captain of West Bromwich Albion, and his former Fulham colleague, Johnny Haynes, have played most important roles in the revival of England's international fortunes. In this article Robson discusses the 4-2-4 plan which England used last season, and how his conversion from inside-forward to wing-half enabled him to fit into the plan, and started him on a new international career.

THE remarkable success of the England international team in the past season was largely the result of employing the 4—2—4 tactical team plan of team-manager Walter Winterbottom. My part in the plan, as right-half, was to stop inside-forwards scoring, and to link with Johnny Haynes, England's captain and hard-working genius behind the attack.

I linked with Johnny when I was with Fulham, but then I was a goal-scoring inside-forward. It was this link, and the fact that it brought goals, which caused me, originally, to be capped for England.

I am the attacking wing-half in our England scheme whereas Ron Flowers, of Wolves, acts as "double" centre-half with Peter Swan.

But first I want to tell you how it came about that I switched from inside-forward to wing-half, how it has affected my play (and improved it), and to quote a few examples of other notable inside-men who have become even better half-backs.

Because of the "roaming" character of the two jobs, most inside-forwards can play at wing-half, and vice versa. Usually, however, it is the inside-forward who makes a better job of being a wing-half than the wing-half does of the inside-forward position.

Look at some of the inside-forwards who have excelled at wing-half in recent years . . . Don Revie, Bill Slater, Len Phillips, Roy Bentley, Billy Wright, Vic Groves, Archie Macaulay. Bentley, Wright and Slater made even better centre-halves as they grew older.

It was Vic Buckingham who persuaded me to try wing-half. He didn't exactly put it like that because, at the time, he was West Bromwich Albion's manager and the Albion had a serious team problem.

It was during the period when Ronnie Allen and Johnny Nicholls were coming to the end of their highly successful dual "spearhead" role in the attack. At the same time, big Ray Barlow, who had been the constructive "link" behind Allen and Nicholls, lost his speed and it was decided to move him to centre-half.

That left a gap at right-half, which was where I came in. It proved a very good move, indeed.

You see, I had been hardly coming up to expectations at West Bromwich. Albion had paid Fulham £25,000 for me—one of the biggest fees in the club's history, I believe—and I just wasn't fitting in.

Certainly, I couldn't get the goals as I used to at Fulham and, in fact, when Mr. Buckingham suggested the switch to wing-half, I was out of Albion's League side.

At first, I wasn't too keen, and found it hard to adjust myself to my new job. I spent a lot of time in practice games, learning how to "stand off" an opponent, when to tackle or "jockey" and how to "time" a tackle.

As I had always been a good and rapid distributor of the ball, that aspect of the wing-half business didn't particularly bother me—but the tackling part of it did.

You cannot hope to be a good wing-half unless you can get the ball off the other fellow—this is the most important part of the job!

I played my first game as a wing-half for the Albion against Blackpool on Easter Saturday, 1959. I will always remember the match—my wife gave birth to our first child on the same day!

I had been up at four o'clock in the morning to rush her to hospital and I wasn't feeling quite as match-fit as I should have been. But everyone seemed to think I had had a good game and from then on, I settled down more and more each week.

At this stage of my career, I was interested only in establishing myself as a first-team player at West Bromwich. I had virtually forgotten about any further England honours for I had been out of the national limelight for too long . . . so I thought!

I had last played for England as an inside-forward in the 1958 World Cup matches in Sweden. Frankly, I had not expected to add to my five caps.

But in 1960, I was playing so well at wing-half for the Albion that there were suggestions in the Press that I should be in the England team again.

As I had played for the Football League team at right-half against the Scottish League at Highbury, in March, 1960, it seemed that my new position had become acceptable to the international selectors.

But Ronnie Clayton was holding down the England job and he was also the skipper. I did not see, then, how he could be displaced. However, after the home draw with Yugoslavia, in early May, the England selectors decided to make changes and I was given the right-half berth for the match against Spain, in Madrid.

We lost that game 3—0, but I kept my place for the game with Hungary, in Budapest a week later. Although we were beaten again, that was the start of an unbroken England half-back line consisting of myself, Peter Swan and Ron Flowers.

I can't mention Flowers without paying tribute to the fine way in which he has adapted his game to suit the England 4-2-4 plan.

Ron, by natural inclination, is an attacking half-back, like myself. At Wolverhampton that is the game he plays. Yet in the England team he is required to play a "dual" centre-half role and spend all his time on defence.

So well has he done this difficult job that the success of Walter Winterbottom's 4-2-4 plan was assured last season.

I am perfectly happy in the half-back line now and I wish I had made the switch much earlier in my career.

One of the happiest features of this move was the renewal of my partnership with Johnny Haynes. Surely, he must be England's skipper for many seasons to come!

His display when we beat Scotland 9—3 last April was just great.

What makes the wing-half job so attractive to so many players? I have been asked this question more than once since my conversion.

Well, I'll let you into a secret—when you have the ball, there are more people around you can give it to!

READING: Standing: McLuckie, Neate, Evans, Meeson, Lacey, Reeves. Sitting: Buck, Wheeler, Walker, Shreeve, Goodall.

ROCHDALE: Standing: Milburn, Powell, Jones, Bushby, Aspden, Thomson. Sitting: Barnes, Cairns, Bodell, Anderson, Collins.

BLACKBURN ROVERS Standing : Bray, Woods, Leyland, Bimpson, Dougan, Whelan, McGrath.
Sitting : Thomas, Dobing, Clayton, Douglas, MacLeod.

▲ October 1960

BURNLEY F.C. Standing – JOYCE, CONNELLY, ELDER, BLACKLAW, CUMMINGS, MILLER, ANGUS.
Sitting – McILROY, POINTER, ADAMSON, ROBSON, HARRIS.

▲ July 1962

WIMBLEDON – THE MOST EXPERIENCED SIDE IN THE COUNTRY

DOUG FLACK

IT is no exaggeration to say that Wimbledon are the most progressive club in the Isthmian League.

Thanks to the generosity and sound business ability of their chairman, Alderman Sidney Black, their headquarters, with an imposing entrance hall and club house, and a new tea lounge, are as well appointed as those of many professional clubs.

Their ground can hold 25,000 spectators comfortably. The south stand has recently been rebuilt and the installation of floodlights on the well-drained pitch is another welcome innovation.

The team has been kept together so well by their popular coach, the former Reading professional, Les Henley, that there are seven players in the first team who have played over 100 games for the club.

There are six amateur internationals in their talented team—right-back John Martin; right-half Bob Ardrey; Roy Law, England's captain and centre-half; Les Brown, the former Dulwich Hamlet star, who took over at outside-right from young Roger Warnes; inside-right Brian Martin; and that experienced campaigner, Geoffrey Hamm, who played at inside-left for Woking when they won the Amateur Cup in 1958.

Their team also includes two Irishmen—left-half Ted Murphy, whose wonder goal enabled Tooting to draw with Nottingham Forest, the ultimate winners, in the third round of the F.A. Cup in 1959, and the club's top scorer, tall, lanky Eddie Reynolds.

Left-back Brian Rudge has turned out many times for Surrey and the clever left-wing pair, Mickey Moore and Brian Keats, both ex-Bromley men, are also County players.

When 19-year-old goalkeeper Mike Kelly was injured for several weeks Wimbledon found Eddie McAlpine a most efficient deputy.

By and large, I reckon the present Wimbledon team the most experienced amateur eleven in the country. The club have been members of the Isthmian League since 1921.

AFTER struggling for a long period, Corinthian-Casuals, in 1956, appointed former Fulham goalkeeper, Doug Flack, as coach. The next season they reached the final of the Amateur Cup and in the following campaign the semi-final.

This speaks for itself. Indeed, Doug's popularity, tactical talks, and general dressing-room personality have helped considerably in transforming Casuals into one of the best-balanced and most formidable amateur sides in London.

WIMBLEDON A.F.C.: Standing—Ardrey, Rudge, J. Martin, Murphy, Kelly, Law, Reynolds. Kneeling—Moore, Hamm, B. Martin, Warnes.

▲ May 1962

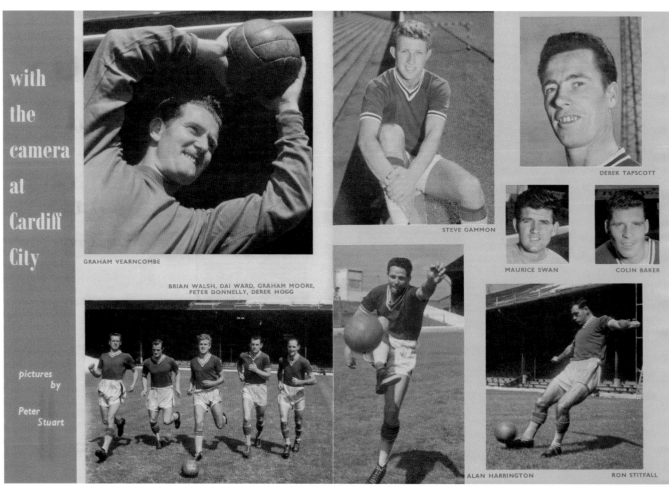

with
the
camera
at
Cardiff
City

pictures
by
Peter
Stuart

GRAHAM VEARNCOMBE

BRIAN WALSH, DAI WARD, GRAHAM MOORE,
PETER DONNELLY, DEREK HOGG

STEVE GAMMON

DEREK TAPSCOTT

MAURICE SWAN

COLIN BAKER

ALAN HARRINGTON

RON STITFALL

▲ October 1961

GALLERY
OF
THE
STARS

Pictures by PETER STUART

ALAN MULLERY
Fulham

COLIN TAYLOR
Walsall

JIMMY LEADBETTER
Ipswich Town

PAT CRERAND, Celtic and Scotland

BOBBY TAMBLING
Chelsea

RON FLOWERS, Wolves and England
GERRY SUMMERS, Sheffield United

▲ April 1962

'THE SALT OF THE EARTH'

SHOWPIECE of schoolboy Soccer is the international at Wembley which every year is filled to capacity with an excited crowd of 95,000 youngsters and parents.

It is the culmination of a season's voluntary work by thousands of teachers who have given many hours of their leisure to coaching boys in the basic skills of the nation's favourite winter sport.

The game itself? Ask anyone who has seen a Wembley schoolboys' international and he will tell you that the standard of play in incredibly high, and a delight to the Soccer purist. England's opponents there, on the last Saturday in April, will be Wales.

As you can well imagine, this big Wembley occasion entails a lot of organisation. Parties come from all parts of the country, by coach or train, and bookings for this transport have to be made many months ahead.

No praise is too high for those schoolmasters who take on the onerous task of bringing a party of 20 or 30 youngsters, aged between 10 and 15, on the long trek to Wembley. For some of them it means a round trip of 500 miles, travelling through two nights. On top of that, meals have to be arranged and the boys kept interested during the hours before and after the game—and, of course, out of mischief!

★　　★　　★

"These unknown schoolmasters are the salt of the earth," says Mr. Sidney Tye, secretary of the English Schools F.A., and it is entirely due to their co-operation that we have been able to keep this an all-ticket match."

The Wembley game hauls in just on £19,000, and the E.S.F.A. estimate that they will get about £9,000. Practically all the tickets are sold through the affiliated district associations who get a rebate on their sales. Rebate payments swallow up £3,000 of the E.S.F.A.'s profit, but there is a condition governing this "bonus"—the money must be spent entirely on Soccer development.

It is the Wembley "gate" that provides the E.S.F.A. with their main source of revenue. Remember, they do not get a penny from any outside organisation; it is their proud boast that they have stood on their own feet since the association was formed 57 years ago.

It was in 1950 that the E.S.F.A. decided to stage the first schools international at Wembley. Interest in Soccer generally, was then at its peak and schools internationals were attracting 40,000—50,000 gates at some of the big professional club grounds—like Maine Road, Manchester and Newcastle.

★　　★　　★

Would it be a flop at Wembley? Many E.S.F.A. officials thought it was too much of a gamble. But the 55,000 attendance exceeded all expectations. There was also an unseen audience of probably a million viewers, for this was the first boys' international to be televised.

What the viewers saw on their screens was Soccer of the highest quality. It firmly established the schools match in the Wembley calendar.

The England team on that historic occasion is invariably taken as the yardstick in comparing the merits of subsequent sides. How many readers can recall the eleven boys who thrashed their Scottish counterparts 8—2?

England's star that day was a pint-sized inside-right with a wayward fringe of hair. His name? JOHNNY HAYNES. Since then, in a span of eleven years, Johnny has scaled the Soccer heights,collecting youth and under-23 honours on the way. Now he is England's captain and Fulham's skipper.

Then there was RAY PARRY (inside-left) who was transferred to Blackpool early this year from Bolton, with whom he won a full England cap and an F.A. Cup medal.

EDDIE CLAMP (left-half) of Wolves is another member of the side who has achieved full international status. He also possesses a League championship medal and a Cupwinners' medal.

RON COPE (centre-half) wears the No. 5 shirt in Manchester United's League side.

Soccer now has little interest for RON WARD (goalkeeper). He was on Chesterfield's books for a time and, as a youth, was offered a trial by Arsenal. After completing his National Service, Ron became a bricklayer, in Yorkshire, and now prefers cricket.

FRED COOPER (right-back) played occasionally in West Ham's League side as Noel Cantwell's deputy, but dropped out of the game a year ago to take over a public house in Stratford.

MALCOLM SPENCER (left-back and captain) joined Wolves' ground staff. He is now a metal worker and plays as a part-time professional for Evesham United in the Birmingham League.

BRIAN TWAITES (right-half) had trials with Crystal Palace and Arsenal, but decided to join his father in the hairdressing business. He now runs his own saloon in Tunbridge Wells.

MICHAEL CHARLTON (outside-right) was all set to make a career with Chelsea after winning F.A. youth honours until a motor-cycle accident put an end to his Soccer ambitions. He took a job as a salesman with a cosmetics firm and is doing very well. His father is a headmaster in Aldershot.

GEORGE BROWN (centre-forward) drifted out of the game after service with Liverpool, Chesterfield and Peterborough.

Lastly, JIM SCOTT (outside-left) joined Burnley and still plays in their reserve side—at half-back.

▲ May 1961

▲ November 1959

▲ August 1961

▲ December 1960

▲ August 1959

I was dropped before I started!

UNLIKE a lot of goalkeepers who were forwards or half-backs as schoolboys and later went into goal either because they were the biggest boys in the side, or someone was injured, I took to goal-keeping from the start.

But it was not an encouraging start. *In fact, after I had been picked to play for Sheffield boys I was dropped because I had a bad match in a Yorkshire Schools Cup-tie.*

When I left school I became an apprentice bricklayer. I played no serious football, but one day a chance visit to the local recreation ground caused me to go back to the game.

A Sheffield works club, Millspaw Steel Works, were short of a goal-keeper and they asked me to play for them. Soon after that I was spotted by a Chesterfield scout.

He invited me to have a trial with their juniors, and as a result I signed amateur forms for manager Teddy Davidson and played for Chester-field's Northern Intermediate League XI.

Not until I was promoted to the Central League team did I really know what it was to be at the receiving end of a shooting barrage.

In successive matches I played against Manchester United and Wolves reserves! It was grand experience for a youngster, believe me.

While with Chesterfield's juniors I was proud to be a member of the team which reached the final of the F.A. Youth Cup.

In the first 'leg', against Manchester United at Old Trafford, we were 0—3 down by half-time, but pulled back to 2—3. The excitement was intense when we lined up again to play the deciding leg at Saltergate.

We scored a quick goal to make the aggregate score 3—3, and not until the last minute of extra time did United get the deciding goal. That was one of the most thrilling games in which I have ever played.

United had a star-studded team of youngsters which included Bobby Charlton and Wilf McGuinness.

In 1956 I went into the Forces and was posted to Germany. There I enjoyed some really good football, although I could not get a place in our regimental side because the soldier in possession was Norman Cole, of Portsmouth.

But I played regularly in inter-unit games—and, incidentally, while in Germany I met the girl who is now my wife.

Whenever I went to England on leave I played for Chesterfield's reserves, and when I left the Army I was signed as a full-time professional. Apparently, the management had been getting some good reports on my play in the Army!

I had a season for Chesterfield in the Third Division, and then I heard that Leicester City were interested in me, and Gerry Sears, our left-back.

Mr. Matt Gillies, who had taken over from Dave Halliday, signed me for Leicester, and in September, 1959, I made my first-team debut, taking over from the injured Dave McLaren.

The game was against Blackpool, at Filbert Street—an evening match —and we drew 1—1. For me, it was quite a peaceful introduction to First Division football—for which I was very thankful.

I played in the next game, against Newcastle, and then was injured and out of action for three weeks. I was recalled against Manchester City, at Maine Road, and after that I retained my place.

Last season was an exciting one for me when I took part in Leicester's F.A. Cup run which ended when we went out to Wolves, the eventual winners, by 1—2.

It was an unlucky 'own-goal' by full-back Len Chalmers which put us out, and we were very disappointed, especially as we had taken four League points from the Molineux men that season.

In fact, we had one of our best wins of the season when we beat the Wolves 3—0, at Molineux. Ironically enough, on the Saturday immediately following our Cup defeat we met them in the return League game, at Filbert Street, and again beat them very convincingly.

Johnny Anderson, now with Peter-borough, gave me plenty of useful tips at Filbert Street, and, of course, I have learned a lot from manager Matt Gillies.

Leicester have always had a reputation for producing good goalkeepers, and I am anxious to keep up that tradition.

▲ January 1961

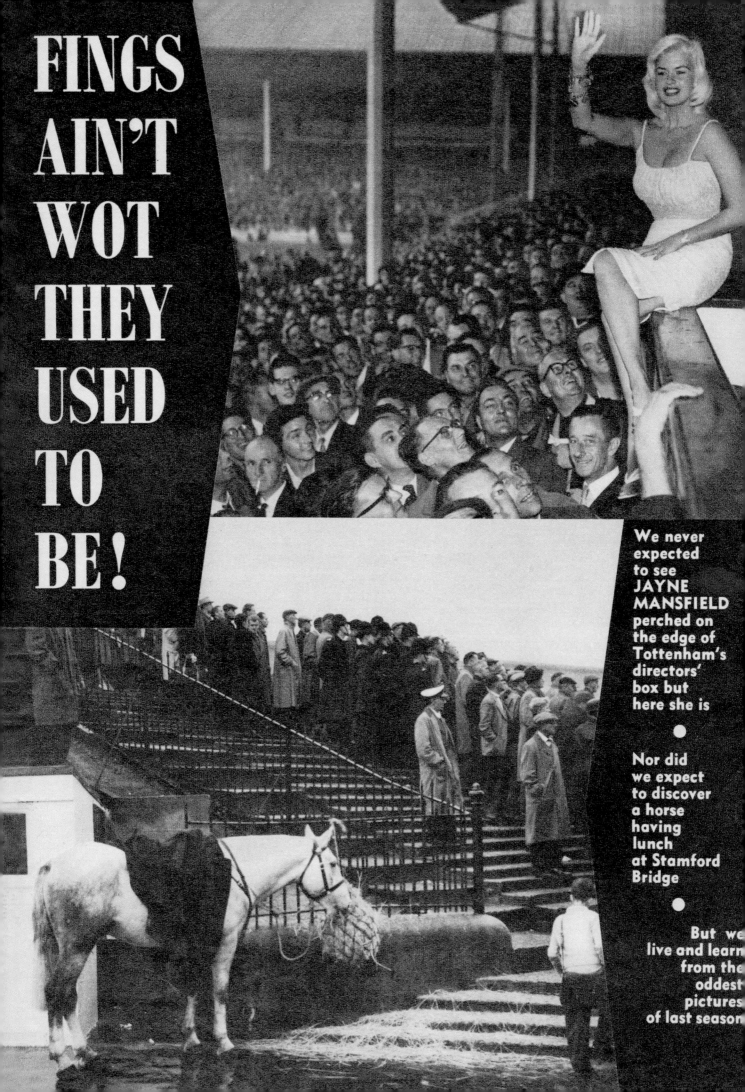

FINGS AIN'T WOT THEY USED TO BE!

We never expected to see JAYNE MANSFIELD perched on the edge of Tottenham's directors' box but here she is

•

Nor did we expect to discover a horse having lunch at Stamford Bridge

•

But we live and learn from the oddest pictures of last season

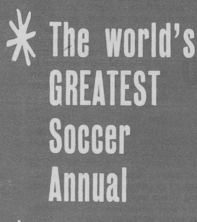

IT'S SELLING OUT FAST
... so get your copy NOW

DON'T RISK DISAPPOINTMENT

* The world's GREATEST Soccer Annual

* Packed with wonderful pictures

CHARLES BUCHAN'S 1961-62

SOCCER GIFT BOOK

from all bookshops and newsagents

In case of difficulty write to Charles Buchan's Publications Ltd., 161-166, Fleet Street, E.C.4

CLUB LETTER

by LESLIE YATES

161-166
Fleet Street,
London, E.C.4.

Dear Fellow-Members,

Whatever claims may be made for the British in Soccer there is one which none can dispute: that our crowds are the best-behaved in the world. We take pride in that fact.

At Ibrox or Molineux, Old Trafford or Ninian Park, we make as much noise as any, are as fiercely critical, certainly more knowledgeable. Saturday afternoon enthusiasm is often a good outlet valve for what may have been pent up during the rest of the week.

But there IS a limit to it and that has been grossly exceeded by the thoughtless practice of invading the pitch to acclaim a goal scored in a high-tension match, like a Cup-tie.

And regretfully the biggest culprits are the youngsters.

It is now a common practice to see hordes of boys pour on to the pitch at the end of a game. It is caused by youthful exuberance. It is still wrong.

The police and club stewards have quite enough to do with their normal task of keeping things in order. The task of clearing a pitch of people after a game should not be added to it. They certainly should not have to do so in the course of a match.

Besides damaging the pitch these cavorting youngsters are an ideal screen for any misguided fool who might feel he had a grievance against a player, or a match official.

That may sound like taking a too drastic view, but it could happen.

This invasion of the pitch is a practice which has sprung up post-war . . . we cannot remember it happening before. In the past two seasons we have had referees threatening, and rightly, to abandon games because of these intrusions. Clubs have been directed to make special appeals against the practice.

The "invaders" should spare a thought for others. Such foolish actions may deprive them of their pleasure. The surplus energy should be more wholesomely employed.

Sincerely yours,
THE EDITORS

"**P**AY PACKET" is a vanishing phrase in big football. Many players are now paid so highly they receive monthly cheques, or direct payments are made into their bank accounts.

Arsenal are among the clubs who credit the players' bank accounts. But to George Swindin, their manager, there is nothing novel about it.

"When I was a young player with Bradford City, in the early thirties, our wages were paid direct into the bank each week," he said.

This system was adopted by the Yorkshire club to encourage players to save.

Now it enables clubs to avoid the handling of thick wads of bank-notes!

In all divisions

LINDY DELAPENHA, the Mansfield Town inside-right, has been in League football since 1948. He comes from Jamaica and learned his Soccer on the sands at Kingston.

He signed for Portsmouth after leaving the R.A.F., but most of his career has been with Middlesbrough.

Delapenha moved from Portsmouth to Middlesbrough in 1950. In the summer of 1958 he went to Mansfield and has now played in all four divisions of the Football League.

TRANSFERS have been completed in some peculiar places—sometimes in dressing-rooms, sometimes on railway stations.

Setting with a difference for a transfer was that of right-winger Jimmy Campbell, from West Bromwich Albion to Portsmouth, during the summer.

"I signed Campbell in the car park outside Southampton's ground," says manager Freddie Cox.

"I had arranged to meet Gordon Clark, Albion's manager, and Jimmy at Southampton Central Station. But as Gordon also wanted to call on the Southampton club, we drove to the Dell.

"While he was in Southampton's office, I signed on Campbell outside the ground."

Worth a goal

"**W**E should have one of the best home records in the League," says Alec Stock, manager of Queen's Park Rangers. "A pitch like ours should always be worth a goal start."

Rangers' pitch is one of the smallest in the League, and most visiting teams take a little time to get used to it.

Manager Stock speaks from first-hand experience. As a Rangers forward in pre-war days, he remembers how much extra ground he had to cover when playing away from home.

BILL LANE, Brighton and Hove Albion manager, will never forget the first time he saw Dave Hollins, his first-choice goalkeeper. It was in the kitchen of the Hollins family, at Merrow, near Guildford.

Bill went there to sign left-winger Roy Hollins. While talking to Roy, the player's 11-year-old brother, Dave, walked in.

"I'd like to be your goalkeeper one day," piped up young Dave.

A few years later his wish came true. And this season he has played for the Welsh Under-23 team.

All-rounder

MR. AUBREY MOORE, the Football League referee from Lowestoft, keeps fit during the summer by playing lawn tennis and cricket.

He plays regularly for Kirkley Cricket Club, and has represented Suffolk County at lawn tennis.

Mr. Moore, who lives in a house overlooking the sea, trains on the beach during the football season.

On religious grounds he declines matches on Good Fridays.

IN launching the Port Vale Social Club, the Burslem club have taken a leaf out of the Continental book. Vale Park is now more than a football ground. It is also a centre for social entertainment, and keeps the supporters of Vale in touch throughout the summer.

The new social club is on the site of the old gymnasium. Steward is Billy Russell, pre-war Chelsea right-half, and father of the Sheffield United inside-forward.

Selected from 1959–62

No spectator

ALTHOUGH Charlie Hurley, Sunderland's Eire international centre-half, was keen on playing Soccer from an early age, he saw only one big match before becoming a professional with Millwall.

Charlie remembers the game well. He travelled from his home at Rainham, Essex, to see Spurs play Wolves at Tottenham.

Spurs were then enjoying a great era of prosperity, with their push-and-run style of play, under the management of Arthur Rowe.

Hurley cannot explain it, but he admits that apart from that isolated match, he felt no urge to watch big football.

Youths only

THE young players on the books of West Bromwich Albion are given plenty of coaching, but the senior professionals are left alone.

Gordon Clark, the West Bromwich manager, sees no useful purpose in coaching experienced players.

"More harm than good can be done," he says. *"Most professionals know their weaknesses, and try to correct them themselves.*

"With teenage players it is a different matter. They can often be moulded on the right lines if taken in hand early enough."

SANDY KENNON, Norwich City's South African goalkeeper, is going strong this summer with his four-piece band. Known as Sandy Kennon and his Blazes, the band comprises piano, bass, drums and guitar.

"We don't go in for rock and roll, but popular modern music is our line," says Kennon, who sings with the band.

The band fulfil engagements most Wednesday and Saturday evenings. They travel all over Norfolk, and sometimes into Suffolk.

SOUTHEND UNITED'S supporters are making themselves heard again this season. Their battle-cry "Up the Blues" had encouraged the team from the early days of the club's existence, until last year. Then Southend changed their blue shirts for an all-white strip.

Yelling "Up the Whites" did not come naturally to the Southend crowd, so this season the club have gone back to blue.

It was almost certainly coincidental, but Southend had a poor playing record in their one season as a white-shirted team.

SPURS have an unusual wall ornament in the tunnel leading to the dressing-rooms at White Hart-lane.

It is a name-plate, 'Tottenham Hotspur', which was removed from the railway engine of that name when it was scrapped at Doncaster in December, 1958.

This was one of several old London and North Eastern Railway engines named after League football clubs.

The 'Tottenham Hotspur' locomotive was christened in May, 1937, by the late Mr. Charles Roberts, Spurs' chairman for many years, at Hoe Street Station, Walthamstow.

ALTHOUGH Manchester United don't hesitate to enter the transfer market for players of established reputation, they continue to produce top-notchers for their own nursery.

An outstanding case is Norbet Stiles, who has won golden opinions by his skilful play at right-half.

Stiles—known as "Nobby"—is a local product who played for Manchester and England Schoolboys.

He is yet another in the impressive line of wing-halves developed by Matt Busby, United's manager.

CONWAY SMITH, the Halifax Town inside-right, has an unusual off-field occupation. He helps in the breeding of mice and guinea-pigs at a farm in Huddersfield for laboratory research.

Smith, a part-timer with Halifax, also helps his mother to run a confectionery shop in Huddersfield.

MARK LAZARUS, Wolves' outside-right, comes from a boxing family. His brothers Harry and Lew made a name in the ring under the name of Lazar.

Mark also tried his hand at boxing, but failed to make much headway. Football came a lot more naturally to him.

Lazarus started with Leyton Orient, who transferred him to Queen's Park Rangers early last season. He is the type of player who is always ready to listen to advice.

ONE of the best discoveries of last season was Billy Bremner, the 17-year-old Leeds United outside-right. Bremner turned professional for Leeds in December, and his inclusion in a team fighting against relegation was a tough introduction to big football.

A Scottish schoolboy international, he developed with Gowanhill Juniors, and Jack Taylor, the Leeds manager, believes Bremner will strike his best form next season.

The experience he gained in the closing weeks of last season removed some of the rough edges from his play.

WHAT is wrong with English football? Frank Broome, former England and Aston Villa forward, now managing Southend United, has a theory. He believes the poor standard of reserve-team football has caused the decline.

"In my playing days with Villa before the war, the reserve team was composed mainly of players who were knocking on the door of the first team," he said. "And the same applied to most clubs in the League.

"It meant that few first-team players could be sure of their places.

"Now it is a different matter. Few first-team players are being pushed to greater effort by good reserve players, and this has led inevitably to a lowering of the general standard."

Lack of financial incentive is the probable explanation. Fewer young players are prepared to make a career of Soccer unless they can have a senior place.

ALAS, POOR ACCRINGTON!

by John Macadam

THE day of the New Deal for football is marked upon the calendar. It was decided by the defection of Accrington Stanley F.C., who looked around, counted their blessings and decided there were not enough.

Like other unfavoured clubs, particularly in the North of England, Accrington Stanley were plugging away and losing a lot of money in so doing.

They were £60,000 in debt when their directors decided to call it a day, and my bet is that other clubs in the same unfortunate position are going to come to the same conclusion.

Gillingham, Exeter City, Chester and Hartlepools all disclaimed any fear of the future but the plain fact is that that fear hangs heavily over the heads of many of the lowly clubs of the Football League whose administrators are now face to face with the very problem from which they are wont to avert an anxious eye.

The Football League is the one-eyed man in the country of the blind, but, alas, it is not King. It fumbles around without authority.

The Football League is one-eyed in several things. It is one-eyed in its addiction to the abortive League Cup.

It thought it could borrow from the Scots and make a success of this pale imitation of the Association's great competition, but the League clubs do not like it; it is in fact an embarrassment to them.

The crowds do not like it and abstain from these matches by the many thousand. In fact, First Division clubs have the humiliation of performing these Cup matches before Third and Fourth Division-sized audiences.

The players are even less inclined to attend these Cup affairs which bring them in scant cash, and expose them to the possibility of serious injuries from minor encounters.

In other words, every match is a reserve match in this Cup that nobody cheers.

Well, if the League can be as one-eyed as this, and in many other things which one could well mention but decently does not, then who are they to stop the rot which Accrington Stanley have started?

Money has begun to dictate in football, and only money at the gate will keep the game on a level keel.

The Welfare State, racing, the repellent, phoney, all-in wrestling and snatches of football highlights tempt a lot of people to stay away from their local football grounds, particularly humble ones like Accrington Stanley, to watch the great outside world of sport on television.

A man and his dog—and the end of Accrington Stanley as a Football League club. Cold, desolate, empty, heartbreaking, for this groundsman and everyone else.

and the others in the same breath as you would talk of Tottenham, Burnley, Manchester United, Benfica, Real Madrid.

World-wide Soccer has left far behind the tram tracks of Accrington to move off to the jet age in which a World Football League is not so far away.

Don't forget that we now have at the hub of world Soccer affairs, as President of FIFA, the figure of Sir Stanley Rous—not to be confused in any way with Accrington Stanley—who has always been the great visionary of Soccer, and sees the game as what it is.

He envisages it as a world game and not

FROM NOW ON IT IS...

The survival of the fittest

You cannot blame these absentees. Too long has the Football League geared its speed of progress to the Accrington Stanleys.

Such an attitude is understandable in the Football Association who are steeped in tradition, but it does not sit easily on the shoulders of such characters—successful businessmen—as John Moores and Bob Lord, of Everton and Burnley respectively.

These men are realists, they are men of Twentieth Century football and they will shed few crocodile tears over the departure of Accrington Stanley and all the other small-time clubs who will assuredly follow them into obscurity because they cannot keep pace with the big-money aspect of modern football.

You cannot talk of Accrington Stanley, Gillingham, Exeter, Torquay, Hartlepools

something that dwells in the back streets and the open lots. In fact, only the best is good enough—and I am afraid that only the best can survive.

So, with the deepest regret, Accrington Stanley must go and must be followed by all the other lagging clubs.

They are the heavy brake on the natural progress which will take the Football League into a realist world in which football will be a truly global competition, and in which British teams like Burnley, Spurs, Manchester United, Everton and Glasgow Rangers and Dundee will all aspire to a level which is their right, and which the public are entitled to observe.

There is no point in playing the Canute act with this tide. Stanley have made it too obvious that it is irresistible.

▲ May 1962

SECOND DIVISION CHAMPIONS

LIVERPOOL   Standing—Milne, Yeats, Furnell, Moran, Byrne, Leishman. Sitting—Callaghan, Hunt, Ian St. John (with club mascot), Melia, A'Court.

FOURTH DIVISION CHAMPIONS

MILLWALL   Standing—Trainer J. Blackman, chairman F. Purser, Terry, Anderson (now Scunthorpe United), P. Brady, Davies, Gilchrist, McQuade, R. Brady, manager Ron Gray. Sitting—Obeney, Townend, Burridge (now Crystal Palace), Jones, Broadfoot.

SCOTTISH CUP WINNERS

GLASGOW RANGERS   Wilson, McKinnon, Baxter, Millar, Caldow (holding the Cup), Brand, Shearer, McMillan, Ritchie, Davis, Henderson (crouching).

▲ August 1962 | August 1962 | August 1962

HONOURS 1959-62

1959-60
Division 1 Burnley
Division 2 Aston Villa
Division 3 Southampton
Division 4 Walsall

Scottish 1 Heart of Midlothian
Scottish 2 St Johnstone

FA Cup Wolverhampton Wanderers
Scottish Cup Rangers
Amateur Cup Hendon

Charles Buchan's Best XI Ron Springett
(Sheff Wed), Jimmy Armfield (Blackpool),
Ray Wilson (Huddersfield), Maurice Setters
(Man Utd), Peter Swan (Sheff Wed),
Dave Mackay (Spurs), John Connelly (Blackburn),
Peter Broadbent (Wolves), Joe Baker (Hibs),
Cliff Holton (Watford), Peter McParland (Villa)
Manager Joe Mercer (Villa)

European Cup Real Madrid
Inter Cities Fairs Cup Barcelona
European Championships USSR

1960-61
Division 1 Tottenham Hotspur
Division 2 Ipswich Town
Division 3 Bury
Division 4 Peterborough United

Scottish 1 Rangers
Scottish 2 Stirling Albion

FA Cup Tottenham Hotspur
League Cup Aston Villa
Scottish Cup Dunfermline
Amateur Cup Walthamstow Avenue

CBFM Readers' Top Ten Players
1. Johnny Haynes (Fulham)
2. Danny Blanchflower (Spurs) 3. Jimmy Greaves
(Chelsea) 4. Dave Mackay (Spurs) 5. Cliff Jones
(Spurs) 6. Bobby Charlton (Man Utd)
7. Jimmy Armfield (Blackpool) 8. Denis Law
(Man City) 9. Jimmy McIlroy (Burnley)
10. Ron Springett (Sheff Wed)
European Cup Benfica
Cup Winners' Cup Fiorentina
Inter Cities Fairs Cup Roma

1961-62
Division 1 Ipswich Town
Division 2 Liverpool *(top)*
Division 3 Portsmouth
Division 4 Millwall *(centre)*

Scottish 1 Dundee
Scottish 2 Clyde

FA Cup Tottenham Hotspur
League Cup Norwich City
Scottish Cup Rangers *(bottom)*
Amateur Cup Crook Town

CBFM Readers' Top Ten Players
1. Johnny Haynes (Fulham) 2. Ron Springett
(Sheff Wed) 3. Jimmy Adamson (Burnley)
4. Jimmy Greaves (Spurs) 5. Danny Blanchflower
(Spurs) 6. Dave Mackay (Spurs) 7. Ray Crawford
(Ipswich) 8. Cliff Jones (Spurs) 9. Ron Flowers
(Wolves) 10. Jimmy McIlroy (Burnley)

European Cup Benfica
Cup Winners' Cup Atletico Madrid
Inter Cities Fairs Cup Valencia
World Cup Brazil

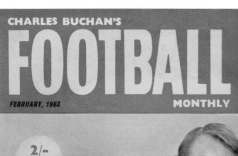

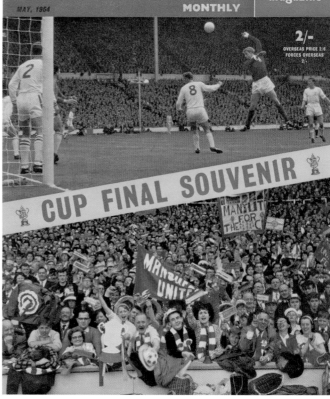

CHARLES BUCHAN'S

FOOTBALL

MONTHLY

The World's Greatest Soccer Magazine

FEBRUARY, 1963

2/-
OVERSEAS PRICE 2/6
FORCES OVERSEAS
2/-

CALVIN PALMER
Nottingham Forest

CHARLES BUCHAN'S

FOOTBALL

MONTHLY

The World's Greatest Soccer Magazine

MAY, 1964

2/-
OVERSEAS PRICE 2/6
FORCES OVERSEAS
2/-

CUP FINAL SOUVENIR

CHARLES BUCHAN'S

FOOTBALL

MONTHLY

The World's Greatest Soccer Magazine

JUNE, 1963

2/-
OVERSEAS PRICE 2/6
FORCES OVERSEAS 2/-

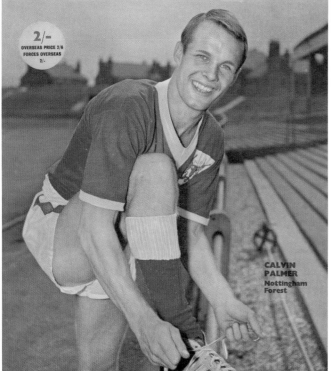

CUP FINAL SOUVENIR

CHARLES BUCHAN'S

FOOTBALL

MONTHLY

The World's Greatest Soccer Magazine

SEPTEMBER, 1964

2/-
OVERSEAS PRICE 2/6
FORCES OVERSEAS 2

JOHNNY HAYNES... *Does England need him?*

CHARLES BUCHAN'S
FOOTBALL
MONTHLY
The World's Greatest Soccer Magazine
NOVEMBER, 1964
2/-
OVERSEAS PRICE 2/6
FORCES OVERSEAS 2/-
PETER THOMPSON
Liverpool

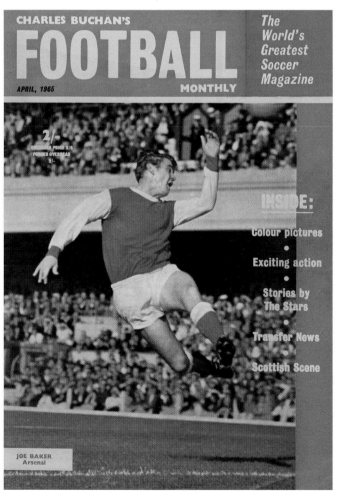

CHARLES BUCHAN'S
FOOTBALL
MONTHLY
The World's Greatest Soccer Magazine
APRIL, 1965
2/-
OVERSEAS PRICE 2/6
FORCES OVERSEAS 2/-
INSIDE:
Colour pictures
•
Exciting action
•
Stories by The Stars
•
Transfer News
•
Scottish Scene
JOE BAKER
Arsenal

1962-65

A bumper 64 page issue of *Charles Buchan's Football Monthly*, now priced 2s, welcomes Oxford United to the Fourth Division, while League Secretary Alan Hardaker warns that following a spate of pitch invasions and bottle throwing incidents 'there seems to be a dangerous element creeping into the game'. Even so he hopes that Britain is still a long way from Continental and South American-style barbed wire perimeter fences.

Nuclear confrontation is averted by resolution of the Cuban missile crisis. A late-night revue called *That Was The Week That Was* brings political satire to British television. On the large screen, Sean Connery makes his debut as Agent 007.

Pat Collins reports that England's new boss, Alf Ramsey, accepted the post only after insisting on his right to pick the team 'without worrying about the recommendations of an over-blown selection committee'.

England's subsequent 2-1 defeat by Scotland at Wembley in April 1963 is described as 'the worst England team I have ever seen'.

A newly appointed Pools Panel is kept busy as over 400 League and Cup matches are postponed during the Big Freeze of early 1963. Dr Beeching announces swingeing cuts to Britain's rail network. The Beatles gain their first Number One. Mods and Rockers go on the rampage at south coast resorts. War minister John Profumo resigns over his dalliance with Christine Keeler.

Tottenham are the first British team to win a European trophy, beating Atletico Madrid 5-1 in the Cup Winners Cup. Dundee reach the European Cup semi-finals.

Football's Retain and Transfer system is ruled illegal after George Eastham wins his test case against Newcastle United. Harold Wilson leads Labour back into power. US president John Kennedy is shot in Dallas. Nelson Mandela starts a life sentence on Robben Island. Tottenham's John White is killed by lightning on an Enfield golf course. *The Sun* newspaper is launched.

At Coventry, new manager Jimmy Hill unleashes a Sky Blue revolution. Disc jockeys entertain the crowds. A new stand with restaurant, saunas and bowling alley is planned. Don Revie, manager of Second Division champions Leeds, defends his team against accusations of rough tactics.

Pat Collins predicts a European Superleague by the 1970s. 'Clubs like Everton and Manchester United will not foot £100,000 transfer bills solely for the possible rewards an English season might bring.'

In August 1964 the new BBC 2 channel broadcasts an experimental programme called *Match of the Day*, featuring highlights of Liverpool v Arsenal. Available only in London, it attracts just 20,000 viewers.

Peter Swan, Tony Kay and David Layne are exposed by *The People* for having conspired to fix a Sheffield Wednesday match as part of a betting ring. The trio are banned, while the ringleader, former Charlton player Jimmy Gauld, receives a four year jail sentence.

'Never has there been such ferment and upheaval,' comments the magazine in February 1965. 'Players against referees, managers against the FA, directors against officialdom.' Attendances have dropped by 20 million since the post war boom. 'As the squabbling gets louder the raft sinks lower...'

Fifty year old Stanley Matthews plays his last game, for Stoke, and is the first footballer to be knighted.

Although it has been known since 1960 that England is to stage the 1966 World Cup, only in mid 1965 is financial support forthcoming. Sir John Lang admits, 'I don't think Her Majesty's Government were aware of the dates until recently. At least we've had nothing official about it.'

You are wishing for the moon, Mr. Richards!

by
PAT
COLLINS

TO make a better showing in the World Cup of 1966, right here in our own backyard, England must, apparently, do the following: sack Winterbottom; sack Haynes; make England players more dedicated; keep them together longer; bring in a League club manager, or managers; let Stanley Matthews and Tom Finney take charge of the international sides.

ALSO, AS MR. JOE RICHARDS SAYS, PUT COUNTRY BEFORE CLUB.

Don't stop me if you have heard any or all of this before. It's the remark from the League President-cum-Chairman of the England selectors which makes me smile.

For on the day we were wondering about the news from Rancagua and England's fate against the tough Argentinians, I was smog-bound in the thick haze of cigar and cigarette smoke which hung over the League's A.G.M. in London.

Maybe it had no real part in the business on hand—club business—but I thought it would have been nice to hear a well-wisher there make some goodwill comment about England's game, to show that the gathering was in Chile in spirit, at least.

But it was not given a thought. And in the two hours of talk . . . procedure, plaint and proposal . . . not a syllable was uttered about improving England's football, from the playing or watching angle.

The only time England were mentioned there was a smug satisfaction that the F.A. had agreed to pay the wages of players on representative duty. Then followed a request for the League to do likewise for inter-League games!

Mr. Bob Lord, of Burnley, and Mr. John Moores, the Everton chairman, almost a double-act in which they were continually bobbing up and down, teamed-up on the above.

Country before club? I wonder if they realise how their clubs benefit DIRECTLY from calls which put their players in the "star" class.

Willingly or otherwise, clubs have accepted this "star" system, as shown by the different pay scales which now operate. It is on the international and representative field that names are made, not at Turf Moor, Goodison, Molineux, or anywhere else.

Last season, the Football League lost 639,852 customers. We may sometimes sigh that there are not more personalities in the game, but the international-tag does help to boost gates, especially in away games. However, as always, the clubs want it both ways.

My thoughts went back to that League meeting when I heard of the play-safe, defensive games which marred the World Cup as a spectacle in Chile. For who could be more cautious than English League clubs?

Even those sobering figures of a further attendance slump could not make them take the plunge and try the four-up and four-down proposal of the Management Committee. This proposed broadening of the competition may not be entirely the magic wand needed to bring back the crowds, but it DOES merit a trial.

Perhaps the play-safe clubs knew they were flouting the hopes of many in turning it down, and that would explain the decision to hide their votes under the cloak of the secret ballot, a decision which justly angered Mr. Richards.

I don't see any patriotic lead coming from League clubs to aid England's international cause. It will still be "club before country" come what may.

One of the things I regret—while appreciating what is behind it—is the first opposition to the F.A.'s decision to let clubs sign youngsters still at school. England have envied other countries who have taken boys from the cradle and brought them along in a club social atmosphere. Might not the idea work here? I feel that with earlier coaching and training, England—and Scotland, Ireland and Wales—could go a long way towards turning out more athletic youngsters, particularly in the way of speeding them up. For one of the things I believe we most lack in our British game is speed. It shows at top-level competition.

I don't want a brood of sprinters. I know there is not much point in moving fast without the ball. But one of the reasons why Jimmy Armfield is among the best full-backs in the world is his speed. He goes where he wants to, fast. And he has an attacking flair because he has the speed to recover.

It is also because of his speed that I would have liked to have seen John Connelly on England's right wing in Chile.

The Continentals often score over England where all else is equal, when pace, just pure pace, comes into the reckoning.

If they are taken at an earlier age it should be possible to sharpen up the youngsters. The skills, ball control, heading and the rest, are matters for later coaching.

Two final thoughts on the last World Cup. First, wing-half Ron Flowers, with two penalties, was England's top-scorer—the biggest indictment of a woe-begone attack.

Second, the strange twist by the men on the spot when they acclaimed Bobby Charlton as England's only world-class forward. Just a few weeks before he left for Chile the majority were of the opinion that he was lucky to be in the England side.

Strange, isn't it?

▲ August 1962

GETTING AROUND

with PETER MORRIS

OUR REFEREES ARE THE BEST

—AND IF THEY ARE GETTING TOUGHER THEN I AM ALL FOR IT

ALTHOUGH British referees are indisputedly the best in the world, our treatment of, and attitude to, them on the domestic scene baffles me.

The Football Association issued pre-season instructions to their referees to "stand no nonsense". And referees, who always yearned for official backing like that, have been "standing no nonsense"—rightly so.

The result? Forty players ordered off (as I write) in English Soccer and the names taken of 400. Not all those offenders are within the Football League, but certainly all senior professional Soccer in England is covered.

This represents a considerable increase on punishments doled out at the same period last year. It suggests that the great mass of petty offenders and "tough eggs", alike, are being told firmly where they get off—literally so.

But does the rest of the world of football approve of the big clean-up? Not on your life!

Referees, always wrong in the mind of some people, are now bigger villains than ever . . . because they are doing their jobs efficiently!

Three times this season I saw matches in which the referee INSISTED that defenders stand off the regulation ten yards for free kicks. He was booed and slow handclapped by spectators apparently unaware of the rule, and heckled by players who are ignorant, seemingly, of the rules of the game which gives them a fat living.

Not so long ago I was at a Midlands match in which there were literally dozens of nasty little fouls, childish displays of bad temper, blows thrown by some players at their opponents.

Two players were ordered off; two had their names taken and the same should have happened to at least one other, in my opinion.

Now I know there are bad referees,

"homers" and so on. I know, too, that weak or indecisive refereeing can ruin a match; irritating players and spectators alike.

After this particular brawl, I thought the officials and players of both clubs would have been a little crestfallen. But, no!

Listening to the after-match talk, you would have thought that the referee (efficient, strong-minded, perhaps erring slightly on the over-fussy side) was the biggest rogue in the whole sorry business.

Managers who should have known better defended their players with tongue in cheek. Directors were over-ready to lay the blame on a referee who had done no more (and no less) than his duty.

The two players who had been sent off later apologised to each other for losing their heads in the heat of the moment. I

"I must warn you, ref., I am a fully paid-up member—and if it's one off, it's all off!"

wonder if either of them thought of begging the referee's pardon?

It is all too easy to parrot cry: "refereeing is getting worse." Old-stagers who insist that Jack Howcroft and his like never had this trouble, forget, conveniently, that whistlers kept the peace in those halcyon days BECAUSE they *were* tough. And when players did get marching orders, they received far heavier penalties than today.

So there you are! There has been a lot of drivel talked by responsible persons, slandering referees in general.

But I say: "referees—well done . . . keep it up for the good of the game."

THE big money of professional Soccer has carried the game into "A Career For Your Boy" class and may even get into the classified columns of those quality newspapers which go with bowlers and umbrellas.

I forecast that one effect of this will result in a surge in the recruitment of many more talented grammar schoolboys, "red brick university" graduates and even, possibly, some public schoolboys.

This will be a wonderful thing for the game. The higher degree of intelligence gained MUST automatically raise standards of play.

It is significant that Danny Blanchflower and Bill Slater, two of the post-war period's most accomplished players, are both university graduates; thai Jimmy Armfield, the new England skipper, is a product of one of the north's better grammar schools.

MY moan (October) about the distribution of F.A. Cup Final tickets brought a swift response from the "We Want Wembley" movement—a band of determined fans who hope to make the F.A. Cup Final Committee see the error of their ways.

Committee member Mike Curly informs me that more demonstrations are planned outside Lancaster Gate following a previous informal discussion with F.A. official, Mr. E. B. Miller, who had promised to put forward the committee's views to the right quarter.

Major Harry Wilson Keys, forthright chairman of West Bromwich Albion F.C., also put forward a proposal that in future the Cup Finalists' quota should be increased from 15,000 to 20,000. It was heavily defeated.

The "We Want Wembley" movement is bound to grow. Eventually, the F.A. cannot help but bow to the inevitable and start looking after the real fans instead of an (out-dated) Establishment which clutters up valuable space at Wembley.

BOBBY MOORE, West Ham and England

ARTHUR ROWLEY

"Football Monthly" presents this page as a tribute to ARTHUR ROWLEY. On September 17, at Millwall, he equalled the British League goal-scoring record of Jimmy McGrory when he scored his 410th goal. On September 26 he broke the record at Shrewsbury. This is how he equalled the record:

Season		Games	Goals	Club
1946-47	...	2	0	West Brom
1947-48	...	21	4	,,
1948-49	...	1	0	,,
1948-49	...	22	19	Fulham
1949-50	...	34	8	,,
1950-51	...	39	28	Leicester
1951-52	...	42	38	,,
1952-53	...	41	39	,,
1953-54	...	42	30	,,
1954-55	...	36	23	,,
1955-56	...	36	29	,,
1956-57	...	42	44	,,
1957-58	...	25	20	,,
1958-59	...	43	38	Shrewsbury
1959-60	...	41	32	,,
1960-61	...	40	28	,,
1961-62	...	41	23	,,
1962-63	...	9	7	,,
		557	**410**	

GEORGE ARTHUR ROWLEY, a 14-stone native of Staffordshire, is a man of power and purpose. Also a man of his word. For, when on September 26, beneath Shrewsbury Town's lights, he set up a British League goal-scoring record, he did it with his right foot. The one they said was only to stand on, a "swinger".

Just before the interval big Arthur (the George is silent in Soccer), hammered home a 25-yarder against Millwall. It was his 411th goal, and it broke the 24-year-old record set by dapper Jimmy McGrory (410), now managing Celtic.

And it lifted the 36-year-old football wanderer farther above the great goal-getters like Hughie Gallacher (386), "Dixie" Dean (379), Hugh Ferguson (362) and Steve Bloomer (352).

Player-manager Rowley is a record-maker, not a record-keeper. This burly scoring machine who has moved around by way of Manchester United, West Bromwich, Fulham, Leicester and so to Shrewsbury, has no memory of the goal which started it all and shrugs off the rest by saying: "I'm just the fellow who finishes off moves by the others."

When he got his 410th goal on September 17, to equal McGrory—also against Millwall—he remarked: "Good, now we're two up". That goal also came from his right, the "swinger".

It prompted one of the few personal references to the feat which set everybody talking . . . "I shall try to get the record the same way, just so they can't say I'm left-footed only."

He did just that.

He is one of three footballing brothers from Wolverhampton. The local League club—more alive than most to talent on their own doorstep—did not notice the Rowleys. And although Manchester United saw the glint of talent in elder brother Jack, and fashioned him for Cup, League and international honours, they let young Arthur, an amateur with the club, move on.

His goals brought promotion to Fulham, Leicester City (twice) and then Shrewsbury Town.

But, though he is setting the target still higher for the goal-getters to come, any goals he gets these days are designed to help Town's fortunes—not to bolster Arthur Rowley's stock.

P.C.

GOAL-SNATCHER IN-CHIEF

◄ September 1963 | December 1962 ▲

... the road with a record

it turned out...

KEN BROWN
LES and
DENNIS ALLEN
DAVE CONEY
DICK WALKER
AND ME

by TERRY VENABLES
Chelsea

IT is a fair journey from Dagenham to Tottenham when you are a schoolboy. But I made the trip regularly by train. For I was a Spurs supporter. And for two seasons, I missed hardly one first-team match at White Hart Lane.

There was one Spurs player in particular who captivated me; entertainment value apart, it was a sheer education to watch him perform. He was Danny Blanchflower. What a model for any budding young wing-half!

In watching Danny I realised that Soccer is indeed an art. His cultured play and powerful influence on the rest of Spurs' team were an inspiration to me.

I was really "sent" by Spurs in those days. Yet when the time came for me to join a big club, I preferred Chelsea.

Spurs were interested, but I was looking ahead. Because of Spurs' glittering array of talent I felt opportunity might be limited for me at White Hart Lane.

Prospects of an early chance at Chelsea seemed brighter. And no eager young player wants to lose time in getting into the act.

There was another reason for my leaning to Chelsea. Bert Murray and Alan Harris, who had played in the England Boys team with me, had already joined the club. That meant I would be among old friends from the moment I arrived at Stamford Bridge.

As a Chelsea junior I came under the supervision of Dick Foss—a stroke of luck.

Dick is the ideal type to rub the rough edges off a young player. And as he had played at wing-half for Chelsea, I was given expert instruction on the special needs of my own position.

I think I can say I was useful on the ball in those early days with Chelsea, but my defensive qualities left something to be desired. I thought too much about attacking. To do a wing-half's job properly I had to sharpen my tackling.

Dick Foss did a lot to remedy this defect in my play. And I have also had a lot of valuable instruction from Tommy Docherty, our manager, on the same point.

Anyone who saw Tommy play knows how strongly he tackled. I've been more than glad to listen to him.

I was right in guessing I would get an early chance with Chelsea. I made my League debut before I was old enough to turn professional, in a First Division match at West Ham in February, 1960. We lost 4—2, and I did not have a particularly good game.

But it gave me the taste of big-match atmosphere. As a League player I had "arrived". Strange that my debut should be at West Ham, the League ground nearest to my home!

Environment has a lot to do with the urge to make good in Soccer. Here again I was lucky. I come from Bonham Road, Dagenham. And football-wise, that's a road with a record.

Ken Brown, West Ham's English international centre-half; the brothers Les and Dennis Allen, now with Spurs and Reading respectively; and Dave Coney, Bedford's right-back, all come from there.

I am younger than these players, but I used to play in the local park with them. I think my own development was speeded by playing among older boys who had the ability to make the professional grade.

Dick Walker, the old West Ham centre-half, now scouting for Spurs, also comes from Bonham Road. He used to watch us kicking about, and was always ready to pass on the tips.

Football is full of thrills and memorable occasions. I think the greatest moment of my Soccer life was when I first stepped out at Wembley for England Boys against Scotland.

The crowd was around 90,000, and to me, a schoolboy, it all seemed fantastic. I felt overwhelmed by the occasion, but once the whistle had sounded I was too occupied with the match to give thought to the setting. We won 3—1.

My next biggest thrill? You don't have to think hard about that, do you? It was the night last season when we caned Portsmouth 7—0 in our final match to gain promotion to the First Division.

It was our biggest win for 52 years and I got a penalty goal. As you probably read in the newspapers at the time our supporters went wild with delight.

It had been a hard season for them as well as for us and I am glad we were able to reward them for their loyalty.

Now for the Spurs—and Stanley Matthews again!

▲ July 1963

by JIMMY BLOOMFIELD
Birmingham City

Cockney-born

footballers rarely

leave "the smoke",

but I did and I

say now . . .

LONDON? I DON'T MISS IT A BIT!

WHEN I read that stars like Peter Brabrook and Johnny Byrne refused to leave London when Provincial clubs were willing to pay big money for their transfers I recalled the time when the very idea of quitting "the smoke" also would have appalled me.

It has seemed to me that all the top players eventually were drawn to London clubs where the crowds and the glamour were supposed to be greater. Hughie Gallacher, Alex James, and in recent years, Danny Blanchflower, Dave Mackay and many others, seem to have proved the point.

Others, like Brabrook, not to mention Jimmy Greaves, of course, are "Cockney-born" footballers who would seem out of place outside the metropolis. I felt like that once.

I am London born-and-bred, and having learned my Soccer with the amateurs, Hayes, and then Brentford, I felt that I could do no better, and look no further, when I had the good fortune to be signed by Arsenal. Yet, now, here I am, away from London and enjoying my football better than ever in a city that was once completely alien to me and to my wife.

The point I am making is that it is a mistake to assume that all that is brightest and best (and happiest) in football is to be found only in the metropolis.

I have found it to be very different since I joined Birmingham City.

And I am not missing London a bit!

I had a great life with Arsenal for a long time. Things were not so bright there at the period when I moved, but it was still a wrench to leave Highbury.

The idea of playing for a Provincial club had never occurred to me. Quite frankly, I don't think it ever does to the majority of London-bred footballers. As I have said, the talent has always seemed to go to town from the North and the Midlands, rather than vice versa.

But for one Londoner, at least, a move north was more beneficial than I could have imagined.

There were differences, at first, of course. I made my début for Birmingham in London — against Tottenham at White Hart Lane. We were thrashed 6—0 by the League and Cup "double" side and as I waved my new team mates goodbye after the game, I wondered whether I had done the right thing after all.

Birmingham had paid a biggish fee for me and I realised that great things would be expected of me. But my first game in a blue shirt had not been a very auspicious occasion.

I need not have worried. I had a wonderful welcome when I appeared for the first time at St. Andrew's and I quickly realised that the Birmingham crowd were much more tolerant than at Highbury.

When the possibilities of my move to Birmingham had been put to me, I had thought at first that it would be a good idea still to live and train in London.

My wife, Suzy, changed my mind. She suggested that if we were to move, a complete break from London would be best. She was absolutely right.

I soon found that in Birmingham folk are friendlier, the supporters closer to you. And your name *meant* more to the ordinary terrace fan when you met him AWAY from the ground. Unless you are a star they forget you in five minutes in London.

There is more feeling for Birmingham City as a TEAM, representing England's second city. Local patriotism is much more pronounced than in London where they tend to go for personalities rather than the clubs.

Because of the lower cost of living, a First Division "regular" in Birmingham is generally better off than his London counterpart, although some of the Spurs players, I understand, seem to be in a wage class by themselves.

My form has improved considerably since I joined The Blues, although much of what I have learned about inside-forward play was taught to me by Ron Greenwood, now West Ham's manager, but coach at Arsenal for part of my time there.

I knew that I had been signed by Birmingham's manager, Gil Merrick, to do a definite job. And, apart from an aggravating spell when I was out for a few weeks with a broken forearm at one of the most vital stages of the 1961-62 campaign, I believe I have managed to do that job.

It was just when I had struck up a slick understanding with my speedy wing partner, Mike Hellawell, that I broke my forearm.

Soon afterwards, we were drawn at home to Spurs in the Cup. It was a match in which I would have dearly loved to have played. There was some talk that I might be fit, but I had to sit in the directors' box at St. Andrew's and watch one of the most thrilling Cup games I have ever seen.

After looking well-licked at one stage, The Blues fought back magnificently to level at 3—3, urged on by that fabulous St. Andrew's Cup anthem: "Keep Right On To The End Of The Road"—the song which took Birmingham through to Wembley in 1956.

But it wasn't enough this time. I was passed fit to play in the replay on the following Wednesday evening, but we lost and my Cup dreams faded.

But there is always another year . . . and another year after that!

▲ November 1962

OUCH!

You can almost hear the whistle of breath from Gerry Young, of Sheffield Wednesday. His stomach got in the way of this shot by team-mate Colin Dobson during the match with Manchester United.

Snapped against a massed, roaring background of Roker Park fans, Charlie Hurley (No. 5, striped shirt), heads past Gordon West, Denis Stevens and Brian Labone, to start a goal-scoring movement which put Everton out of the Cup.

SNOW ?

I had never seen the stuff . . .

and suddenly

I was asked to play in it!

by ALBERT JOHANNESON, Leeds United

WHEN I was at school in Johannesburg only one English club interested me—Manchester United. Even from that distance I was a great United fan. I didn't think of any other side—until the day I received an invitation to go to England to have a trial with Leeds United.

No one was more surprised than I was to receive that request. A career in English football had been a dream. I was full of envy when my pal, Gerry Francis, went off to Elland Road. It was Gerry who got me my chance.

Leeds didn't see me play until I arrived in England in January, 1960. They had acted on Gerry's recommendation.

It was a strange experience, moving from Johannesburg to Yorkshire, particularly as I landed here in an English winter. In those early weeks I felt I would never get used to this new life. Many times I wished I had stayed at home.

But now, in my third season here, I know I could not have made a happier choice. I have been made to feel at home and have been readily accepted.

The early days of settling in were the hardest. I had to go through all the early training stages, like any other young player, but everything seemed so different. And I felt it more because I had in my mind the fact that United had gone to a lot of expense to bring me over—I felt I just had to do well.

But all the time I was trying to get used to heavy pitches, matches in sludge and rain and, to crown it all, when I was told that my chance in the League team was at hand there was the threat of snow!

I had never seen the stuff, let alone think of playing in it.

The match was against Scunthorpe at Elland Road in April, 1960. I prayed that it would not take place.

What a crazy set-up! There was I, longing to get into the first team to make my mark, yet hoping that when the chance came it would be put back.

Nobody was more relieved than I when that game, due to be played on the Tuesday after the usual crowded Easter programme was ruled off. I played against Swansea a few days later, we got a draw, and I think —because I was so determined to do well— that it was just about the best game I have played so far.

I am now regarded as a winger, although most of my previous games were as an inside-forward. When training I had preferred playing out on the wing and that is how I changed my position. It suited the club.

Last season I suffered my first injury of any kind, a groin injury which put me out of action for three months.

It seemed to me that the trouble would never clear up and I felt pretty low about everything. I was not used to being inactive and found it hard to go for treatment—and to have to wait and wait.

It is great to be among the fine players here at Elland Road. They are a fine bunch and they help me a lot, particularly on match days.

I am a bundle of nerves on such days and I cannot relax until we go onto the pitch. It is there that the more experienced lads pass a few words here and there to make things easier for me.

Finally, I must give credit to two grand people who helped me to settle down—Mr. and Mrs. Winely, with whom I have had digs since I came here.

Gerry Francis was living with this kindly couple, and I shared with him. Even now, when he is a York City player, he stays with me. It is a home from home for us.

◄ January 1963 | April 1964 | ▲ November 1962

LEEDS UNITED : Standing:- Willie Bell, Paul Reaney, Fred Goodwin (now with Scunthorpe), Gary Sprake, Brian Williamson, Norman Hunter, Ian Lawson. Sitting:- John Giles, Billy Bremner, Jim Storrie, Bobby Collins, Don Weston, Jimmy Greenhoff, Jack Charlton. The Trophies:- The West Riding Cup and the Football League Second Division Championship Cup.

▲ March 1965

TOTTENHAM HOTSPUR : Standing—Baker, Allen, Norman, Brown, Henry, Smith, Mackay. Sitting—Medwin, Greaves, Blanchflower, White, Jones.

▲ May 1963

SHEFFIELD WEDNESDAY: Back row—Hardy, Johnson, McLaren, Hill, Griffin, Young. Centre row—O'Donnell, Wilkinson, Swan, Springett, Mac Anearney, Ellis, Layne. Front row—Finney, Holliday, Kay, Dobson, Fantham, Megson.

▲ November 1962

COVENTRY CITY: Back row—Kirby, Hudson, Wesson, Meeson, Mitten, Hill. Centre row—Barr, Smith, Kearns, Manager J. Hill, Sillett, Humphries, Newton. Front row—Farmer, Curtis, Hale, Bruck, Machin, Rees.

▲ November 1964

the game's the same . . .

Above, a scene at *White Hart Lane*. Thousands of the Tottenham faithful pack the terraces and stands to watch the ultra-sophisticated play of their favourites. This is football in the £100-a-week, Jaguar, class.

Not far away (see below) is a place where, for many top footballers, it all began—Hackney Marshes, a vast open space in East London where every Sunday 111 games are played on pitches so close to each other that spectators can watch several matches merely by turning their heads—and barking dogs are utterly confused by the number of balls to chase.

But whether at Tottenham or Old Trafford, in street, on waste land or marsh—the spirit of this great game is the same.

'He's a nice wee player,'
they said (about me),
'but too small'

I SHALL never forget the day I was transferred from Falkirk to Spurs. It was a big enough thrill to join such a famous club, but at that time—October, 1959—I was not to know what brilliant successes lay ahead.

I was in the Army at Berwick at the time and Tommy Younger, then managing Falkirk, telephoned to tell me to meet him in Glasgow.

I knew it was about a transfer, but it was not until several hours later that Tommy told me I was booked for Tottenham.

Naturally, I was delighted. And if I had known that the next three seasons would produce a Cup and League double, a further F.A. Cup triumph and then the winning of the European Cup-winners' Cup, I doubt if my hand would have been steady enough to sign the forms!

Things could have worked out a lot differently. In fact, there was a time when it seemed that the bright lights of Soccer were not for me.

At school back home in Musselburgh, I was an outside-left. I was very small. The wing, it seemed, was the safest place for me.

I remember people saying . . . "he's a nice wee player, but too small." Praise perhaps . . . but not very encouraging.

By the time I left school I was taller, but still very slight. I joined the Prestonpans Y.M.C.A. team and moved to inside-forward. It seemed I had the stamina for that position in spite of lack of size.

When I was playing for Bonnyrigg Rose big clubs began to show an interest.

Johnny Love, then managing Walsall, happened to be staying at a nearby mining village. Someone must have put a word in for me. Anyway, Johnny turned up at my home at a time when I was actually training in the lobby.

"Is your brother in?" he asked.

That tells you how small I was. The Walsall manager mistook me for a younger brother!

Once that little misunderstanding was put right he made me a really good offer. But the prospect, coming out of the blue like that, scared me a bit. My mother was out and I told him I could do nothing until I had consulted her. I was told I would hear again a few weeks later. But nothing happened.

It is strange how much can hinge upon so little. If my mother had been at home that day, I may have become a Walsall player.

There have been other might-have-beens in my football life. Motherwell gave me a run in the reserves against Queen of the South. We won 2—1, and I scored the first goal.

Bobby Ancell, Motherwell's manager, was

by
JOHN WHITE
Spurs and Scotland

willing to take me on the ground staff at Fir Park. But as he was running only two teams he could not guarantee me a game each week.

Much as I wanted to get on in football I was unwilling to sit on the sidelines for even the odd week in three. I wanted a regular game, so I stayed with Bonnyrigg.

Then there were Middlesbrough. Bob Dennison, then the club manager, had me down on trial; Alan Stenhouse, who later signed for Motherwell, came with me.

We played in the reserves. Again I scored. Mr. Dennison seemed pleased with me, but again I was told I was very small.

I left Ayresome Park with instructions to do plenty of walking and skipping, and get a good quota of sleep. I heard nothing more from Middlesbrough.

Looking back, I know these experiences —discouraging though they were at the time—were conditioning me to the topsy-turvydom of football. Progress was proving difficult . . . but it meant that recognition was all the sweeter when it came.

Alloa gave me my first big chance. And then I was transferred to Falkirk.

My movement up the Soccer scale had been gradual, but climbing steadily through the grades must have helped me. No step was too steep at a time when I was developing my game.

I had moved from juvenile to junior class in Scotland; a harder grade. Then came the move to the Scottish Second Division, where I had to compete with players of keener Soccer intelligence.

It is a good thing for a player to come up through smaller clubs. He learns to appreciate the luxury of playing for a really famous

club. The first thing I discovered on joining Spurs was how great it is to have first-class players around you.

Movement off the ball and creating space is an important part of an inside-forward's job. By playing in a top-class team my ability was sharpened.

Bill Nicholson, our manager, has told me this part of my play impressed him when he first watched me. At that time my play was instinctive, and I was not thinking deliberately of my movements.

Under his guidance, however, I have developed my "off-the-ball" play. He has made me realise how important it is.

So I now think about it. And if I am doing the wrong thing, I am quickly aware of it. This keeps me up to scratch.

In the old days in Scotland I was playing a type of game that came naturally to me. But often, I would lapse during a match because I was not conscious of the vital importance of taking up a correct position when a team-mate was playing the ball.

The set-up at Tottenham is out of this world. The training programme is carefully planned, and always interesting. And on a match day at White Hart Lane, with the vast crowd close to the pitch, the atmosphere is tremendous.

It is a great distinction to play for Spurs, and every member of the team gives all he has to retain that distinction.

There have been many wonderful moments in these past few seasons. But there are always fresh fields to conquer. My burning ambition is to help Spurs win the European Cup.

YOU have been warned!

by PAT COLLINS

THE words on the right were written in the September, 1962, issue of "Football Monthly" by Alan Hardaker, secretary of the Football League. And now, 15 months later?

There are barricades behind the Everton goals.

Elsewhere there are prowling plain-clothes detectives moving along the terraces . . . vigilantes being sought to report on miscreants they spot in the crowd . . . and police dogs patrolling round the pitch.

That is League football today in England.

Now the moats and wire fences all round the pitch may not much longer be the prerogative of the South Americans. When they come, then we shall need only the baton-twirling police and the fire-hoses . . . to bring us down to their standards.

It is shocking. Handfuls of hooligans spattered around League club grounds are holding something like half-a-million ordinary football followers to ransom.

Here a few bottles, there a maniac with a dart. Lunatics who vent their spleen with brawls on the terraces on grounds other than their own, idiots who throw toilet rolls on the pitch, yobbos who wreck excursion trains.

Put together, it makes a savage, sad story.

And put together like that it unfairly brands English Soccer fans as an undisciplined mob, ripe for the cage—like zoo animals.

Where do we start to apportion the blame, or to find the answer?

F.A. secretary Denis Follows is quoted as saying: "If spectators are to be asked to improve their behaviour on the terraces, then first there must be better behaviour down on the pitch.

"The players must put their house in order first."

'It is to be hoped that we are still a long way from the ultimate in Continental and South Americanism—a barbed wire fence!'

From Joe Richards, the League President, we hear: "I am certain the public at large is not responsible for this disgraceful behaviour.

"We must attack the unruly few who are bringing shame to Soccer throughout the country."

Players . . . SOME in the crowd. Others will accuse weak and inefficient referees. The truth is hard to get at. We are ALL in it some way or another.

An alarming number of players has already been sent off this season. But is the game dirtier than before? I don't think so, although it is more intense as much more hangs on the result.

Thank goodness referees have got tougher!

What IS happening is that we are getting too many Soccer prima donnas—players who cannot stand being penalised or who want every other tackle on themselves penalised—who show their feelings. Supporters then take their side and so the bad feeling mounts.

I would have every referee cut out arm-waving dissent by players as quickly and as ruthlessly as any verbally expressed dissatisfaction. There is too much of it these days.

And I would have suspensions and fines at least doubled, nay trebled, to hit guilty

parties right where it hurts most. Some of the punishment handed out has been ludicrous.

Players should not be suspended for days, but for matches.

When they, and their clubs, are hit that way they would think twice before going into tantrums.

The players AND the clubs could and should take the first steps towards better discipline. It is gamesmanship more than really vicious fouls which cause most upset.

I know that referees have been told to take a firm hand about it—for nothing upsets a crowd more—but clubs MUST give a lead to their players.

Mr. Richards speaks of the "unruly few". As yet they are but a few. But they are growing. Here is the hardest task of all . . . seeking out those rowdies.

The F.A. can close grounds for a period. Such action is harsh on the majority, the ordinary, sensible football fans. If a thug has no compunction about tossing a stone or a bottle he is hardly likely to be conscience-stricken about depriving others of their pleasure.

The closing-down of grounds is crude, rough justice, but nobody has yet come up with a better remedy.

There is no easy solution. The situation calls for everybody concerned with the game to look harder at himself to see where he can help to calm things down.

PLAYERS must cut out the theatricals, the dissensions and any bend-the-rules antics.

MANAGERS must give a lead and insist on a better code of field conduct from their teams.

REFEREES must punish even harder the slightest question of their authority so that the fans in turn will come to accept what is good for the game.

And YOU, the Soccer fan, can show a little more tolerance, a little less misguided partisanship.

The alternative could well be shredded Soccer-watching . . . through chicken-wire every week. And, perhaps, none at all on some Saturdays, at some grounds.

Something new in English football — barricades at Goodison Park.

▲ January 1964

▲ November 1962

SLAZENGER CHALLENGE 4-STAR

The finest football boot ever made in this country. Designed with European flair; made here by craftsmen; the Challenge 4-Star *outclasses the best Continental boots*. One reason: *it fits like a glove*; tough yet flexible leather grips and fits perfectly. Another reason: *the completely flat sole* — for absolutely certain balance, finest control.

Best leather, padded and lined tongue: **108/-**
Also available: 3-Star moulded rubber sole with screw-in studs: **79/6**
2-Star moulded multi-studded rubber sole: **61/3**

Soccer Supremacy

Slazenger
THE NAME TO PLAY WITH

SLAZENGER CHALLENGE 4-STAR

Superb ball from a famous range. It's tough, hand-sewn throughout; keeps its shape and size. A match-making ball.

Available in tan, white, orange or lemon laceless or laced with vaive bladder.

Slazenger
25
★★★★
CHALLENGE

▲ August 1962

JIM BAXTER IS NO. 1

Controversial Confident Casual

...a Master Footballer

by W. G. GALLAGHER

SCOTLAND'S player of the year? Unquestionably, in my opinion, the country's most controversial football operator, is Jim Baxter, left-half of Scotland and Rangers.

Reared in the pits of his native Fife—the Kingdom—he became a teenage senior with Raith Rovers, one of the many fine prospects signed by the club's manager, then Bert Herdman.

On joining Raith he came under the influence of international full-back Willie M'Naught, and that was a happy association for Baxter. Willie took the deepest interest in Jim and in a big way aided the youngster in the development of his natural skill.

He was wing-half with the Fife club, but Rangers, when they paid something in the region of £17,000 for him, had a notion he could be exploited at inside-forward.

But the No. 6 jersey was the one he liked best, the one in which he could be most successful.

He ousted the regular left-half Billy Stevenson—now with Liverpool—and proved he was easily Scotland's star performer in the position.

For many, many years my greatest among left-halves was Jimmy M'Mullan, Partick Thistle and Manchester City, one of our 1928 Wembley Wizards.

But now, if I were asked to pick a Scotland team to beat the world Baxter would be in to the omission of M'Mullan.

I believe that the Fifer will establish himself as one of the master footballers of all time, in the Scottish game.

In his early prominence he was criticised on the grounds that he could not tackle. Certainly, it is seldom that he goes into the tackle but equally true it is seldom that he requires to. He is such a wonderful reader of a game that moving into position for successful interception is almost instinctive with him.

But it is when he is in possession that one is made to realise the greatness of his football skill. It used to be said of the famed boxing champion Joe Gans that he could "duck and deliver" in the space of a handkerchief. Baxter can trick three opponents within the same limited confines.

Just as he seems to find it easy to divine the intentions of those opposed to him so does he make it difficult for the fellows in the other jerseys to guess what his next move will be.

He breaks through solo when he is expected to pass, he passes when he is expected to break through solo. AND HE NEVER SENDS THE BALL TO A COVERED MATE.

Everything he does, too, he accomplishes with a confident ease that borders on the casual. He never seems to be in difficulties, never gives the impression of being worried to the slightest degree. He is the supreme football craftsman.

Slim Jim they call him, and his lean figure is accentuated by the thinness—compared with other players—of his legs below the knee.

Not for Baxter yards of bandages, padding of cotton wool, shin-guards. "All that stuff," he once told me, "does away with the sense of touch."

I believe that Baxter is in the £100,000 class, but seemingly I am alone in that opinion, for not a single offer, not even a £50,000 one, has been received by Rangers since the club some months ago disconsolately decided, after persistent requests by the player, to put him on the transfer list.

He was among the most astonished of men when time passed without a wealthy English or Continental combine making a bid for his signature. And it was during those closing three months of last season, when he was "up for sale", that he emphatically proved how great a player he is.

His Wembley achievement alone, it was predicted, would lead to negotiations for his services, but the season closed with Slim Jim a very mystified young man.

He admitted that he was after the big money that is to be had in England, he confessed to being chawed that Stevenson, whom he ousted from the Rangers' team, was getting wages far in excess of his own, at Goodison Park.

It may be that as this appears in print Baxter will be transferred—although I do not think so—but I am crossing my fingers in the hope that the ex-miner remains on the Northern side of the Border.

He is needed here, one of the few personalities who can help maintain the fans' interest in the game, providing as he does the highest form of football entertainment.

Which brings me to wonder why players established in the first team at Ibrox wish to leave Rangers.

The wages and bonuses they now pay are in excess of those of most of the English clubs, and over a season are not so far behind those of the few Saxon combines who pay as much as £5,000 per annum for their stars.

However, that is a matter removed from the original purpose of this contribution—the naming of Scotland's player of the year.

Slim Jim Baxter is my man and I confer the accolade on him ungrudgingly, and with the feeling that he has no rival for it.

Baxter on his knee after scoring the first of his two goals for Scotland against England at Wembley.

▲ June 1963

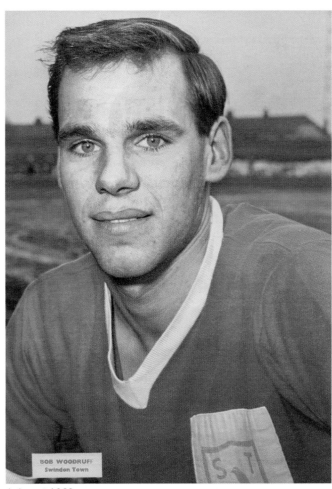
▲ August 1963

▲ March 1965

▲ August 1964

Plenty of volunteers for Queen's Park

QUEEN'S PARK, the famous, tradition-soaked, Scottish amateur club, have known better days. Former members of the Scottish First Division, Queen's Park were winners of the Scottish Cup in each of the first three years the competition was held. Now they struggle in the Second Division before gates of around 3,000.

Yet, in spite of their slump, Queen's still hold plenty of appeal for the young amateurs of the Glasgow district.

"When Mel Donaldson, our first-team goalkeeper, was doubtful for one match this season, we had 23 players from whom to choose his deputy!" said secretary James Gillies.

Soccer first

DEREK WARD, the Stockport County inside-right, has a busy life. In addition to playing and training with Stockport, he runs a taxi service at Longton in the Potteries.

But football comes first. On the night before a match he will take no job that will keep him out after ten o'clock.

Ward, who was a winger with Stoke City, joined Stockport in the summer of 1961. His younger brother, Terry, is a full-back with Stoke.

Jimmy knows

THERE is never any need for an argument about the laws of the game in Aldershot's dressing-room, for Jimmy Sirrel, Aldershot's trainer, is smart enough on football's knotty points for any quiz programme.

He referees all Aldershot's mid-week practice matches, and is as familiar with the problems of the job as any fully-qualified referee.

Businessman

TONY CLAYPOLE, the Northampton Town full-back, puts his spare time to good use. Last October he started a self-drive car hire service, and the business has developed faster than he expected.

He is now running three self-drive cars and one taxi, and during the close season will be able to give more time to the venture.

Claypole even operates an all-in summer holiday scheme from Northampton. The customers get a caravan holiday on Canvey Island, and a car trip both ways.

Keeping busy

BUD HOUGHTON, the Oxford United inside-right, will have a busy close season. During the freeze-up he started a window-cleaning business with Ron Atkinson, the Oxford right-half.

It proved a success and during the summer they will have more time to develop their side-line.

Houghton and Atkinson will even take their holiday together. They have planned to tour France by car with their families in July, and hope to stay in the Cannes district for a time.

Played with Buchan

FEW motorists calling for petrol at a service station near Spurs' ground are aware that the pump attendant is a former English international wing-half.

Although always willing to exchange a cheery word on football, he avoids reference to his own playing days.

Seth Plum is his name, and it was in season 1922-23 that he played against France in Paris for an England team that included Charles Buchan, Percy Barton and Kenneth Hegan. England won 4—1.

Plum, who lives in Tottenham and watches Spurs occasionally, was then a Charlton player. He moved to Chelsea, and played in the same team as Andy Wilson, George Smith and Bobby McNeil.

He's 'made' it

THE switch from Fourth to First Division is not easy for any player. Apart from the higher standard of skill expected, there is greater tension.

Jeff Astle, the West Bromwich Albion inside-forward, can feel satisfied at the way he bridged the gap after leaving Notts County at the end of September.

It took Astle time to settle down, but by mid-season he was displaying First Division class.

Astle joined Notts when he was 15. After four months as an apprentice fitter in a coal-mine, he jumped at the offer of a ground-staff job at Meadow Lane.

No Midlander

BOB FERGUSON, Derby County's left-back, comes from Dudley . . . but not the town near Wolverhampton. Bob's Dudley is a mining village in Northumberland.

For years people have thought of him as a Midlander, but his only connection with that part of the country is his father's link with West Bromwich Albion.

Bob Ferguson senior was once an inside-forward with Albion and for that reason young Bob regarded himself as a West Bromwich supporter in his schooldays.

Ferguson, who gave up his apprenticeship as an electrician to join Newcastle United, spends a lot of his spare time on rough shoots with a 12-bore shotgun around the Derbyshire farms, to rid them of vermin.

POOLE GO INTO 'SHOW' BUSINESS

(but only before games)

DOUG MILLWARD, who left Ipswich Town during the summer to become player-manager of Poole Town, has introduced a bright new idea. In his League days with Ipswich and Southampton, Doug always disliked the idle pre-match kick-about.

"It has no value to player or spectator," said Millward. "That's why I am turning my team out fifteen minutes before the kick-off time with instructions to entertain the crowd.

"I believe spectators enjoy an exhibition of ball control. In a match there is little call for the subtle flick or extra trick that most players can perform.

"Our pre-match exhibitions are an attempt to entertain. We are even having a penalty-kicking competition, and I'm ready to try anything else."

Millward is a versatile player, at home at wing-half, inside-forward or centre-forward.

" I'd go home, only it would be even more boring there ! "

Coaches Dutch

THE national coach to the Dutch Football Association this season is an Englishman—Dennis Neville, who comes from Harrow in Middlesex, and was a half-back with Fulham before the war.

Neville is now in his tenth year as a coach in Holland. After several successful years with the Sparta club of Rotterdam, he is now with Scheveningen, near The Hague.

He regularly visits England to renew contacts and to keep abreast of developments in British football.

INJURY often ruins a player's career, but in the case of Fred Pickering, the Blackburn Rovers player, it was the stepping-stone to success.

Pickering was injured when playing at full-back, his former position, in a reserve match against Manchester City. After giving him treatment, Jock Wightman, Blackburn's assistant-trainer and pre-war left-half, moved Fred to centre-forward just for "nuisance value".

He scored two goals and did so well that he was in Blackburn's first team as centre-forward within a few weeks. He has stayed in that position ever since.

Pickering never refuses to sign an autograph book. "I remember when I used to scramble after signatures as a schoolboy at Blackburn," he says.

SURF-RIDER

RON SAUNDERS, the Watford centre-forward, plans to try his hand at surf-riding this summer. Saunders is taking his family in June to Newquay, one of the best spots for surf-riding on the Cornish coast, for a holiday. He will also spend a lot of time swimming and playing tennis.

Signed from Portsmouth last September, Ron has been a big success with Watford. A Birkenhead man, he has also played for Everton, Tonbridge and Gillingham.

Full marks

SID BISHOP, the Leyton Orient centre-half, is a great believer in physical fitness. Bishop gives his parents full marks for putting him on the right lines when he was a young player with Orient. "Early to bed was a firm rule at home," he said. "From Wednesday onwards each week, I went to bed between 9.30 and 10 o'clock.

"I commend it to all young players with Soccer ambitions."

Who are you?

ALEC STOCK, manager of Queen's Park Rangers, has a problem. His reserve wingers this season are Roger and Ian Morgan, from Walthamstow. They are 16-year-old identical twins! They are so much alike that manager Stock and his staff are constantly asking them to identify themselves. And when they are on the field there is scarcely a spectator who can tell the difference.

Roger is the elder . . . by ten minutes.

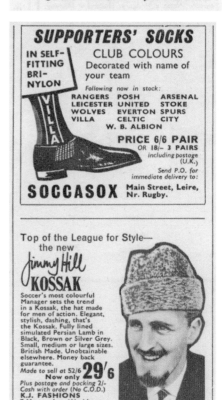

Selected from 1962–65

by ALAN BALL, Blackpool

IF YOU WANT TO GET AHEAD

— KEEP WALKING!

WHEN I was about 14, my burning desire was to have a bicycle—which is what you would expect of a healthy school-boy. But despite my pleas, my father was strongly against it. If I had cajoled him, I would no doubt have got one. But I saw the sense of his argument.

Ever since I was 10 years old, my dad—his name, too, is Alan, and he played professionally for Birmingham, Oldham, Rochdale and Southport—had trained me with a view to taking up Soccer as a career.

"Cycling is good exercise," he used to say. "But walking is much better for you."

I accepted his judgment and even today, although the proud owner of a car, I still obey on the odd occasion when dad asks me to walk somewhere, rather than take the car.

And I'm reaping the benefit of his good advice. He is, of course, still in the game, as manager of Nantwich in the mid-Cheshire League, after ending his playing days as player-manager for Oswestry.

He was my inspiration when as a boy I played for Farnworth (near Bolton) Grammar School at inside-forward. After leaving school I signed for Bolton Wanderers and played several games for the colts, but was told (via my father) that I just wasn't good enough.

My dad has never said who made that decision—and I've never asked him. I don't want to know . . .

I was disappointed, of course, but my youthful spirit wasn't daunted. I was then 17 and when on holiday with my parents in Blackpool, I blithely went along to Bloomfield Road, asked for Mr. Ronnie Suart, and asked for a trial.

My request was granted. I went for a Monday night game with 21 other trialists and at half-time was asked to sign as an apprentice. I couldn't sign the form fast enough!

And I shall never forget my first game for Blackpool. It was against Burnley "A" at Lytham—*and they licked us 6—1!* Still, I must have had a satisfactory game, for I was kept in the "A" side for the whole of that season.

At the start of the following season (1962-63), a huge chunk of luck came my way. The first team right-winger Mandy Hill (he had succeeded Stanley Matthews), was injured in pre-season training and I was selected to play in this position against Liverpool in the opening match at Bloomfield Road.

I had rarely played on the wing before, but I kept the position for five games, until Mandy had recovered, when I was returned to inside-forward in the "A" team!

After three or four matches I was promoted to the reserves for the rest of that season and didn't have another run with the League side until early last season.

The side didn't make a very good start to the season and for a home game against Manchester United I was given the inside-right berth. Fortunately, I had a good game, and apart from injuries, have held the position ever since.

Not that I bother to try to remember any good games I might have. I am paid to play well.

But I worry about the bad ones. There shouldn't be any, and when it happens I try to analyse where I went wrong.

My father, the boss Mr. Suart, and his assistant Mr. Eric Hayward, have drummed into me that I should always keep going, build plenty of stamina to last the full 90 minutes, fight for, and learn to control the ball—and get goals.

This I am trying to do every minute I am on the field, and I can't speak too highly of those people who have helped me, and who are still doing so.

But now I have a definite objective. If it is within my capabilities, I am determined to play for England in the 1966 World Cup series.

At the end of last season I toured with the Under-23 side to Israel, Hungary and Turkey. Unfortunately I didn't get a game. But it gave me a taste of the international scene, and I liked it. So I was delighted to get picked against the Welsh Under-23s this season.

But if I work hard and still have the support of my dad, Mr. Suart and Mr. Hayward—then between us we can do it!

▲ December 1964

THE CHAMPIONS

EVERTON: Back row - Parker, Gabriel, West, Vernon, Labone, Meagan. Front row - Scott, Stevens, Young, manager Harry Catterick, Temple, Kay. The trophies - Championship Cup and Charity Shield.

STOKE CITY Second Division Championship team: Standing— trainer L. GRAHAM, CLAMP, ASPREY, O'NEILL, ALLEN, manager A. WADDINGTON. Sitting— MATTHEWS, VIOLLET, STUART, MUDIE, McILROY, RATCLIFFE (now Middlesbrough). On ground—BEBBINGTON, SKEELS.

VICTORIOUS HAMMERS: Back row—Bond, Standen, Moore, Hurst, physiotherapist Jenkins, manager Greenwood (with Cup), Brown, Boyce, Brabrook. Front row— Burkett, Sissons, Byrne, Bovington. Below, acknowledging the East End multitude.

▲ February 1964 | December 1963 | July 1964

HONOURS 1962-65

1962-63
Division 1 Everton *(top)*
Division 2 Stoke City *(centre)*
Division 3 Northampton Town
Division 4 Brentford

Scottish 1 Rangers
Scottish 2 St Johnstone

FA Cup Manchester United
League Cup Birmingham City
Scottish Cup Rangers
Amateur Cup Wimbledon

CBFM Readers' Top Ten Players
1. Denis Law (Man Utd) 2. Dave Mackay (Spurs)
3. Stanley Matthews (Stoke City) 4. Jimmy
Greaves (Spurs) 5. Bobby Moore (West Ham)
6. Roy Vernon (Everton) 7. Tony Kay (Everton)
8. Bobby Tambling (Chelsea) 9. Jimmy Armfield
(Blackpool) 10. Bobby Charlton (Man Utd)

European Cup AC Milan
Cup Winners' Cup Tottenham Hotspur
Inter Cities Fairs Cup Valencia

1963-64
Division 1 Liverpool
Division 2 Leeds United
Division 3 Coventry City
Division 4 Gillingham

Scottish 1 Rangers
Scottish 2 Morton

FA Cup West Ham United *(bottom)*
League Cup Leicester City
Scottish Cup Rangers
Amateur Cup Crook Town

CBFM Readers' Top Ten Players
1. Bobby Moore (West Ham) 2. Denis Law
(Man Utd) 3. Charlie Hurley (Sunderland)
4. Johnny Byrne (West Ham) 5. Jimmy Greaves
(Spurs) 6. Gordon Milne (Liverpool)
7. Bobby Charlton (Man Utd) 8. Ron Yeats
(Liverpool) 9. Nobby Lawton (Preston)
10. George Cohen (Fulham)

European Cup Inter Milan
Cup Winners' Cup Sporting Lisbon
Inter Cities Fairs Cup Zaragoza
European Nations Cup Spain

1964-65
Division 1 Manchester United
Division 2 Newcastle United
Division 3 Carlisle United
Division 4 Brighton & Hove Albion

Scottish 1 Kilmarnock
Scottish 2 Stirling Albion

FA Cup Liverpool
League Cup Chelsea
Scottish Cup Celtic
Amateur Cup Hendon

CBFM Readers' Top Ten Players
1. Denis Law (Man Utd) 2. Bobby Moore
(West Ham) 3. Bobby Charlton (Man Utd)
4. Jackie Charlton (Leeds) 5. Jimmy Greaves
(Spurs) 6. Bobby Collins (Leeds)
7. Peter Thompson (Liverpool) 8. Nobby Stiles
(Man Utd) 9. Ron Yeats (Liverpool)
10. Stan Anderson (Newcastle)

European Cup Inter Milan
Cup Winners' Cup West Ham United
Fairs Cup/UEFA Cup Ferencvaros

Cut out the 'missionaries'

FOR heaven's sake, use your influence to stop our clubs making 'missionary' tours of the U.S.A. during the close season. One of these days the Americans will take up Soccer seriously. When that happens, a team of footballing 'Harlem Globetrotters' will descend on us and the World Cup will have a permanent home in the U.S.A. — T. O'LOUGHLIN — 12, Conway Close, Middleton, Manchester.

West Bromwich go to America this year. Other English clubs which have successfully toured the U.S.A. include Liverpool, Manchester Utd., Spurs and Everton.

Good idea

WHY not some new attractions among seasonal representative matches? For instance, why not Division I v. Division II or Division III v. Division IV? On paper, Division I should beat Division II.

But the latter possess more stars than folk realise. There's Johnny Haynes and Graham Leggat, of Fulham, Alan A'Court, of Liverpool, Brian Clough, of Middlesbrough — all internationals, to name but a few — JOHN MOTSON — Fulford School, Bury St. Edmunds, Suffolk.

Why not, indeed!

▼▼▼▼▼▼▼▼▼▼▼▼

Nostalgia

UNABLE to match the continentals in football ability, we decided that at least we would be their equals in dress. Now, in the briefest shorts, sleeveless, plunging-neckline shirts and all-white stockings our young footballers with their crew cuts look as fine a bunch of perfectly trained athletes as you could wish for— until the ball comes into it!

Is it too much to hope for the return of the long-sleeved, collar-attached jersey . . . the baggy pants . . . the bulging stockings? I seem to remember there were some great players attired in that style.—R. J. HOLMES—48, Newham Drive, Grimsby.

More nostalgic memories of Alex James, Dixie Dean and Co.

I HEARTILY agree with Joe Mercer ('Football Monthly', May), British football *IS* the best. When Barcelona beat Wolves the headlines were all for the Spaniards. But when Birmingham drew with Barcelona we had only brief reports of the game in the newspapers.

It seems to me that if we do well we get scant praise and if we lose we are dragged through the dust—PETER RIMMER—90, Larkfield Lane, Churchtown, Southport, Lancs.

This is not true of all newspapers.

He remembers 1914-18

PLEASE allow me to congratulate you on the production of "Football Monthly"—it is magnificent. I enjoy reading it so much for it brings back wonderful memories to an old stager who has been exiled "down under" since the end of the 1914-18 war.

I recall playing against Charles Buchan in France during the Great War. It was a match between the Cavalry and some Guards details and I was centre-half for the Cavalry. Charles scored a magnificent goal that day—one I'll never forget.

We had some grand players turning out for us in those days—Alf. Quantrill, of Derby County, J. J. Quinn, of Clyde, and Jack Fort, of Millwall, were among them.

Blackpool were out here this summer. They played some delightful football and we were all thrilled by Stanley Matthews who reminded me of Billy Meredith and Fanny Walden.—John Whear—24, MacArthur Street, Fairfield, New South Wales, Australia.

It was great to hear from you John. Charles Buchan DOES recall that long ago match in France and will be writing to you personally.

━━━━

These crowds are disgusting

THE present behaviour of football crowds is absolutely disgusting. Unless drastic action is taken, England, as host nation in the 1966 World Cup series, will earn a poor reputation in world football.

Please, let us have no more ugly incidents that mar so many of our games.

A. G. P. WILKINSON, 34, Felland Way, Reigate. Surrey.

━━━━

MR. HILL, YOU ARE SO WRONG ABOUT BUS CONDUCTORS!

JIMMY HILL, chairman of the Professional Footballers' Association, has been quoted as saying that the minimum wage of a bus conductor is £14. He should get his facts right.

Flat rate for a conductor for a 42-hour week is approximately £9 10s. (18s. higher in London area). That would mean working 15 hours' overtime to reach £14!

Mr. Hill would be better advised to campaign for more attractive football to merit higher wages for professionals—J. E. FENSOM—66, Perry Road, Sherwood, Nottingham.

The players say they were fighting for a principle—not the money!

Lady's plea

I AM a regular reader of "Football Monthly", which I consider to be excellent. But why do you always assume that Soccer is only masculine in its interest? I am 13 and a supporter of Nottingham Forest. The sign over an entrance gate at the City ground reads: "Boys and H.M. Forces". I feel stupid every time I have to pass through this gate. Why can't the thick-headed male realise that more and more women are becoming followers of our great game— MISS J. STANLEY — 15, Conifer Crescent, Clifton Estate, Nottingham.

We feel the time will come when clubs will realise that the ladies must be catered for, and will design new stands accordingly. Wolves are planning a new super stadium with this in mind.

"If we don't talk about football, what is there to do?"

AT the Burnley v. Rheims European Cup game I stood between two old men, both long-standing Burnley supporters. At half-time, the old fellows had to lean against me for a rest.

Why can't League clubs set aside a section of the cheaper part of their grounds and provide seating for older supporters who find 90 minutes a long time to stand and cannot afford a stand seat?

Some of these old-timers have stood in rain and snow for more than 50 years to support their clubs. Surely they merit a little consideration? Certainly they have never thought of going on strike!—A. MIT-CHELL—22, Picadilly Road, Burnley, Lancs.

We agree wholeheartedly with this suggestion. Mr. Mitchell wins our prize letter award of a Ronson C.F.L. electric razor.

He disagrees with Charles Buchan

MANY times I have disagreed with Charles Buchan's "Opinion" column in "Football Monthly". But none more so than with his criticism of managers who dare to write in the official programme about the weaknesses of their team in general and players in particular.

Why Mr. Buchan should deprecate the manager who has the 'guts' to tell supporters what he thinks about his players is beyond me. Surely a manager has the right to expose the player who couldn't care less about his contribution to the side.

What about those players who receive payment from newspapers to write their views and who refer to the shortcomings of club management!

I'm sure Charles Buchan equally deprecates this, too.

Most managers would not take advantage of the club programme to criticise their own players unless it was painfully necessary. Good luck to them and more power to their pungency.—J. H. TAYLOR—22, Lytham Drive, Heywood, Nr. Manchester.

Since programmes and newspaper articles are read by the public, Charles Buchan feels that criticism of players by managers, or vice versa, should be conducted in private for the good of the game.

But for his outspoken attitude towards a topical Soccer matter, Mr. Taylor wins our monthly prize award of a RONSON SUPER TRIM electric razor.

A FRIENDLIE KINDE OF FIGHTE . . . !

WHILE browsing through my library the other night, I came upon Stubbes' "Anatomie of Abuses in the Realme of England".

The index indicated that "football playing" was an "abuse" in Mr. Stubbes' time, so, bearing in mind the reports of the innumerable suspensions and bookings of present-day players for supposedly bad behaviour which fill all too easily the sports pages of our daily newspapers, I turned back eagerly to see how the Laws and Greaves of the 1580s had behaved themselves.

The passage began with the entreaty: "Lord, remove these exercises from the Sabaoth", which sounds fair enough until you remember that Sunday in those times was the only day in the week when the English yeoman could escape legally to the playing fields.

It continued: ". . . it (football) may rather be called a friendlie kinde of fighte than a play or recreation--a bloody and murthering practice than a felowly sport or pastime."

Apparently, the really accomplished player "lyes in waight for his adversarie, seeking to overthrow him and picke him on his nose . . . so he may have him downe."

Injuries, naturally, were not infrequent: ". . . sometimes their necks are broken, sometimes their backs, sometimes their legs . . . sometimes their noses gush with blood sometimes their eyes start out . . ."

Let us not be too hasty, then, to condemn our footballers as a bunch of brawling, quick-tempered hooligans. We rely almost entirely on our ancestors for our religion, government and laws. We have accepted their heritage without a murmur.

Thank heavens the modern footballer has not.

E. CLOUSTON
("A defender of the faith").
Oakleigh, Banchory, Kincardineshire.
(For this stout defence, and for the research which brought forth such interesting comment, a "Ronson 21" electric razor goes to reader Clouston for the prize letter of the month.)

Quit London!

NO wonder England were beaten by Sweden at Wembley. The crowd hardly raised a cheer for them—probably they were saving their voices to shout for Arsenal, Spurs, West Ham and Chelsea on the following Saturday.

If England were to stage international matches in the North and the Midlands, they'd get the vocal support they deserve.—J. KILSHAW—125, Nuthurst Road, West Heath, Birmingham, 31.
You are probably right.

He reads us

WE are introduced to Rugby on arrival in the First Form, with no alternative for our games lessons—unlike a nearby Grammar School which allows several sports. Once, boys of our school formed an independent Soccer team. They were not allowed to use the school ground. Yet at present half of it lies unused.

Because of the ban they played only away games. Now Rugby reigns supreme.

Soccer is not played at our school because it might lower the intellectual level. But our Head takes your magazine each month!
THREE DISGUSTED SCHOOLBOYS, Derby.

The huggers

JOHN MACADAM would impose a £5 fine on any player who hugs a teammate . . . I dislike the hugging, but Macadam misses the point.

Surely it is of little importance if players hug each other, so long as they try to play good, intelligent football? Often a player who does the most hugging is the one who puts most enthusiasm into his game.
B. CHEAL
26, Springwell Road, Tonbridge, Kent

Seat them !

SOCCER rowdyism starts from the terraces. Seated people in the stands are well behaved. So the cure—no terraces. Seats everywhere. no standing.

If a hooligan threw a bottle, etc., from a seat, he could be more easily spotted. Also, more seating would attract people who like Soccer, but not squashing or standing.

B. J. OWEN,
70, Prestbury Avenue,
Prenton, Birkenhead.

Beat Them !

HOOLIGANS . . . "give them a damned good hiding", said Alan Hardaker. Hear! Hear! If they behave like children, interfering with other people's enjoyment and wrecking trains, let them have a child's punishment.

Tan their backsides—hard! Very few will want a second dose.

G. HALL,
94, Clifton Hill, London, N.W.8.

Selected from 1958–65

CHARLES BUCHAN'S
FOOTBALL MONTHLY

APRIL, 1966

WORLD CUP
ENGLAND, 1966

2/6d.

PELE, Brazil

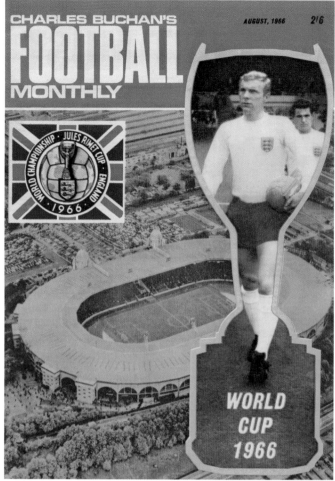

CHARLES BUCHAN'S
FOOTBALL MONTHLY

AUGUST, 1966   2/6

WORLD CUP 1966

CHARLES BUCHAN'S
FOOTBALL MONTHLY

MAY, 1966

WORLD CUP
ENGLAND, 1966

2/6d.

GEORGE COHEN (Fulham), left, and
GEORGE BEST (Manchester United)

CHARLES BUCHAN'S
FOOTBALL MONTHLY

MARCH, 1967

2/6

JIM BAXTER
Sunderland

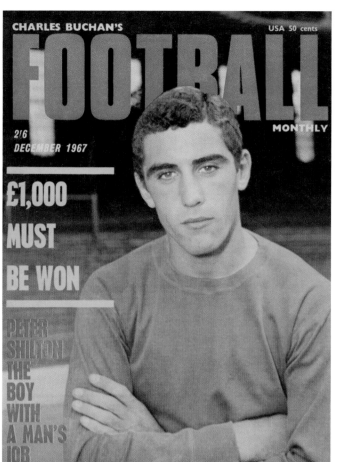

CHARLES BUCHAN'S FOOTBALL MONTHLY

USA 50 cents

CHARLES BUCHAN'S

FOOTBALL

2/6
DECEMBER 1967

MONTHLY

£1,000
MUST
BE WON

PETER
SHILTON
THE
BOY
WITH
A MAN'S
JOB

CHARLES BUCHAN'S

FOOTBALL

USA 60 cents

MAY, 1968
3/-

MONTHLY

SPECIAL: *Matt Busby, Man and Manager*

CHARLES BUCHAN'S FOOTBALL MONTHLY
1965-68

After years of lobbying, substitutes are finally allowed in senior English football. Charlton's Keith Peacock is the first, at Bolton in August 1965.

In Vietnam, the war escalates. In 'Swinging' London, it is announced that at all World Cup venues the players' tunnels will be protected by mesh, and drinks served only in cardboard cups. A week after it was stolen, the Jules Rimet trophy is found by Pickles the dog.

On the morning of the 1966 Cup Final Everton fans gather in Downing Street and sing 'ee-aye-addio, Harold's still in bed'. Later that day Everton win the Cup. Liverpool are League Champions.

Readers of *Charles Buchan's Football Monthly* rage against the hooligans. At Millwall 'they hurled stones and pennies at the small contingent of Hull supporters, who included women and children.' Charlton fans are attacked by a 200 strong 'jeering, singing mob' at Blackburn. Chelsea's Ron Boyle is knocked out by a missile thrown from the crowd in Rome.

England 'did not bestride the competition as did Brazil in 1958,' reflects Pat Collins, after the hosts' 4-2 World Cup victory over West Germany. Instead, 'It was a professional job carried out by professionals who were prepared by professionals under a professional overlord who let no feelings get in the way...' He refers to Alf Ramsey's decision to drop Jimmy Greaves.

The Kray twins are arrested. A slag heap kills 116 children in Aberfan. Plans for a new city called Milton Keynes are announced.

Boys' Own Paper ceases publication after 88 years. *Charles Buchan's Football Monthly* ups its print run to 250,000 and carries its first adverts for men's cosmetics (by Max Factor) and trainers (by Gola). Other adverts urge readers to Buy British after five typists in Surbiton

launch the 'I'm Backing Britain' campaign to boost the economy.

Scotland beat England 3-2 at Wembley. Celtic become Britain's first holders of the European Cup, in Lisbon, while in Nuremberg Rangers lose out in the Cup Winners Cup Final. Kilmarnock reach the semi-finals of the Inter Cities Fairs Cup.

In the aftermath of the World Cup, Football League attendances rise by one million. The 'Summer of Love' is followed by the launch of Radio One. Che Guevara is gunned down in Bolivia, while in Montevideo Celtic fine each player £250 for their part in a stormy World Club Championship against Racing Club of Buenos Aires.

Leeds finally win a trophy after beating an 'earnest but artless' Arsenal in a 'squalid and shabby' League Cup Final at Wembley.

Tory Minister Enoch Powell warns of an impending 'river of blood' if immigration is not stemmed.

Peterborough are demoted for illegal payments. Port Vale, under manager Sir Stanley Matthews, are expelled for similar breaches, but are immediately re-elected.

Wholesale changes to football are recommended in a major report drawn up by the Warden of Nuffield College, Oxford, Norman Chester. One suggestion is a levy on pools betting to fund community facilities.

Football Monthly opens its pages to female fans. 'You never hear of girls wrecking trains,' writes Sheila Neal of Sunderland. Mrs Doris Trott of Bishop Stortford insists 'It didn't need a World Cup to stir my enthusiasm.'

Ten years after the Munich disaster, Manchester United emulate Celtic by winning the European Cup, beating Benfica 4-1 at Wembley

French students riot in Paris. Soviet tanks bring to an end the Prague Spring. Basil D'Oliveira is left out of England's touring party to South Africa.

HALF-A-MILLION

An impression of Old Trafford's new stand.

Getting ready for the World Cup!

In last month's issue, Eric Taylor, general manager and secretary of Sheffield Wednesday, wrote of the preparations his club are making for the World Cup Finals, to be held in England next year.

Now, Les Olive, secretary of Manchester United, writes of the plans of his club to impress our visitors. They include a £300,000 new stand . . . waiters . . . carpets . . . special boxes . . . lifts . . . all mod. con.—to impress with the best.

BY the time July, 1966, and the World Cup, comes around, we at Old Trafford will have spent three years on preparations for our part in this event.

We are proud that we were chosen by the Football Association to stage World Cup games, and we intend to do everything possible to uphold the prestige of Manchester—and to make our contribution worthy of the North West. My club want to help to make this event a most memorable one, for the World Cup is not likely to be staged again in England for a long time.

Top of our list of ground improvements is the erection of a magnificent cantilever stand which will undoubtedly set a new standard of comfort in every possible way.

This stand has been in mind for some time, but the World Cup series has prompted the club to press forward sooner than expected—even at the cost of reducing our ground capacity during the time of building.

Now almost completed (the main part will be ready for the start of the 1965-66 season!) it will finally accommodate 10,000 fans in specially designed tip-up chairs with curved seats and backs, and 10,000 standing under cover.

One new and interesting feature will be the installation of 34 private boxes each of which will hold six people.

These have been taken up by business houses in the city to entertain their clients in the best possible surroundings—a sort of Soccer-Ascot if you like.

There will be a waiter-service available for refreshments, and a private lift will transfer spectators from ground level to the boxes which will be approached via a luxuriously-carpeted lounge. The boxes will be heated, and high-class refreshment bars will be installed.

When all is done it will indeed be a far cry from the old-time conception of the football fan standing in the open in all kinds of weather, shouting himself hoarse.

In fact, it will be the equal of anything that the world Soccer-traveller will find no matter where he goes.

But, of course, there is much more to World Cup facilities than one new stand—

▲ September 1965

(and more!)

**by LES OLIVE
secretary of Manchester United**

has a lot of experience in football. They will have the assistance of representatives of G.P.O., Thos. Cook & Sons (travel agents), their own Press and public relations officer, representatives of the local government and different organisations in the city.

The object of this committee is to ensure that visitors to Manchester, especially foreign visitors, should leave with the best possible impression.

Everyone here is on trial

Hotel accommodation, restaurants, entertainment facilities, transport, car-parking arrangements, stores and shops, and the people of the city will all have a part to play in making our visitors feel welcome.

Many foreigners will be taking their annual holiday in Britain and combining it with watching the championship matches.

They will tour the country between games, and the treatment they receive is of the utmost importance. Everyone in the area will be on trial—even the man or woman in the street, who may be stopped and asked for information.

You will see that the task of this committee is formidable and it is hoped that the aid of the civic authorities, leading commercial interests, Press representatives, and all local bodies will give their support in order that justice to our city can be done.

We look forward to the challenge of this event, to presenting the international teams playing for this great championship, and to bringing Soccer stars and personalities to Old Trafford for the benefit not only of our own supporters, but of football followers in the North-West.

It is our privilege to do this and we shall do all in our power to make the World Cup games a huge success.

no matter how large or luxurious. When completed, ours will have cost more than £300,000 but by 1966 we will have spent, in all, more than £500,000 over the past 15 years on improvements at Old Trafford.

Two corner paddocks have been rebuilt and cover has been erected behind the Stretford goal. Our main stand (destroyed by enemy war-time action), has been rebuilt and its design will prove a tremendous boon in accommodating visiting radio, television, and Press representatives.

We will have to remove seats to extend the Press box to take at least 400 Soccer writers, and we shall have to provide them with working and rest rooms.

We will require at least 300 telephone lines, a communications room, radio and

TV interview rooms, and platforms for TV and film cameras which will show pictures of the matches in all parts of the world.

Luckily, we have sufficient space in which to erect these temporary structures on the first-floor level underneath our "A" and "D" stands.

Our time-table is set, our plans are ready, and we shall do our best to ensure that Manchester United offer nothing but the best in comfort and facilities at a time when the eyes of the world will be on Britain.

A liaison committee has been formed under the chairmanship of Mr. S. T. Pilkington (vice-president of the Lancashire Football Association). The secretary is Mr. J. M. Howarth (another vice-president of the Lancashire Football Association). Each

"Darling, wouldn't it be nice to spend a few days in Sheffield with your mother in July?"

▲ January 1966

WAKE

TONY PULLEIN is secretary of the National Federation of Football Supporters' Clubs. This is World Cup time, here. He calls for more support from the fans for England, the hosts. His cry is . . .

ENGLAND have a worse World Cup record than Wales, U.S.A. and Cuba! England are 21st in the ratings, but I suppose our insular fans will remain complacent so long as we are higher than Scotland, who can only equal the worst of the 37 countries who have ever reached the final stages of the competition.

Englishmen couldn't care less

This is Alf Ramsey's tragic problem.

Englishmen couldn't care less how the side fare during this vital build-up period for the World Cup so long as they get a ticket to see Scotland, who have never, in all their history, been such nonentities in the wide Soccer world.

The public criticises League clubs for not putting country first, but ideals are forgotten when it comes to *supporting* country first.

If we assume that winning the World Cup reflects 100 per cent success, losing in the Final 50 per cent, finishing semi-finalists 25 per cent, and quarter-finalists 12½ per cent, we can assess the merits of all countries who have appeared in the final stages of the seven completed competitions.

England have twice reached the quarter-finals (12½ per cent success on each occasion) and twice been eliminated before that stage.

Therefore, the average for four appearances in the last sixteen is 6.25 per cent. Top four countries are Uruguay (56.25), West Germany (45.8), Brazil (41.1) and Italy (40).

Cuba, N. Ireland and Wales (each 12.5)—though it should be remembered they have appeared in the Finals only once—U.S.A. and Chile (8.3) and France (7.5), are all higher than England.

If this makes dismal reading as we enter the last lap for this country's greatest footballing occasion, the fans' record is probably even worse!

I would place their performance at the Austria game at Wembley, when they booed the players off the pitch with such an appalling lack of sportsmanship as to make me feel I never wanted to be part of a Wembley crowd again.

Sick and tired of Scotland

Unless a spectator is aware of footballing technique and standards throughout the world, how can he assess — and be qualified to criticise—the England side?

▲ January 1966

UP, ENGLAND!

Look at the paltry crowds who have turned up for some fine internationals over the past five years.

Fifty-five thousand v Uruguay —top country in the charts!— 33,000 v Luxembourg, 35,000 v France and Switzerland, 45,000 v Belgium, 50,000 v Hungary, 50,000 and 65,000 v Austria.

But always there are 100,000 to watch Scotland, whom many of us are sick and tired of seeing year after year.

There are a few *real* supporters, though. Not many, but they are genuine.

Five thousand belong to the England Football Supporters' Association which was formed in 1963 at the suggestion of Mr. Walter Winterbottom and has since been represented at *every* England match, except during the 1964 South American tour. That was beyond the pocket of even the most avid fan.

new year. Sometimes I wonder if efforts to raise more spirit are worthwhile. Official cheerleader Ken Baily has been welcomed on to all the famous stadiums in Europe except the one where his presence matters most—Wembley.

He was "lunched" by Swiss F.A. officials, given V.I.P. treatment in Portugal, Sweden, France . . . and thrown out of Wembley!

Mr. Baily, a proved favourite of the Wembley crowd when he did make one or two brief appearances, has never created trouble anywhere in the world.

He is merely trying to create an English national fervour similar to that of Scotland and Wales. But that sort of thing is just "not done" at Wembley or so it seems. Soccer fans are inclined to hang the millstone of a purely mythical "tradition" around Mr. Ramsey's neck. They are continually reminding him of Eng-

land's great past "achievements" which he must live up to.

I have searched my record books for these great feats, but in vain.

True, we were unbeaten by foreign sides for many years . . . before they had all learned how to play!

But I could go out today, invent a new sport, build myself up to perfection and probably beat anyone else in the world until they twigged the technique.

Let us remember that England have never won anything in top competition.

Forget the "tradition." Give Mr. Ramsey the backing he deserves. And if he wins the World Cup, let us hail it as the greatest Soccer achievement ever.

No jumping on the bandwagon

Planes have been chartered to France, Portugal, Switzerland, Sweden, Netherlands, N. Ireland, Eire and Scotland. Small groups have visited Czechoslovakia, Yugoslavia, East and West Germany . . . and even the U.S.A.!

A holiday tour is planned for next June's tour games in Europe.

The association has purchased £4,500 worth of World Cup tickets for people who were members exactly a year before the Finals were due to start. There will be no jumping on the bandwagon; bookings have closed.

A special World Cup song has been written for the association by Alexander Silver, of Watford, and records and sheet music are expected on the market in the

Ken Baily. An ardent England supporter, parades at Basle, Switzerland. Free translation: "Long Live Switzerland, Long Live England. Shout for both!"

ALLAN McGRAW
Morton

W & S Ltd

Everything makes a profit at Altrincham or they want to know WHY!

by GERRY DAWSON

THEY are as different as chalk and cheese — in appearance, in personality, in likes and dislikes. They are not quite the direct opposites that are popularly supposed to make ideal partners—but they are different enough to be extremely good for each other.

This shows in the success they have enjoyed as business partners, and in the fact that they are making an equally good job of putting Altrincham F.C. on the Soccer map.

They are Noel White and Peter J. Swales, better known as White and Swales Ltd., record, radio and television retailers, and respectively vice-chairman and chairman of Altrincham F.C.

By profession they are accountants—both worked for the same firm. With £50 between them they decided ten years ago to "have a go" and opened a music shop in Altrincham. They added records and record players and radio and television naturally followed.

They now have 15 shops, and, being former players themselves — Lancashire-born Swales played inside forward for Ashton United, White had three years as centre-half with Chester—they were naturally interested in Altrincham F.C., the Cheshire League team.

By 1961 the club was in a bad way financially, the ground was in bad shape, the team doing badly and the future gloomy.

They decided to step in—and once the decision was made they applied the same sound, tough—almost ruthless—methods that had built up their business.

They loaned £6,000 to the club to clear its immediate debts. They took up £2,000-worth of unissued shares, and by guaranteeing wages succeeded in preventing the club's complete professional staff from walking out.

They replaced all the then directors (except Len Pollitt a haulage contractor) with themselves and three specialist members of their own staff. They were now in business—right at the bottom of the ladder again.

Knowing only too well that names make news, they brought in ex-Newcastle, Manchester United and Blackpool inside forward Ernie Taylor; Paddy Fagan from Manchester City and Tommy Banks from Bolton. They made Paddy player-manager, but three weeks later he was injured and never played again.

They next appointed Charlie Mitten as manager after his spell with Newcastle and he stayed a couple of seasons. When Charlie left they had a re-think. Maybe the best man for a non-league club was a manager who knew the non-league set-up, inside out. They picked Freddie Pye—a successful scrap-metal dealer, who had played with Accrington Stanley, but who made his biggest mark in winning two Cheshire League championship medals as a wing-half with Hyde United.

With two business-men at the helm, and an equally good business-man running the team, things began to happen. They reached the third round of this year's F.A. Cup, and met Wolves at Molineux.

"Our ambition, naturally, is League Football at Moss Lane, but not just yet. We still have a lot to do," they told me. That gives a clue to their methods, achievement and foresight. Already they have smartened up the ground and installed three new refreshment bars.

They have built a £38,000 social club; organised a weekly pool which started with a £45 top prize that is now £350, and which has raised £50,000 for the club in five years. They have put in first-class floodlights.

"The club has just finished paying back to us the original £6,000 that we loaned—and every year so far we have shown a profit, including increased gate money, receipts from pools and raffles, from the sale of jockey-style caps (we've sold 1,000 of these), and of club ties which are steady sellers." say W. & S.

"Everything has to show a profit—or we want to know why, but the only real guarantee of success is a winning team, and—thanks to Freddie Pye we've had that too this season."

Yes—W. & S. are a team all right, and a very successful one at that, proving that there is only one way to run a successful football club—as a business.

ts training. Standing: Cohen, Stiles, Baker, Thompson, Wilson, Reaney, Greaves, Harris, Hunter, Hunt. Charlton, Newton, Ball, Hurst, Bobby Charlton, Moore.

IT MUST

SAID PAT COLLINS LAST MONTH

SUPER-FITNESS, brilliant back-stage planning, superb teamwork and great fighting heart made England the new kings of world football, and gave them a safe, unfettered passport to the finals of the Jules Rimet Trophy in Mexico in 1970.

In winning, they provided 400-million world-wide TV viewers — the greatest audience ever — and a nerve-wracked, nail-biting 93,000 Wembley crowd with the most dramatic, most exciting and unforgettable of the eight World Cup finals so far staged.

In the end, in the last of the three weeks of football fiesta, all the early doubts, misgivings and criticisms were thrown back in the teeth of England's critics — at home and abroad — as the team that Alf Ramsey built, the men he stood by and who backed him all the way, proved worthy champions.

The satisfaction, even more, my pride on being right about the eventual winners — does not dazzle me into lauding their magnificent achievement as being that of some miracle side.

They did not bestride the competition and their competitors as did Brazil in 1958.

Even England's warmest admirers could not be fully satisfied by the team's early efforts as Uruguay, Mexico and France were headed on the first steps towards the Final.

But the great test was met — and passed — in the last eight days when Argentina, Portugal and then West Germany bowed down before disciplined and determined football by the dedicated disciples of Ramsey.

It was a professional job carried out by professionals who were prepared by professionals under a professional overlord who let no feelings get in the way of a three-year old vow to win the world's greatest football prize.

The Argentinians snarled their way home, taking with them a story of English injustice. To me they had posed the biggest prob-

...AND

(GLORY BE)

IT WAS!

lem to England's progress — until they paid, maybe a little more highly than they deserved, for their lack of discipline. But it was still a self-inflicted wound they suffered.

Portugal, most adventurous, most gallant and certainly the most sporting opponents, with their Eusebio, most dangerous goal-menace in the whole competition, tried everything to blast English hopes.

They failed with high honour in a match to remember, a game as clean and refreshing as the brushing of teeth. They failed and in so doing proved the worth of the men who checked them.

Portugal proved themselves the No. 3 football nation of the

▲ March 1967 | August 1966 | August 1966

▲ September 1966

BE ENGLAND!

Bobby Moore receives the World Cup from the Queen. So for the third successive year he climbed Wembley's steps at the head of a triumphant team. Previously it was for the F.A. Cup, then the European Cup Winners' Cup.

world. The powerful West Germans the No. 2. Bobby Moore and his team, by relegating them to those positions, silenced the fears and released the cheers in those last eight days which vindicated Ramsey's judgement . . . and English football.

Those who slated England's early efforts overlooked the fact that Gordon Banks did not need

to make a worthwhile save until nearly three-and-a-half matches had been played.

That if you can remember, was a snap shot by Onega, the Argentinian. And it is full testimony to the greatest defence in the world.

When Banks was called on he proved undoubtedly the finest keeper in the tournament. It was

generally agreed that the general standard of goalkeeping was low, but Banks made the others, by his magnificent work in those last eight days, insignificant.

The finest English effort was fittingly saved for the last day, the sort of day Alf Ramsey had always promised for England when his forwards really clicked. Until then, under the team plan, those

This is the second when German flags waved madly at Wembley, and German throats became hoarse. Weber gets the equaliser seconds from full-time.

same forwards had proved themselves as additional defenders when needed. But they were not judged in that light. Chances had not been taken.

But on that final day they made and took them against the defence which had been second only to their own. By their efforts they made sure it remained so.

Bobby Moore was, deservedly, voted the player of the World Cup. His was a majestic performance. Jack Charlton, Stiles and

Ball starred way above expectations. Peters' inclusion was a masterpiece of team selection. We knew that Cohen and Wilson had no peers anywhere . . . and they underlined it. Hurst and Hunt, selfless and undaunted, most typified the spirit of the side.

And Bobby Charlton? He was just Bobby Charlton, the forward the rest most feared, often careless with his passing, but always a threat and a tremendous worker for the cause.

Every match paid its tribute to the work of trainer Harold Shepherdson and his assistant Les Cocker. None more than the final when our men ran on while the Germans ran right out of steam.

We salute them all, these men who helped England to lick the world.

And made us
THE CHAMPIONS!

THEY ALL CAME...!

This is a scene at "Football Monthly's" exhibition at Wembley. It was an incessant babble of foreign tongues—and of great interest to all England's visitors from overseas. We were pleased to see them. And we wish them well.

CHARLES BUCHAN'S
FOOTBALL
MONTHLY
THE WORLD'S GREATEST SOCCER MAGAZINE

▲ September 1966

Dea:

Ramsey's choice vindicated

MAY I congratula
England on the
magnificent pe
formance, and in particula
manager Alf Ramsey, architect
that great victory.

He had been criticised right, left a
centre from so-called football critics, a
the majority of the public. Most of tho
who disagreed with his team selectio
were those who wanted to see the
particular favourites on the side. It w
his job to pick the eleven men he thoug
would do best for England. His choi
was the right one!

PADDY DE LA COU
1, Ash Street, Yough
Co. Cork, Ei

Argentinians should study Koreans

I WAS absolutely disgust
with the inexplicable displa
of the Argentinians against Englan
Their behaviour, especially that of Rat
and Onega, was really undesirable and
hope, will never be repeated on a footb
ground again.

I hope that other countries take n
of their punishment. I recommend the
to note the very clean style of play of t
North Koreans.

DAVID WRIGH
Brimfield, 64, High Ro
Buckhurst Hill, Ess

Let winners meet a World Select

AN added attraction to t
ending of the World C
tournament would be for the winni
country to play a selected side from t
15 other nations. This last time, wi
stars like Beckenbauer, Haller, Oneg
Artime, Eusebio, Yashin, Rivera, See
and others to call, it would have been
really star ending to the show.

BERNARD SAUNDE
12, Alderbury Ro
Stansted, Ess

Worth a fiver to watch

THE England v Portugal ser
final was an unforgetta
game, worth a fiver to watch. It h
everything, including great sportsma
ship, particularly from the Portugu
team. Everyone on both sides deserve
medal as big as a dinner plate!

H. SPENC
67, Delce Ro
Rochester, K

▲ October 1966

Sir

... is this month the place where readers have the last word on the World Cup

READERS' LETTERS
FOOTBALL MONTHLY,
161-166 FLEET ST.,
LONDON E.C.4

PELE ... hacked out after 30 minutes.

Robbed of the Pele genius

HOW poor was the standard of refereeing in the World Cup! More often than not the referee did not have control of the game.

In the Portugal v Brazil match the Portuguese defender who kicked Pele out of the Cup was allowed to go unpunished. It was in this match that Eusebio was acclaimed to have taken over Pele's title of the world's greatest footballer. Pele was written off when he played for only 30 minutes of the game.

It was a pity that such a great footballer was hacked out, leaving spectators with a completely one-sided match without any of his genius.

SIMON VAREY,
28, Woodlands Avenue,
New Malden, Surrey.

We must teach them how to lose

MY enjoyment of the World Cup was marred by false accusations made by visiting countries, namely the South Americans and the Italians.

It seems a coincidence that most of those accusations were made by defeated countries returning home in disgrace, particularly the Italians who have made FIFA the scapegoat for their pathetic performance in the competition.

In recent years England has accepted defeat gracefully, making no excuse other than being beaten by a better team.

However, as soon as the home country reaps reward for a tough, pre-championship training schedule, the losing visitors try to escape responsibility for their poor displays and blame the choice of officials and their attitude towards the home country, England.

England has taught the world to play football. Now, it seems, she has to teach them how to accept defeat with honour.

DAVID BUCKBY,
42, Wallis Road,
Kettering, Northants.

Football was publicly ridiculed

AT one stage of the match between England and Argentina I thought that the referee would have to stop the game to buy himself a new notebook and re-fill his pen! He stopped the game all right, by sending off Rattin.

Rattin duly went off and took his team with him. For eight minutes football was held up before the eyes of the world to be publicly ridiculed.

The next day their newspapers accused the FA of "fixing" the match. In Argentina a guard had to be put on the British Embassy and the Press accused us of being pirates (Long John Charlton and Bluebeard Stiles, perhaps?) It was also stated that we had stolen the Falklands (what this has to do with football I do not know).

The comedy continued with FIFA fining the Argentinian FA the princely sum of £83 and censoring Alf Ramsey for remarks not likely to foster good international relations.

All I can suggest is that FIFA and the FA officials be given a dope test!

P. MAGUIRE,
14, Brookcroft Avenue,
Sharston, Wythenshawe, Manchester.

It proved summer's best

THERE are many lessons to be learned from it; the menace of defensive football, the stupidity of bad behaviour and, less obvious, the blessing of summer football.

It has now been proved beyond all doubt that fans and players much prefer football on cool summer evenings and afternoons to sticking out the unbearable weather of our winter. In summer there would not be the usual enormous number of postponements of games.

Regarding cricket, let's face it, the average football fan does NOT follow cricket.

C. W. BOOTH,
"Taybank", Stockton Road,
Easington Village, Peterlee, Co. Durham.

Gordon Banks well on top

ONE of the most surprising features was the poor standard of goalkeeping. Many 'keepers were way below world class and their mistakes often cost matches.

By his consistently good performances, Gordon Banks showed that he can now be rated the world's best. Many of the top Football League 'keepers would easily find places in the international sides of European and South American countries.

The general standing of goalkeeping here must now be the best in the world.

M. EASTERBROOK,
80, Alinthus Avenue,
Wednesfield, Wolverhampton.

RATTIN ... captain of Argentina, who was sent off against England, spent the next day, photographing the Guards.

Glyn Pardoe and Alan Oakes

the country cousins who are . . .

Manchester City's double helping of good fortune

AS a youngster who scored goals and was an England schoolboy international leader, they called him "Lightning." Now they're predicting — and not without cause — that he will win Under-23 honours . . . as a full-back. Such is the way the pendulum of Soccer fortune has swung for Manchester City's Glyn Pardoe.

It's a coincidence, really, that Glyn's cousin, Alan Oakes, is also a Manchester City first-teamer—at wing-half—and that he has been turning in displays which have earned him the title of "Mr. Consistency."

But, for the moment, let's go back to Glyn. City manager Joe Mercer said of him: "He'd been switched from one position to another before I arrived, but trainer Johnny Hart said he would always have Glyn in his side.

"So, when I was faced with a left-back problem, the choice was made for me."

And what a magnificent success Glyn Pardoe has made of the job he was handed. I can recall seeing him playing upfield for City, and pondering doubtfully on whether or not he ever would

GLYN PARDOE

make the top-class grade. I can also recall that when he played at left-back in the "derby" game against Manchester United, of having no doubt that he was the man-of-the-match.

Glyn comes from the Cheshire village of Winsford. As a 15-year-old, he was plunged into Manchester City's first team at centre-forward. Even then, he was no weakling—he weighed 12 stone, and stood 5ft. 10in. tall.

And the reason he was known as "Lightning" was simple . . . for two years, he was the Cheshire schoolboys 220 yards champion—his time was 24 sec.

Glyn played Soccer for Cheshire and England schoolboys, slammed home the goals regularly, and then joined Manchester City—which was a blow to the hopes of almost a score of other clubs.

City had not been slow to recognise Glyn's promise—they had kept close watch on him as a Cheshire schoolboy, as an England schoolboy international leader. So when he left school, he went straight to Maine-road.

You could say that 107 days robbed Glyn Pardoe of one record straight away, when he made his debut as a 15-year-old. For a player called Albert Geldard had become the youngest to make a League bow when, in 1929, he played in a Second Division game.

And Ray Parry, of Bolton, Blackpool and Bury pipped Glyn by 107 days for the honour of being the First Division's youngest-ever debutant.

Now, however, Glyn Pardoe looks set for new honours—in his first-team spot at left back. His speed as a youngster must have played a big part in his ability now to recover swiftly.

Physically, he is strong enough to fear no opponent. And he has added touches of craft and skill to the job, which seemed lacking when he was playing up front.

AS for Alan Oakes, this was another case of Manchester City beating rivals for a lad who showed promise

ALAN OAKES

of becoming a Soccer star. That was way back in April, 1958, after Alan had been skipper of Cheshire schoolboys.

Just as they had done with Glyn Pardoe, Manchester City had been keeping a watch on Alan Oakes—for two years, in fact. And the moment he left school at Winsford—yes, the cousins hail from the same village—Alan was snapped up by City.

The list of clubs disappointed was impressive. But Manchester City were happy. And by the time he was 17, Alan Oakes was fulfilling his early promise by gaining a place in the first team, against Chelsea.

He made his League debut in November, 1959. Then he followed up by putting City through to the third round of the F.A. Youth Cup against Everton. He scored the first goal in a 2-0 victory.

Well over three years ago he was being rated as "the most consistent wing-half in the game".

In February, 1965, he was drafted into attack as an emergency inside-left, and he has maintained his form which has made him such a great clubman for Manchester City.

There is still plenty of time for both players, Glyn Pardoe and Alan Oakes, to win honours at the game's top level. But even if they never achieve such an ambition, Manchester City—and their thousands of fans—will have cause to be grateful to both players.

For one thing, you cannot put a price upon loyalty . . . and when it's coupled with ability, you must thank the fates for giving you a double helping of good fortune.   **I.D.**

▲ January 1968

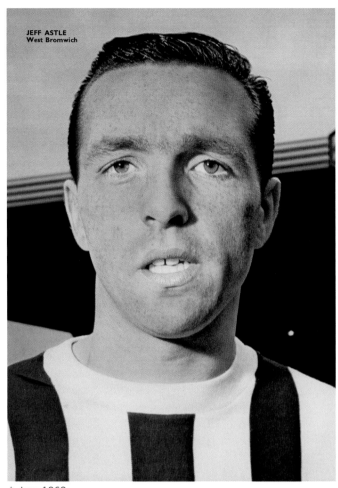

JEFF ASTLE
West Bromwich

▲ June 1968

PETER OSGOOD
Chelsea

▲ June 1968

JOE ROYLE
Everton

▲ February 1968

CHARLES BUCHAN'S
FOOTBALL
MONTHLY
MAY, 1966

TOMMY McLEAN
Kilmarnock

▲ May 1966

REFEREES

has their loyalty reached breaking strain?

A FEW weeks ago it was reported that a few top referees were threatening to resign unless they were given stronger backing by the Football Association in their efforts to stamp out those many undesirable incidents that were spoiling the game and bringing it into disrepute.

They were also concerned at the many incidents on grounds where a minority of unruly spectators had invaded playing areas and adopted threatening attitudes to both referees and players.

Shortly after this came the announcement from the Football Association that Millwall F.C. had been fined £1,000 and ordered to post "warning notices" as to the future behaviour of spectators.

This was not the backing referees had been expecting for an incident at The Den had involved an assault on a referee and was just one of many alarming incidents that had occurred there over a period of time.

Like many others, the Association of Football League Referees and Linesmen did not consider that justice had been done, nor even seen to be done. Within hours it was announced they were advising their members not to officiate at Millwall until adequate protection had been provided.

Happily, this advice was withdrawn when the Football League gave assurances they were treating the matter of protection as one of urgency, not only at Millwall, but on other grounds as well.

But while this particular incident highlights the danger to referees and players on Football League club grounds we are apt to forget the danger to those thousands of other referees who week after week give up some of their leisure time officiating at games on public parks and other open spaces.

Their problem is far greater for they have no police to assist and no wall or railing to prevent spectators coming on to the pitch.

True, in comparison to the number of games played, the incidence of referees being assaulted on these grounds has been very, very, small. But cases have been reported of referees suffering injury from attacks by players and spectators.

Stern action has been taken by County F.A.s and players committing these assaults have, in quite a number of cases, been suspended *sine die*.

Such grounds as public parks cannot, of course, be closed. And it is of little use fining the club concerned because of the misbehaviour of a few spectators.

I do know, however, of one club virtually closed down by a local Council who refused them the use of any of their pitches after a series of incidents involving their spectators.

During the last year or so the number of players sent off and the number of cautions administered by referees has shown an alarming increase but despite

Talking Point

CYRIL JACKSON EDITOR OF "FOOTBALL REFEREE" WARNS OF A SERIOUS LOSS TO THE GAME

firmer action by the F.A. and County F.A.s the figure continues to grow.

Many of these stem from the use of foul and abusive language at or to the referee or opposing player.

Some will say: "The referee is too touchy, he should shut his ears to such language."

But he dare not for he would soon be classed as "weak" by players and it would not be long before fouls crept in and the game possibly get out of hand.

It is easy for the onlooker to say "ignore bad language", but he has not the job of controlling twenty-two men whose sense of discipline often leaves much to be desired.

The referee has for long been the Aunt Sally of Soccer. Blamed for everything that is wrong with the game. Suffering insult from player and spectator alike.

Why then does he continue to referee when his monetary reward, other than those officiating on the Football League and other senior leagues, is but a few shillings?

For many it is a sense of loyalty—to put back into the game as much or more than they took out as players.

But this loyalty has now reached breaking point and many referees, particularly younger men who in the years ahead should be those controlling our top games, are resigning after only a year or so.

At the present moment the loss of referees exceeds the intake and this is causing serious concern for week after week hundreds of games in this country are being played without a qualified official in control.

If this trend continues the time will come when there may be little or no organised junior football with its consequent effect on the senior game.

Referees are beginning to strike against the attitude of players and spectators towards them. If this attitude does not soon change, then the future could be bleak for the game.

Opinion . . .

■ Like Mr. Jackson, we are alarmed at the serious decline in recruiting young referees. At the same time, we can understand why so many League referees feel that everyone is hostile to them—players, crowds, yes, and even managers, directors and Press.

■ Apart from the hooligan problem— and that is rapidly exceeding our worst fears—much of the antagonism towards referees stems from an appalling ignorance of the Laws of the Game and the referee's job.

■ It has been our experience to listen sometimes to league club chairmen (who should know better) ranting about the referee when it has been clear that they are unfamiliar with certain of the Laws.

■ As a result, the unfortunate referee is a victim of the iniquitous League marking system which decrees that he shall be "assessed" by officials of both clubs.

▲ January 1968

Dick Graham, when manager of Orient, explaining to hundreds of fans the club's financial position.

THE BACK-SLAPPING IS OVER — NOW IT'S SHAKING HEADS

JOHN ANTHONY traces the rise and fall of Orient

ONE Spring morning in 1962, the citizens of East London awoke to find a First Division team on their doorstep.

Leyton Orient (then), a humble club of slender resources and considerable ambition, had won a season-long struggle with Sunderland by a single point. Together with champions, Liverpool, they were leaving behind the Second Division.

It was—so they said in Leyton—the start of an era.

And, at first, that's how it seemed. Busby, Nicholson and the rest took their teams to Brisbane Road to argue First Division points, space was scarce on the terraces and the showbiz stars flocked to cheer on the "O's", backslapping the manager with one hand and waving to the photographers with the other.

Today, six years later, all, even the name is changed. Resources are desperately slender, ambition is dimmed and showbiz doesn't call round any more—there aren't so many photographers.

The era was short—and it ended some time ago. Relegation to the Second Division after one season among the aristocrats. Relegation to the Third Division in 1966. Extinction . . . when?

It's a sad story, and perhaps the saddest chapter was written at the end of February this year. Amid angry charges of "desertion", Dick Graham decided he'd had enough of the mess that is Orient and resigned the managership to become assistant manager of Walsall.

"The time to stop doing a job is when you cease to get a kick out of it", explained Graham. "The trend at Orient was to let things drift, to put off decisions until the next day. Gradually, I found myself accepting that state of affairs—and it was then I realised I had to quit.

"I had something at Orient that was the envy of several managers—the security of a five-year contract. But security is useless without ambition.

"People were content to look back on our First Division days and say: 'If only we'd spent the money we made then in such and such a way . . .' but the fact was that we hadn't spent it in the right way. We had to make do with the money available. We had to take moderate gambles in the transfer market.

"That was one of the things that finished me. It got to the stage that when I looked at a player he had to be both a free transfer man, because we had no cash for fees, and an unmarried man, because there was virtually no club accommodation.

"At the time I left, we were down to eleven fit senior players and a few apprentices. I couldn't drop anyone because I couldn't replace them. If we'd been hit by a run of injuries, I'd have had to toss youngsters into the side and risk their futures.

"I found two players who could be bought cheaply and on easy terms. We had to have them quickly. But the board decided against it—and that was the end for me."

Orient chairman Arthur Page declared himself "disgusted" with Graham's action. "It was a shabby thing to do", said Mr. Page.

It was thus, in a storm of frustration and bitterness, of charge and counter-charge that Orient crept closer to the grave.

It's a sad little story, but one which is going to crop up increasingly in the lower regions of the Football League.

Chairman of struggling club hires dynamic manager—manager discovers miracles are impossible without money—manager quits—chairman is left angry and baffled—slide continues.

Orient and their like will find it increasingly difficult to survive in a world whose standards are set at Old Trafford and Anfield and White Hart Lane. The story will be repeated.

But it's difficult not to feel sorry for Orient. They, at least, had a fleetingly glorious past. The perilous present must be hard to swallow.

▲ May 1968

GARY SPRAKE . . . match
held up till he arrived

W HAT a way to make a debut! I was only 16, — not yet a full professional — it was a Saturday morning and I was due to play that afternoon for the Leeds United Junior XI.

The time was 10 a.m., and I was enjoying my usual lie-in, to conserve my strength for the afternoon's game. Then there came a knock at the door. There stood Leeds' coach Maurice Lindley with an urgent message for me to report at once at Elland Road.

First - team goalkeeper Tommy Younger had gone down with tonsillitis at Southampton where the team were to play their Second Division game, so manager Don Revie had telephoned for me to rush down south.

Rush it was!

I was taken by car to Manchester where a chartered two-seater 'plane was waiting to fly me to Southampton. *I was sick for the whole journey.*

I arrived at the Dell at 3 p.m., (the kick-off had been put back pending my arrival), and we started at 3-15 p.m.

It was a double debut, for not only was it my initial game for the League side, it was also the first time I had ever flown.

Some baptism, I can assure you!

The next week I was back in the Junior XI. The following season I had half-a-dozen outings in the reserves. Then, in the next season, came the breakthrough.

The League side had not been doing terribly well and the boss decided to

I WAS 16 . . . STILL IN BED . . . MADE MY FIRST FLIGHT AND WAS SICK!

and that's how I began
says GARY SPRAKE
of Leeds United

give a chance to Norman Hunter, Paul Reaney, Rod Johnson and myself in a game at—of all places—my home town of Swansea.

We won 2-0, and I have been first-choice goalkeeper ever since. It was a strange quirk that my League career really began in Swansea, where I first played Soccer—but not until I was 14.

My first school was Llansamlet

Secondary Modern where Rugger was the school game, and I played at centre. At fourteen I moved to the school's Soccer team (in goal, of course) and a year later, played for Swansea Boys against Newport.

At 15 I left school and became an apprentice fitter and turner at a local works, Smith & Clark. I played for the football team among men and boys much older than I, which resulted in my being chosen for a Welsh Youth team against a Pembroke side.

It was really a trial game for unknown to me, I was being watched at this time by Leeds scout Jack Pickard who eventually took me to Elland Road for a two-week trial — and I signed as an apprentice professional.

At 18, came one of the biggest thrills of my career, when I was chosen for the first time (I've now made around a dozen international appearances) to play for Wales.

I had played one Wednesday for the Welsh Under-23s at Bristol, where we ran England to a 1-1 draw. I returned to Leeds the next day, and on arrival at Elland Road, was told that I had been given my first full cap. I thought they were joking, and I took quite a few minutes to digest the news, and to realise that I had achieved one of my great ambitions.

The game was against Scotland at Hampden Park (this was a bit of a baptism, too!), and though we lost 1-2, we had a good game and I felt that I had at least justified my selection.

That apart, one of the greatest moments of my career was the famous F.A. Cup semi-final at Nottingham when Leeds beat Manchester United.

It was a big disappointment that we lost to Liverpool in the Final at Wembley, but nothing could rob the team of the thrill of beating the mighty Manchester side, and realising that we were booked for Wembley.

The Final, undoubtedly, is a great event and every team wants to win the coveted trophy. But it still is a very big moment indeed to win a semi-final and to know that you are to be a part at least of the great Soccer show-day.

One day we shall go back to Wembley and bring the Cup home to Leeds, although since climbing from the Second Division, we haven't much to show in the way of trophies.

But we are still a young side. We have several times failed at the last gasp, but we have been learning, learning, all the time.

With that extra experience under our belts, and every encouragement from the manager and board, make no mistake, Leeds are going to win something soon.

And most of all we want the League Championship. Twice we have finished second. It must be coming up to our turn!

▲ February 1968

▲ July 1967

▲ June 1967

▲ December 1967

▲ May 1966

SOCCER

Bright boy Brooking!

A FOOTBALL career need never prejudice a young player's education. Trevor Brooking, the young West Ham wing-half, proves the point.

He had eight "O" levels before leaving school, and added another four at day school after joining the London club as an apprentice professional. Now Brooking is taking "A" levels.

He is an Essex boy, who gained schoolboy international recognition in the 1963-64 season after playing for the Ilford, London and Essex representative teams.

His scholastic aims have been given every encouragement by Ron Greenwood, West Ham's manager.

MIDWEEK MOVE

IS SATURDAY now out of date as the traditional day for football? Harry Haslam, manager of Tonbridge, the Southern League club, believes it is.

Mid-week fixtures, with matches allocated to different evenings to avoid the local clashes we now have in the big centres on Saturdays is his plan for the future.

"*It is not so much the challenge of television that is hitting gates on Saturdays*", says Haslam. "*There's a different way of life to-day. Saturday is still all right for the amateurs, but not for professional clubs.*"

The Tonbridge chief is also a firm advocate of summer Soccer.

SCHOOL OF FAME

GRAHAM TAYLOR, Grimsby Town's left-back, attended the same school as two other noted Soccer personalities.

He gained his G.C.E. at the Scunthorpe Grammar School, whose ex-pupils include Alan Wade, the F.A. coaching chief, and Jackie Marriott, star winger for years with Sheffield Wednesday and Huddersfield Town.

Taylor, who played for the England Grammar Schools representative team, and was sought by several clubs other than Grimsby, was a keen supporter of Scunthorpe United in his schooldays.

Please copy

THE ELECTRONIC notice-board on Sheffield Wednesday's ground has been a tremendous success, and a similar installation on all big grounds would be a boon to spectators.

The Wednesday board gives goal-scorers, details of injuries and substitutes, and half-time scores of other matches in large amber letters and figures.

Before the match even "commercials" are flashed on to the Hillsborough board. No crowd in the country gets a better service of on-the-spot information.

ORIENT TV

DICK GRAHAM, Leyton Orient's new manager, has had a television set installed in the dressing-room for his players.

He is convinced that TV relaxes the players and eases the tension before a match.

He also feels that it encourages an easy flow of conversation among the players and by this means promotes a good team spirit.

"I don't over-estimate the importance of psychology in keeping players in the right frame of mind, but anything is worth trying," says Graham.

Keeping in trim

IN each of the last two summers, Alan Spavin, the Preston inside-forward, has acted as sports organiser at Pontin's Middleton Tower Holiday Camp at Heysham.

Spavin, whose home is at Heysham, hopes to return for a third time this summer. He enjoys the work, and it keeps him at peak fitness throughout the close season.

The Preston player's engagement at the holiday camp means plenty of football for the campers. He splits the camp into halves, and picks his own teams for regular matches.

Superstitious

FOOTBALLERS are noted for their superstitions, and Jon Sammels, the Arsenal inside-forward, is no exception. Sammels makes a habit of being the last player to file on to the field.

Jon's quirk is simply explained. He was last man out, by chance, for a match a couple of years ago.

Arsenal won, and Sammels decided it was a strong enough reason for making it a regular habit.

Jon, one of Arsenal's biggest successes in recent seasons, made his one hundredth League appearance for the club last September.

Part of life!

NORTHAMPTON TOWN have an extra-special reason for wanting to keep clear of the relegation zone.

Northampton were relegated from the First Division at the end of season 1965-66. Last season they dropped to the Third.

If they were to finish among the bottom four of the Third Division this season, Northampton would be the first club in League history to plunge from First to Fourth Division without a pause!

It's a remarkable thing that only eighteen months ago Northampton were playing League matches against Spurs, Sunderland and Liverpool.

Edwards—attendant and customer

DENNIS EDWARDS, Portsmouth's inside-forward, has become an expert on Sauna and steam baths.

Two afternoons each week he takes charge at the baths, at Waterlooville issuing tickets and towels and generally attending to the comfort of the customers.

But on Monday mornings Edwards becomes a customer. That is when the whole Portsmouth team turn up for toning-up baths.

UNUSUAL TALENT

RON DAVIES, Norwich City's Welsh international centre-forward, has an unusual off-field talent.

He is a cartoonist of no mean ability, and if he gave enough time and practice to it, could turn his artistic flair to financial advantage.

Davies has studied at art school in his spare time, and is alert to the value of a sideline.

A great favourite at Norwich, Davies joined the club from Luton Town. He comes from Holywell, in Flintshire, and started his career with Chester.

SIDESHOW

BY LESLIE YATES

"Now, remember — no violence!"

It's easier now

HUMPING a kit basket about on their travels is a thing of the past for Bournemouth. This season all the players have been issued with smart, red hold-alls, and movement between railway stations is now a lot smoother.

As the Bournemouth bags are fitted with a waterproof compartment, there is no problem in conveying boots, shirts and shorts after matches played in wet weather.

This idea, introduced by manager Fred Cox, is popular with the Bournemouth players, and may catch on with other clubs.

Over the top!

MR. CLIVE THOMAS, the Football League referee from Treorchy, once added threequarters of an hour to normal playing time for stoppages!

The circumstances were far from usual. Referee Thomas was in charge of a boys' club match on a pitch at the top of a mountain at Blaengwynfi.

It took so long to recover the ball each time it was kicked down the mountainside that referee Thomas was forced to stretch the match over two-and-a-quarter hours.

Mr. Thomas, who is Senior Field Officer and Sports Adviser for the Boys' Clubs of Wales, is now in his second season on the League List.

No washday blues

THE weekly wash is no problem for John Barnwell, Nottingham Forest's inside-right, or for his landlady.

John is a partner in a coin-operated launderette in Melton-road, West Bridgford. He takes his own washing along, and the wives of several Forest players are among his customers.

Barnwell, who made his name with Arsenal before joining Forest in March, 1964, is taking an active part in running the business. And that includes talking football to the customers!

"It's not teenagers I'm against—it's their ridiculous clothes!"

Suits them!

WITH the upward swing in incomes since the removal of the maximum wage, there is now plenty of opportunity for players to launch out in business.

Terry Venables, Ron Harris and George Graham, the Chelsea players, have started a men's tailoring business in Old Compton Street, Soho. All styles fit into their range, but the emphasis is on up-to-date fashions.

With Chelsea's heavy match and training demands, Venables, Harris and Graham are unable to give a lot of time to their business venture, but each is learning as much as possible about the running of a concern that can provide security when their playing days are over.

RON DAVIES
He's a cartoonist

Selected from 1965–68

BOOM TOWN!

Read the City Pages of the newspapers and you'll find Southampton called the Boom Town of the South. They are so in football, too—in the First Division for the first time. And here is Terry Paine being chaired by his idolisers.

IF YOU ARE A SCOUSE

. . . then you will treasure these pictures. They show the world's three top trophies on display in one English city— Liverpool, at Goodison Park where Liverpool won the F.A. Charity Shield against Everton. Right, Roger Hunt (Liverpool) and Ray Wilson (Everton) parade with the World Cup they helped England to win. Below, Ron Yeats (Liverpool) with the Football League Cup, and Brian Labone (Everton) and F.A. Cup.

▲ July 1966 | October 1966

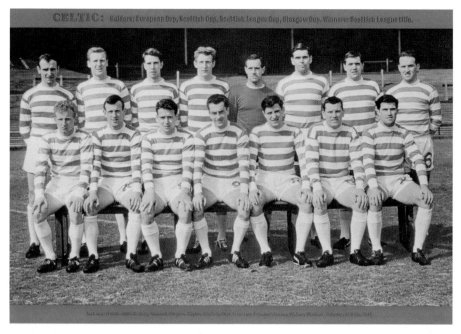

▲ September 1967 | July 1968 | May 1967

HONOURS 1965-68

1965-66
Division 1 Liverpool
Division 2 Manchester City
Division 3 Hull City
Division 4 Doncaster Rovers

Scottish 1 Celtic *(top)*
Scottish 2 Ayr United

FA Cup Everton
League Cup West Bromwich Albion
Scottish Cup Rangers
Amateur Cup Wealdstone

CBFM Readers' Top Ten Players
1. Bobby Charlton (Man Utd) 2. George Cohen (Fulham) 3. Ray Wilson (Everton)
4. Billy Bremner (Leeds) 5. Gordon Banks (Leicester) 6. Alan Ball (Blackpool) 7. Denis Law (Man Utd) 8. Peter Bonetti (Chelsea)
9. John Atyeo (Bristol City) 10. Kevin Hector (Bradford Park Avenue)

European Cup Real Madrid
Cup Winners' Cup Borussia Dortmund
Inter Cities Fairs Cup Barcelona
World Cup England

1966-67
Division 1 Manchester United
Division 2 Coventry City
Division 3 Queen's Park Rangers *(bottom)*
Division 4 Stockport County

Scottish 1 Celtic
Scottish 2 Morton

FA Cup Tottenham Hotspur
League Cup Queen's Park Rangers
Scottish Cup Celtic
Amateur Cup Enfield

CBFM Readers' Top Ten Players
1. Alan Ball (Everton) 2. Peter Bonetti (Chelsea)
3. Jack Charlton (Leeds) 4. Geoff Hurst (West Ham) 5. Rodney Marsh (QPR)
6. Allan Clarke (Fulham) 7. Ron Davies (Southampton) 8. Ian Moore (Nottm Forest)
9. Bobby Charlton (Man Utd)
10. Terry Hennessey (Nottm Forest)

European Cup Celtic
Cup Winners' Cup Bayern Munich
Inter Cities Fairs Cup Dynamo Zagreb

1967-68
Division 1 Manchester City
Division 2 Ipswich Town
Division 3 Oxford United *(centre)*
Division 4 Luton Town

Scottish 1 Celtic
Scottish 2 St Mirren

FA Cup West Bromwich Albion
League Cup Leeds United
Scottish Cup Dunfermline Athletic
Amateur Cup Leytonstone

CBFM Readers' Top Ten Players
1. Bobby Charlton (Man Utd) 2. George Best (Man Utd) 3. Alan Ball (Everton) 4. Jeff Astle (WBA) 5. Brian Labone (Everton) 6. Martin Peters (West Ham) 7. Colin Bell (Man City) 8. Charlie Cooke (Chelsea) 9. Norman Hunter (Leeds) 10. Rodney Marsh (QPR)

European Cup Manchester United
Cup Winners' Cup AC Milan
Inter Cities Fairs Cup Leeds United
European Nations Cup Italy

Soccer reveals our character

JIMMY HILL—a kindly man

I THINK it is time someone said something about the idea foreigners hold that all us British are stolid, dull and unemotional. Any of them who hold this view should go along to a League Soccer match. Let him take a look at the wild delight, the crazy explosion of pent-up excitement, the overwhelming joy when the winning goal is scored.

Can this madman, leaping in the air, embracing his neighbours really be British? Yes, and thanks to Soccer for revealing the true character of the English!

SEBASTIAN C. FAULKS,
The Anglesey,
Wellington College,
Crowthorne, Berks.

(This letter wins £3 3s. for the prize letter of the month.)

Nice of Jimmy

JIMMY HILL of Coventry is not only the world's best manager but also the kindest. When my friend and I wrote asking if we could watch a training session and meet the players, he invited us to come along to see one and also to watch the Coventry v. Wolves match for nothing and take a look round the ground.

S. HOGG,
20, Wade Avenue,
Styvechale Grange, Coventry.

EVERY Monday the boys at our school have football and on one occasion we were all very disappointed when our master was absent. But to our amazement we saw another teacher, Mrs. Langworthy, walking across the yard in a tracksuit and a pair of football boots. I think it is a marvellous achievement when a woman takes such an interest in football.

JOHN NEWMAN,
42 Haig Road,
Stretford,
Manchester,
Lancs.

MAKE THEM PUBLIC

NOT every club has a millionaire knocking on its door—like Birmingham City with Mr. Clifford Coombs—so surely a method of raising funds would be to turn the club into a *public* limited company and offer shares to regular supporters.

A dividend need not be paid in cash, but certain privileges could be granted to shareholders, such as prior consideration for Cup Final tickets and cut-price season tickets.

This would have the effect of giving supporters a financial as well as sporting interest in club affairs. And perhaps one or two of these supporter-shareholders could be elected to serve on the Board.

ROBIN E. HARRIS,
4, Maunsel St., Westminster, S.W.1.

Don't ever change

SUNDAY football? I hope not! What's wrong with the traditional Saturday afternoon? It saves running round the shops with wives and girl friends.

Apart from that, we use up so much energy urging on our teams that we'd never be able to get up on the Monday!

The same goes for Summer Soccer. What about floodlight matches? These are the games that really do generate excitement. So let's stick to the old way.

L. J. HOLT,
26, Hanslope Crescent, Nottingham.

T.V. inconsistency

The TV companies have done it again! This year's European Cup-winners' Cup Final was seen by football fans all over Europe, but not in Britain. Why? If *Dunfermline* had beaten Slovan Bratislava then I expect the final would have been televised.

On May 17, the B.B.C. showed again, by popular demand, the European Cup Final of 1960 for the simple reason that this match was one of the most memorable ever seen. But there wasn't a British team in the Final!

When Manchester United played in last year's European Cup Final didn't we expect the rest of Europe to watch our team? Why shouldn't we watch foreign teams play in their finest 90 minutes?

J. GOY,
37 Granville Road,
Westerham,
Kent.

● *Perhaps your own phrase, "by popular demand," explains it.*

Value for money?

When will fans get value for money? Too often, we have to stand on uncovered terracing in the wind and rain, crushed, due to lack of barriers. On many grounds, toilet facilities are filthy, and it is almost impossible to buy a cup of tea. We are also charged a shilling for a programme.

Pre-match entertainment means listening to antiquated records and the insane chatter of somebody calling himself a disc-jockey.

Clubs who spend £100,000 on a player never consider the spectators who pay for him. Is it too much to ask for a few thousand pounds to be spent on proper terracing?

Success and good football are enough to attract the fans temporarily—but not enough to hold them.

P. DOUGLAS,
19 Maitland Street, Lodge Lane,
Liverpool, L8 OUD.

● *But several clubs are now laying out money to provide more cover and better crowd facilities—in some cases not before time!*

Not the same, please!

RECENTLY, several clubs have adopted shirts, shorts and stockings of the same colour. At first, when Chelsea and Coventry took to all-blue it was not so bad, but now there has been an increasing similarity with Liverpool, Stockport, Cardiff, Bristol City and others.

Traditional styles are being lost.

By all means let this trend be used for changed colours—when necessary—but I would loathe to see every game consisting of one team sporting all-blue and the other all-red.

T. JACKSON,
64, Countess St., Heaviley,
Stockport, Cheshire.

Selected from 1965–71

READERS' LETTERS
FOOTBALL MONTHLY,
161-166 FLEET ST.,
LONDON E.C.4

Break with tradition

ONE thing emerging from recent Wembley Cup Finals is the need for a break with tradition and the dispensing of community singing before the kick-off.

No-one seems to be interested in singing "She's a Lassie from Lancashire" etc., in this modern age. Indeed, the poor chorus master has difficulty at times in making himself heard above the continuous chanting.

For my part, I find these everlasting chants most boring and wonder if the performers are really there to watch football or to listen to the "Top of the Chants".

I can only suggest that a more visual pre-match entertainment would relieve some of the boredom.

C. JONES,
22, Newfield Gardens,
Marlow, Bucks.

Skill first

WEEK AFTER WEEK in winter many games are ruined by the weather, which can turn a pitch into a mud-heap or ice-rink.

Pure skills are of secondary importance in such conditions and the emphasis is on force.

Football should be a game of skill, and skill should be the foremost consideration in what is primarily an entertainment. Take Manchester United, for instance.

Over the last two seasons United have won nothing. Yet look at their attendance figures. This is wholly due to the magnetic personalities of players like Best, Charlton and Law, etc.

The Manchester public turn up in such startling numbers to Old Trafford because they feel they are going to be entertained.

There would be more likelihood of this happening elsewhere if clubs would lay down the Tartan surface instead of continually using the vulnerable grass one.

The richer clubs could surely afford it, for in the long run the idea would certainly be most economical. The poorer clubs could be helped by the Football League.

I put forward this argument because if something is not done to put a greater emphasis on skill, then football will decline wholesale.

M. WARREN, Silkstone, Nr. Barnsley, Yorks.
● *Artificial pitches could make Soccer artificial.*

Limit crowds

IT is time for a maximum gate to be fixed on all Football League grounds. Clubs do not seem interested in the comfort and safety of supporters but rather in how many they can cram into a confined space.

An official body could be responsible for inspecting grounds and setting the maximum gate.

Surely it is better that 30,000 spectators should watch a game in comfort than that 40,000, jammed tight, should hardly see the game and only then in great discomfort?

T. COATES,
2, Church Parade, Sacriston, Co. Durham.

SPORTING CROWD

SLOUGH

WHEN Slough visited Hounslow in an Athenian League match, the Slough supporters accidentally broke a section of the stand. Being honest and good sports, they told the Hounslow officials and had a whip-round to pay for the damage.

For their honesty — and therefore lack of funds — they had to walk all the way back to Slough — which is quite a long way.

NICHOLAS CARR,
35, Thurston Rd., Slough, Bucks.

LUTON TOWN

I AM a supporter of Luton Town but readers who might scoff should remember the 1958-59 season when the leading teams in the country always feared a visit to Kenilworth Road where the Hatters gave them a run for their money.

Luton also reached the F.A. Cup Final that year but were beaten 2-1 by Nottingham Forest.

Further back came our most glorious win when we beat Bristol Rovers 12-0 with Joe Payne slamming in 10 goals — an unbeaten record in English League football even today.

Luton had one of the best home records in the Fourth Division last season but their away showings let them down.

I hope that in coming seasons there will be more "Oak Road Shouters" at away matches and then eventually we will get back into the First Division among the giants.

JOHN HEGLEY
38, Byron Road, Luton, Beds.

THEIR HOME record is mediocre; their away record embarrassing, but to me Luton Town, low in the Fourth Division, are the most important team in Soccer.

I am at Leeds University and whenever Luton are in this part of the world I watch them — when I'm at home I don't miss a game.

On Saturdays when I have not been able to watch them, the condition of tension and anxiety I attain has to be seen to be believed.

NICK OWEN,
18, Kirkdale View,
Ring Road, Leeds 12.

Referees

ONCE AGAIN the question of part-time or professional referees has arisen.

Why should young men throw up secure jobs to take on professional refereeing? Or is refereeing to become an occupation until pension age?

Will professional referees be paid on the same scale as the George Bests of this world?

Will professionalism mean better refereeing?

Surely our referees do their Saturday afternoon stint for the pure love of the game and not financial reward. I'm all for an increase in referees' fees but the idea of professional referees is as ludicrous as having two "whistlers" for one game.

J. McGOLDRICK, Littleton Dairy,
Gatehouse of Fleet, Douglas Castle.

Costs

In January's issue, you reveal that League attendances are down by a million.

Is it any wonder? I am 16 and in December I went along to Turf Moor to watch Burnley play Manchester City. This is what it cost:

(a) Admission — 6 shillings. (The cheapest as only under-14's allowed in as juveniles.)
(b) Programme cost 1 shilling.
(c) Bus to ground — 2 shillings.
Total: 9 shillings.

Young boys and girls cannot afford this. I think the League should increase the age for junior admission to 18 years.

I. CAMPBELL, 20 Conway Drive,
Fulwood, Preston.
● *What do other readers think?*

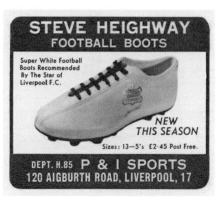

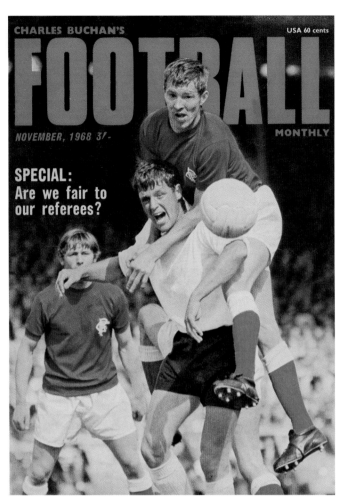

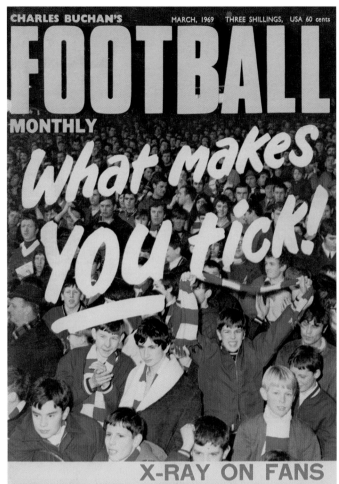

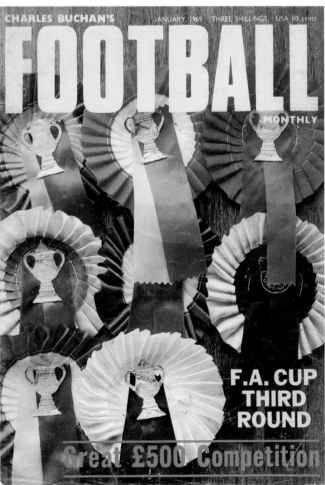

1968-71

CHARLES BUCHAN'S FOOTBALL MONTHLY

NOVEMBER 1970
THREE SHILLINGS (15 NP)
USA 60 cents

Is our Soccer overloaded?

LYNDON HUGHES
West Bromwich
ALUN EVANS
Liverpool

CHARLES BUCHAN'S FOOTBALL MONTHLY

JULY 1971
17½p U.S.A. 70 cents

SALUTE TO ARSENAL:
"UP THE GUNNERS!"

SPECIAL: SOCCER
ON THE BREADLINE

Six months after the death of Jim Clark at Hockenheim, British racing drivers, Jackie Stewart, Graham Hill and John Surtees finish in the top three at the US Grand Prix. Virginia Wade wins the US women's tennis title. In Mexico, student riots, Black Power protests and the 'Fosbury Flop' make for an eventful Olympics.

Leeds are the first British winners of the Inter Cities Fairs Cup. The formation of the Northern Premier League paves the way for a pyramid of non-league football. Leicester break the transfer record by paying £150,000 for Fulham striker Allan Clarke, who later becomes the first winner of a new *Football Monthly* award for Man of the Match, at the 1969 FA Cup Final.

The magazine now has a sister weekly publication, *Goal*. Also on Fleet Street, Australian media mogul Rupert Murdoch buys control of his first British title, *News of the World*.

Boeing launches its Jumbo Jet. Concorde makes its maiden flight. Pelé scores his 1,000th goal, in Rio. Neil Armstrong takes a giant step, on the moon. Violence at a World Cup qualifier between El Salavador and Honduras sparks a four day border war. Ann Jones wins Wimbledon. The Rolling Stones perform a free concert in Hyde Park.

'This is the age of mediocrity in football,' writes Leslie Vernon. With so many games drawn, even the pools are losing their appeal. According to Pat Collins, English football is becoming as defensive as Italy. 'We laughed when we said it couldn't happen here.'

Third Division Swindon beat Arsenal in the League Cup Final. Leeds win their first League title. But despite a record total of 67 points and only two defeats, they manage only 66 goals, the lowest total since 1924.

Sir Matt Busby retires at Old Trafford. Monty Python makes its first appearance. Anti-apartheid demonstrators invade the pitch at Twickenham. The Beatles split

Cambridge United gain election to the League, having 'enlisted the aid of dolly girls flaunting the club colours to parade outside London's Café Royal as the delegates arrived'.

Bobby Moore is accused of theft in Bogota. He later captains an England team that squanders a 2-0 lead against West Germany at the World Cup in Leon, Mexico.

Ted Heath moves into Downing Street. Football League Secretary Alan Hardaker says 'responsible sponsorship can become one of football's major developments over the next decade'. Apart from the new Watney Cup, the Ford Sporting League will award points for goals, but deduct them for bookings and sendings off. Ford is investing £150,000. Peter Morris is not happy. 'Maybe the players will be expected to have the name of the product emblazoned on their shirts!'

An annual football directory, sponsored by Rothmans, is launched. Jack Charlton tells Tyne-Tees television, 'I have a little black book with two players in it. If I get the chance to do them I will.'

Sixty six people die on Stair 13 of Ibrox Park after an Old Firm derby. The first British soldier dies in Ulster. *Football Monthly* highlights the plight of Blackburn, who owe £128,000, and Bolton, relegated to the Third Division, where they join fellow fallen greats, Aston Villa.

In this three year period English clubs win five out of nine possible European trophies. Among them, Arsenal emulate rivals Tottenham by winning the League and Cup Double. Brian Clough admits that after spending the summer in a television studio commenting on the 1970 World Cup he was physically and mentally drained. 'I shan't make that mistake again,' he promises Derby supporters.

WHAT WENT WRONG AT OLDHAM?

THE target was Europe in the Seventies! At first, it seemed an outrageous aim for a club which had just squirmed to safety from a Third Division relegation issue. But Oldham Athletic, their status assured, felt there were valid reasons for such bold talk at the end of the 1965-66 anxiety campaign.

The enthusiasm was there, clearly indicated by the following of 14,000 fans at some of their closing matches in 1965-66 as they struggled to dodge the drop. The ideas were in abundance, as shown by major reconstruction of the club's antique facilities for players and staff—and shown, later that year, by the design of an ultra-modern cantilever stand to cost £180,000 and seat 6,500 fans in readiness for the assault on Europe in the Seventies.

Most important of all, the money was there. It was being poured in willingly by wealthy chairman Ken Bates, a 35-year-old Londoner with vast business interests.

So it wasn't all hot air. Ken Bates had arrived at Oldham as their only saviour on December 22, 1965—at the height of another typical crisis in the cotton town's Soccer affairs. And right from the start he led the generous spending.

Centre-forward Frank Large was bought from Carlisle for £10,000; full-back Bill Asprey was purchased from Stoke for a similar fee; right-winger Ian Towers arrived from Burnley costing another £17,000; Dennis Stevens was signed from Everton for a further £20,000; Reg Blore was snapped up from Blackburn Rovers for £8,000.

It's a long time since the Third Division saw a spending splurge like it.

And then, the deal which Bates considered his master move—the capture of ex-Irish international Jimmy McIlroy as the new Oldham manager. Two months after signing a five-year contract at Boundary Park "Mac" decided to assist the team in their relegation plight, and Stoke City agreed to permit it.

That was the scene. New players, new paint, fresh ideas—for instance, the introduction of the club's own match-day magazine—and a local population aching for success.

INSIDE SIX MONTHS THE DOUBTS WERE REGISTERING; INSIDE ONE YEAR THE CRITICS WERE MANY; AND EXACTLY TWO YEARS AFTER JOINING THE BOARD CHAIRMAN BATES BLUNTLY TOLD THE PUBLIC... "'LATICS HAVE COST ME £100,000, BUT I WILL NOT SPEND ANOTHER PENNY."

The chairman, like the fans, had become disenchanted. A dream had collapsed in two years, and in the squabbling months that followed it seemed inevitable that changes had to come.

They did. In the opening weeks of this season manager McIlroy quit his post and with his brother-in-law Bertie Neill, who had been the first team trainer-coach with 'Latics, he moved back to Stoke City.

THE FANS BLAMED THE CHAIRMAN. He made demands on them, like increased admission charges, reasoning that he was no benefactor and if they "*wanted to pay Cheshire League prices they would have to watch Cheshire League soccer*." He upset them because he committed one of modern football's capital sins . . . he was TOO honest in what he said.

Once he told the fans . . . "to hell with you snipers who are always taking aim at Oldham." He stood no nonsense with ditherers, volunteer helpers who wanted to work hours which suited themselves, and had a reply for every criticism. He spent hours replying to letters of abuse in the local paper and all the time his critics increased.

Many of them driven there by the chairman's unyielding attitude and cold business-like manner. Others by the team's failure to get the results which had been the golden dream when Bates arrived.

The chairman was not prepared to offer the manager's scalp as a sacrifice, and it antagonised some fans that at the height of one long lean run he did something more than many chairmen dare in the Football League . . . he gave a vote of confidence to his manager, and backed his policy to the hilt.

THE CHAIRMAN BLAMED THE FANS. He said they were not prepared to back the club in sufficient numbers. Indeed, attendances slumped as low as the 3,500 mark in the bitterest days, making a mockery of his original plans to turn Oldham into a super Soccer centre.

It angered him that the public showed so much indifference and, to his mind, always wanted something for nothing.

At first, he had only alienated the supporters who felt it was wrong to remove Gordon Hurst from the manager's chair without a chance, and replace him with McIlroy. Success would have overcome the deed—but success never came.

He upset the town's pensioners by insisting there could be no price reductions and that the improvements had to be paid for by everybody; he quarrelled with the old Supporters' Club because he felt they were not raising sufficient revenue, and so he set up his own pools system which was soon thriving. Bates even claimed that his own directors had

▲ November 1968

PAUL DOHERTY fills in the background to a Third Division club which became too ambitious

let him down, and the result of one match-day row was that school headmaster Eric Beard resigned from the Board.

The feuds increased, the funds grew less. And still Bates dominated the scene, simply because he was a man of decision and had the kind of money which could make or break the club. But sadly, he was a man too advanced for the public he dealt with.

His fortune was attained in a high-speed world where quick thinking mattered. He set many of his standards by this.

THE MANAGER WAS BLAMED, TOO. He was allowed to spend heavily for a Third Division club, starting the 1966-67 programme with a £25,000 outlay to Stoke for winger Keith Bebbington and centre-half George Kinnell, followed by a £15,000 deal with Bournemouth for goalkeeper David Best.

But just as success seemed to be attaching itself to the club, he also sold. Kinnell, now a free-scoring forward, moved to Sunderland, then another top-scorer, Large, was sold to Northampton. He made profits on each deal.

Even so, the Oldham public could not understand the reasoning.

But McIlroy was determined to carry through a youth policy, and in his pursuit of this aim appeared to be more sensitive to the faults of his senior professionals.

It made no sense when he sold another leading scorer, Bob Ledger, to Mansfield. But the financial situation had so deteriorated, that he couldn't refuse Preston's £35,000 for Ken Knighton in March this year. . . And in the summer he picked up £12,000 for another of the club's recognised marksmen, Ian Towers, who moved to Bury.

Oldham seemed no home for players with proven scoring ability—Laurie Sheffield, another player with a goal-getting reputation, moved on to Luton only six months after being signed.

And all the time "Mac" put his trust in the youngsters—a fact which irritated his senior professionals. And most of his prospects were acquired from Ireland, his home-land, which gave the fans another reason to be bitter in their resentment. It was untrue, but they felt it was a case of "jobs for the boys".

He likened left-back Michael Nolan to a second Alex Elder. And two years later released him. Tony Foster and Noel Quinn, both from Eire, were quickly promoted to the first team—and just as quickly released.

McIlroy was learning management the hard way . . . and at Oldham's expense. The chairman gave him full control, a brave offer to a stranger to a fiercely competitive world.

The former Irish international inside-forward did not believe in hard physical training when he joined Oldham. His opinions changed almost one year later . . . but one year had been lost.

He felt the youngsters should be given their fling, and was later admitting "*I have made demands which are too heavy for my youth policy to support.*" Again, more precious time had been wasted.

When Bates decided to move home last summer from Cheshire to the British Virgin Islands, over 5,000 miles away, it was apparent that McIlroy would have to take all the strain himself—and that never promised to be a proposition.

Certainly, success would have covered many of the mistakes and demands made by Bates and his manager. His admission prices would have even become acceptable.

But they never obtained it—and Oldham paid the price for investing so much power in men inexperienced in the ways of a football club. 'Latics could not afford a long wait.

And Bates, I greatly regret to say, suffered because he was prepared to wait while his manager learned.

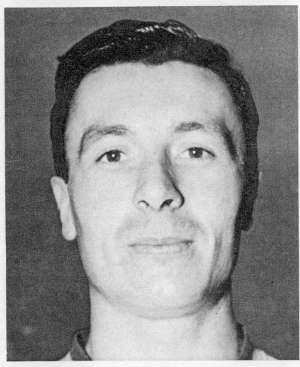

Top, Chairman Ken Bates . . . made demands on fans. Above, Manager McIlroy . . . determined on youth policy and (left) expensive 1966 buys Reg Blore and Dennis Stevens training for Cup tie against West Ham.

▲ December 1968

▲ September 1968

▲ February 1969

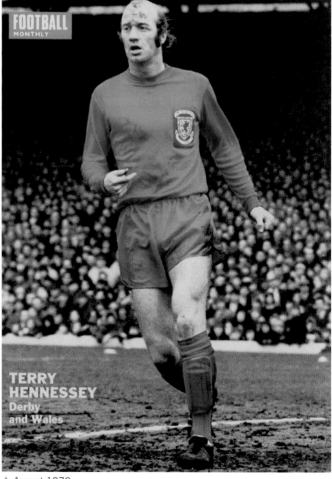

▲ August 1970

A LUXURY HOSTEL, centrally heated, with wall-to-wall carpets, colour television for leisure hours, balanced diets, a sick bay and a "mother" to see to all their needs . . .

That is how the young professionals and trialists with Coventry City are being reared into this plush Soccer world of the sixties.

MANCHESTER UNITED'S latest balance sheet shows a record £120,842 profit. They paid out a massive £194,055 in wages and bonuses. Their credit at the bank stands at £455,544.

THIS IS WHAT IT MEANS TO BE BRITAIN'S MOST SUCCESSFUL CLUB OF THE SIXTIES.

TONY HATELEY is big, strong and dangerous in the air. And without representative honour at any Senior level! But his last move made him the costliest-ever British player with fees totalling £300,000.

HE, HIMSELF, HAS POCKETED MORE THAN £13,000 AS HIS SHARE OF THE FEES.

ALUN EVANS was 18 and unable to make a struggling Wolves League side. Liverpool readily found room for him by paying the first £100,000 transfer for a teenager.

BY CHRISTMAS, Hateley's latest move to Coventry, and that of Evans, who took his place, will have helped the transfer-market to tick past the fantastic £2 million mark reached at the same time last year.

WHAT IT'S ALL ABOUT !

THIS IS THE SLICK SOCCER OF THE SIXTIES! Big-time, brassy, exciting, intense, profane and provocative. Richly rewarding to those who straddle its peaks. Crowds get bigger and more belligerent. Violence increases on and off the pitch.

Over-worked and under-manned police forces, local authorities, clubs, even the psychiatrists, try to find a way to stop the hooligan . . . or the reason for him.

Yet today's game, despite its lunatic and moronic fringe, becomes even more socially acceptable. The big match night is a socialite occasion as once a big fight night used to be.

It has made knights of the sons of an ex-prize fighter (Sir Stanley Matthews), a Lanarkshire miner (Sir Matt Busby) and the son of an Essex smallholder (Sir Alf Ramsey).

It has been done while all are still actively connected with the playing or management side of Soccer. It has been done against all past precedence where only legislative or administrative function had been thinly recognized.

Further out on to the playing pitch it has pinned an O.B.E. on Bobby Moore (for World Cup service) and similar honours on Tom Finney and Ivor Allchurch for exemplary playing careers, besides being all-time great performers. Finney got an O.B.E., Allchurch the M.B.E.

(continued)

TONY HATELEY . . . strong, dangerous and costly.

▲ December 1968

SOCCER IN THE '60s

Soccer in the sixties takes the talented youngster from the back streets and the parks pitch criss-crossing the world, moving as nonchalantly in and out of Europe as among the down-the-road domestic chores of League football.

It's the best home and Continental hotels for the blaise, much-travelled top set of clubs and players. . . .

TRANSFER PERCENTAGE
Legal transfer percentages to players amounted to nearly £250,000 in 1967-68; deals taking in fees of £5,000 or more totalled £4,859,000 as compared with £1,863,000 in 1965-66.

With incomes swollen by ghost-written autobiographies . . . tell-all Sunday newspaper and magazine articles . . . TV match and personal appearances . . . with basic salaries anything from £60 to £100 . . .

With win and incentive bonuses, points bonuses, sliding scale payments for League positions, for attendance, promotion, FA Cup, League Cup and European achievements . . .

With and from all these, the brightest stars of these succulent sixties slip easily into the stockbroker belt of living.

CHELSEA DE LUXE
Chelsea installed six private boxes at £500 each per season. The first buyer went to the club offices within a couple of hours of the announcement.
Now there is a waiting list for them. Each is fully carpeted, has a television set and six armchairs. There is a buffet and waiter service with car-park accommodation.

Soccer today can mean all this just as it can fasten a nation into one big easy chair beside its TV screens in the way that only the greatest Royal occasion can.

As it did to watch England winning the World Cup; Celtic and Manchester United the last two European Cups.

It pulls in the crowds at the new minimum of five bob a head on the exposed terraces. And at £500 a season, with wine and waiter service added . . . in special boxes and bars many theatres would envy.

It pulls in the customers so that the big clubs have long waiting-lists for season tickets and only the mortality rate can hasten the queue.

For important Cup or League matches, for the tougher European ties, all bookable seats are heavily over applied for until you get a picture like this . . .

More than £2½ million had been taken in ticket sales of all kinds BEFORE this season opened.

MORE AND MORE CUP FOOTBALL
Next season (1969-70) about 120 non-League clubs will compete in their own national cup competition—with the final probably at Wembley.

Manchester United (of course!) took £125,000 in season tickets.

Liverpool's reserved seating was taken up for the whole new season . . . with a waiting-list of 5,000 for Anfield seasons.

Promoted clubs like Ipswich, Oxford United and Luton doubled their ticket sale on the previous season.

League champions Manchester City took £20,000 extra in season tickets.

And this was a pretty general picture.

THE MIGHTY MILLIONS
In season 1967-68, League crowds totalled 30,107,298—an increase of nearly a million-and-a-quarter on 1966-67. More girls and women attended matches than ever before.

Match programmes at 1s. a time are the new club money-spinners. In glossy, magazine style, some with colour, they make the old 2d. team sheets look poverty-stricken relations.

Many clubs have increased programme prices by 50 and 100 per cent in the last year or so, with the official *Football League Review* inserted. Eighty of the 92 League clubs' programmes carry the *Review*.

Arsenal, for instance, made a £5,000 profit on their most attractive programme last season. They, and clubs like the two Manchester teams, Liverpool, Chelsea, Everton and Spurs will almost certainly improve their profits this season.

Players and managers sign longer, more lucrative contracts, even if losing managers are axed as readily as ever.

Bobby Charlton recently completed a new contract which could keep him at Old Trafford until he is 39! George Cohen has a four-year contract with Fulham, Rodney Marsh a similar one with Queen's Park Rangers. There are many others.

Cliff Britton has a 10-year contract as Hull City's manager. Don Revie,

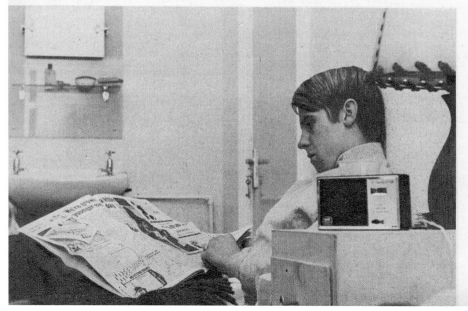

The Knights of Soccer . . . Sir Matt Busby, Sir Stanley Matthews, Sir Alf Ramsey.

Being sent to Coventry these days is almost a pleasure . . . fitted carpets, central heating. Nearly all the lot!

▲ December 1968

with four years of his old contract to run, and having guided Leeds United to the biggest rags-to-riches story of them all, has just signed a new one. For seven years.

300,000 UP
The Football League cup gains in popularity. Last season total attendances reached 1,671,326 with average gates for 110 matches topping 15,000. The Wembley final drew 97,887. Total gates were 300,000 up on 1966-67.

The Football Association made a profit of £435,000 from the last World Cup. England's victorious players received £1,000 a piece, broken down somewhat when they shared it equally with the whole team squad.

The European Cup Final at Wembley last May took £120,000 at the gate, £175,000 with TV fees and the rest added . . . the last FA Cup Final brought in a record £110,000 . . . the second Football League Cup Final pulled in £95,000.

And in winning the European Cup Manchester United earned £200,000.

Fat fees, lumpy wage packets and imposing outside business interests . . . that is Soccer in the sixties for its stars.

Once the height of ambition for no less than an England captain would have been his name proudly displayed over a local tobacconist's or newsagent's shop. Or swapping football talk from behind his own bar.

Now they open garages, petrolstations, boutiques, launderettes, printing-shops, gents' outfitters, besides endorsing endless new football boots, hair dressings, breakfast cereals. They even drink milk . . . for profit.

Big-time, big money, greater incentives. With these, greater responsibilities and expectations.

The days of the star who liked his pint or nip on match days are long past. Only complete dedication, top physical condition and a high consistency of performance keeps the money coming in.

Soccer in the sixties foots a heavy wage bill. It is a ruthless, demanding employer, utterly devoid of old-time sentiment. Now, more than ever

BRITISH RECORD
Biggest crowd pullers of all last season were Manchester United with average home gates of 57,000—a new British club record.

before, a player, and a team, are only as good as their last game.

The fit and the strong survive. It is an open admission that skill alone is not nearly enough. There's no time to stand and admire . . . or be admired. Results don't come that way.

Crowds, the best of them, are not nearly so tolerant. They don't cheer runners-up—only winners. SECONDBEST GETS LITTLE SYMPATHY, SCANT REWARD AND NO PRIZES IN OUR STRIDENT SOCCER IN THE SIXTIES.

Below, Alun Evans, at 18 he cost Liverpool £100,000.

Those who honoured football, and have been honoured. From the top, Tom Finney, Ivor Allchurch, Bobby Moore.

And here is the unhappy side . . . fans who caused trouble and are now putting a shine on the floor of a prison in Manchester.

If I live to be 100 I shall never forget my 19th birthday

by
BRIAN KIDD
Manchester United

WHAT a birthday present! Football has been my life for as long as I can remember, and certainly from the tender age of eight when I first played for my school.

During the following three years I became so obsessed with the game that I even skipped my 11-plus—just so that I could leave school at fifteen. For a year previously I had signed on schoolboy forms for Manchester United.

From the moment I became a full-time member of the United pool of players, my life and career seemed to reach one pinnacle after another.

My first game with the reserves (I signed professional forms at 17) . . . being chosen as substitute for the League side . . . my League debut . . . my first goal for the first team—all were great moments.

But no matter what I have so far achieved, or what may be in store, I don't think anything can match the thrill, the excitement, the overpowering feeling of achievement that my 19th birthday gave me.

It was Wednesday, May 29, 1968, also the date of United's great triumph against Benfica at Wembley in the final of the European Cup!

And I was the lucky one to score the third goal for the Reds—the one that put the issue beyond doubt.

If I live to be a hundred, I shall never forget the sight of the ball hitting the back of the net from my header. Not only do I still dream about it—even in my waking hours I still see the incident as though it had happened only minutes previously.

My chance came as Bobby Charlton headed into the six yard box, I headed it goalwards, goalkeeper Henrique could only palm the ball out, back it came to me—and over his head it went into the net. *What a birthday present!*

That was certainly *my* great moment, just as our victory was for the Boss and for the team. What a lucky guy I am to have been part of this great club success— and in my first season, too!

Mind you, I also had one of my worst moments in that match—and that goes for most of the team. It was when, shortly before the end of 90 minutes, with the score 1-1, we saw that goal-scorer supreme, Eusebio, going through at full speed.

My heart sank, but up came that hero, Alex Stepney, to make a brilliant save which gave us the extra time in which to clinch the victory that had eluded the club for so many long years.

The glamour of that night at Wembley seemed a far cry from my schoolboy days at St. Patrick's School, in Collyhurst, Manchester. I played for the school's fourth team at the earliest possible age (8) and progressed through to the first team and played a full season for Manchester Boys in the side that won the Manchester County Schools Cup.

It was while playing for Manchester Boys that I was spotted by United's famous scout, Mr. Joe Armstrong, who first took me to Old Trafford.

And here I must pay tribute to three people who helped me a lot in those formative years, my school-teachers Mr. James Goggins, Mr. Laurie Cassidy and Mr. John Mulligan—particularly the former who gave me good advice when it came to signing schoolboy forms.

After leaving school, I played a full season in United's "B" team, and at sixteen I became a regular member of the Central League side. At 17 I was chosen as substitute for a League game v. Fulham, but wasn't called upon to play.

Then, in the summer of 1967 I was a member of the United party chosen to tour America, Australia and New Zealand and played in several games as players were switched around.

Then came the opening game of the 1967-68 season, the Charity Shield final at Old Trafford v. Spurs. As David Herd was still out of action with a broken leg, I knew I had a chance. Sure enough, I was chosen for my debut on home soil.

And believe it or not, Mr. Goggins, who was on holiday in Bournemouth, drove the 220 miles to Manchester to see me play—and drove back again after the game to complete his holiday.

With that kind of loyalty and support I just *had* to grab my big chance with both hands. I was lucky, for I was able to hold my place throughout the season, scoring 15 league goals and two in the European Cup—including that fantastic final!

As for the future . . . well, we at Old Trafford (and I'm proud to be able to say "we") have two targets to aim for this new season—to retain the European Cup, and to regain the First Division Championship from our rivals across the town, Manchester City.

This may be aiming high, but we shall strain every nerve and sinew to achieve it. Wish us luck . . .

It's there, in the circle, put there by Kidd against Benfica.

▲ September 1968

TED MacDOUGALL
Bournemouth

▲ February 1971

ERIC McMORDIE
Middlesbrough

▲ January 1970

PETER DOBING
Stoke City

▲ March 1970

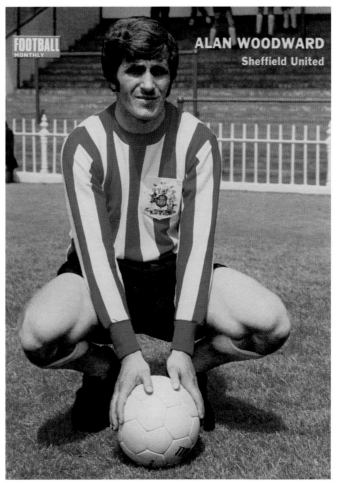

ALAN WOODWARD
Sheffield United

▲ October 1970

HOW would you feel facing mighty Manchester United at Old Trafford after experiencing only four months' League football in the Third Division? Well, that's what happened to me since I joined Watford in September.

What a start! I was thrilled on hearing Watford had drawn Manchester United in the F.A. Cup. There I was about to play on the same pitch as Bobby Charlton, Denis Law, and George Best.

I wonder if these great players knew that as recently as September I was playing on local park pitches in my native Newcastle. Don't laugh . . . it's true! So you can imagine what it felt like stepping out on to Old Trafford with a 63,000 crowd roaring down my neck.

On leaving school at 15, I became an apprentice welder. At that stage, playing football professionally just did not enter my mind. If it had not been for Watford's persuasion I would have been quite happy as a welder back home.

I began playing for Pelton Fell Juniors, initially, as a full-back. Having watched me one Saturday, an Everton scout asked me to attend trials at Goodison Park. I agreed but after spending four days there, asked to be released. I was only 16 and could not take to Liverpool. Harry Catterick was very kind and understanding to me during my short stay.

A few years ago I joined a local pub . . . yes, pub side . . . called Blackhorse. For the two teams I managed to bang in some 140 goals and was settling down to the centre-forward spot.

A Watford scout noticed me in September and recommended me to manager Ken Furphy. After playing in a few practice games I was asked to sign professional forms. Being much older and experienced I jumped at the chance. I still miss the North East but I am grateful to Mr. Furphy for giving me this opportunity.

It was in September that I made my debut against Charlton at Vicarage Road in a mid-week fixture. It was a fairy-tale start for me for I managed to score. Let

BARRY ENDEAN

WATFORD

talks about

a 4-month

'FAIRY TALE'

me describe it. Stewart Scullion our left-winger took a corner. The ball floated towards me, I jumped, headed it and it flew past Charlie Wright. That was the greatest goal I've scored so far and brings me even more joy than my first professional hat-trick against Gillingham a few weeks later.

Playing only for a local side in Newcastle restricted training to two nights a week, and stamina-wise, I wasn't in the best of shape. Training five days a week at Watford has certainly changed this. I am fitter now than I have ever been.

A word or two now about Ken Furphy, for he helped me considerably to adjust myself to London. Ken is the man behind the Watford revival. He is a master tactician. He relies more on gentle persuasion to get the best out of us rather than harsh disciplinary measures. As long as he gets 100-per-cent then he is satisfied.

On joining Watford I realised that on occasions I would be playing in front of large crowds. The crowd of 63,000 at Old Trafford was the worst experience I've had so far. I have never felt so scared before a match. At times, I could not hear what my team-mates were saying.

One continually reads in the Press etc., how big-time atmosphere stimulates players. Well, it had the opposite effect on me. Before the match I was shaking like a leaf.

As a result, I played a "stinker" and at times I was too busy watching open-mouthed the subtle skills of Bobby Charlton. Fortunately the rest of the side played brilliantly.

When Scullion scored after three minutes I was over the moon and even when Law equalised we were not put off our game.

The lads were full of optimism for the replay. It didn't work out just how we planned but we feel we did not disgrace ourselves.

In both matches I played against Steve James. I reckon he's got a great future. But the hardest time I've had against a defender was against Brian Tiler (then at Rotherham). He stuck to me like glue.

For the past few months I have been taking pain-killing injections for a knee injury incurred during training. Still, I shouldn't grumble because I have scored eight goals despite the injury. I don't mind the pain as long as I keep banging in the goals.

Our exit from the F.A. Cup could be a blessing in disguise, for now we are free to concentrate on promotion. We have a grand team spirit and we all believe our present side is too good for the Third Division.

Ken Furphy has had faith in me and I must repay that faith by continually scoring. If I fail, it won't be for want of trying.

I want to add another chapter on my fairy-tale rise to League football by helping Watford to the Second Division in my first season.

▲ April 1969

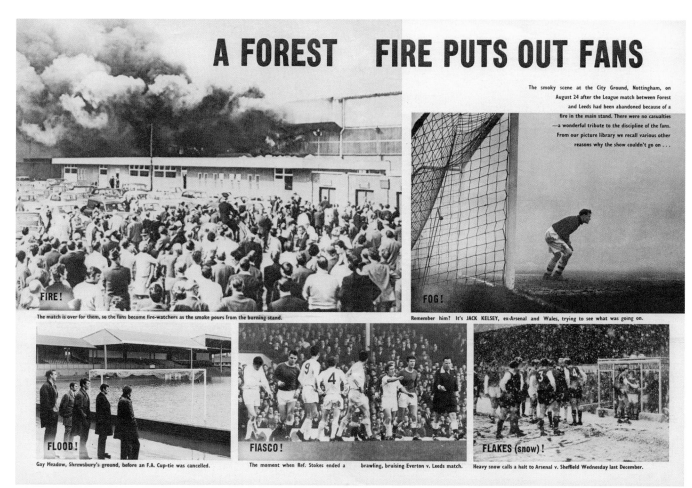

A FOREST FIRE PUTS OUT FANS

The smoky scene at the City Ground, Nottingham, on August 24 after the League match between Forest and Leeds had been abandoned because of a fire in the main stand. There were no casualties —a wonderful tribute to the discipline of the fans. From our picture library we recall various other reasons why the show couldn't go on . . .

FIRE!

The match is over for them, so the fans become fire-watchers as the smoke pours from the burning stand.

FOG!

Remember him? It's JACK KELSEY, ex-Arsenal and Wales, trying to see what was going on.

FLOOD!

Gay Meadow, Shrewsbury's ground, before an F.A. Cup-tie was cancelled.

FIASCO!

The moment when Ref. Stokes ended a brawling, bruising Everton v. Leeds match.

FLAKES (snow)!

Heavy snow calls a halt to Arsenal v. Sheffield Wednesday last December.

▲ November 1968

For newly elected Cambridge United their first League point in a 1-1 draw with Lincoln. Here, Lincoln goalkeeper Kennedy saves from Cassidy at the Abbey Stadium

Against the background of Goodison's uncompleted stand Everton's Joe Royle heads the first goal against Arsenal

At Stamford Bridge, Ian Hutchinson (Chelsea) leaps high but is foiled by Derby's Les Green as Weller and Mackay wait on

ACTION THIS DAY... as the battle for League points goes on again

Heading duel at Old Trafford. the winner— David Sadler over Billy Bremner

Flying header by Spurs' Alan Gilzean for No. 2 against West Ham at White Hart Lane

Soft goal for Sheffield United against Orient as Colin Addison (left) slips the ball between Terry Mancini, Dave Harper and goalkeeper Ray Goddard

▲October 1970

WE ARE THE C-H-A-M-P-I-O-N-S
...AND THE CUP-HOLDERS, TOO!

FOOTBALL MONTHLY

The Arsenal line-up
which made history

Standing left to right: George Wright, trainer, Bob McNab, Peter Storey, Peter Simpson, Geoff Barnett, Bob Wilson, John Roberts, Ray Kennedy, Peter Marinello, Don Howe, assistant-manager.
Seated: Charlie George, John Radford, George Armstrong, Jon Sammels, Frank McLintock, Manager Bertie Mee, Pat Rice, Eddie Kelly, George Graham and Sammy Nelson

▲ July 1971

NEWCASTLE UNITED

FOOTBALL MONTHLY

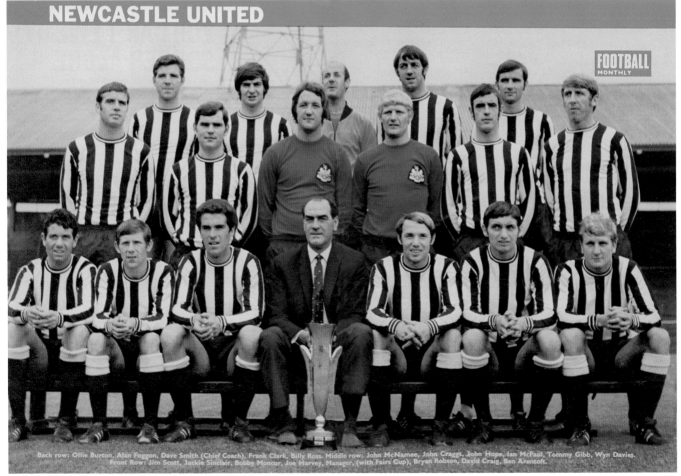

Back row: Ollie Burton, Alan Foggon, Dave Smith (Chief Coach), Frank Clark, Billy Ross. Middle row: John McNamee, John Craggs, John Hope, Ian McFaul, Tommy Gibb, Wyn Davies.
Front Row: Jim Scott, Jackie Sinclair, Bobby Moncur, Joe Harvey, Manager, (with Fairs Cup), Bryan Robson, David Craig, Ben Arentoft.

▲ February 1970

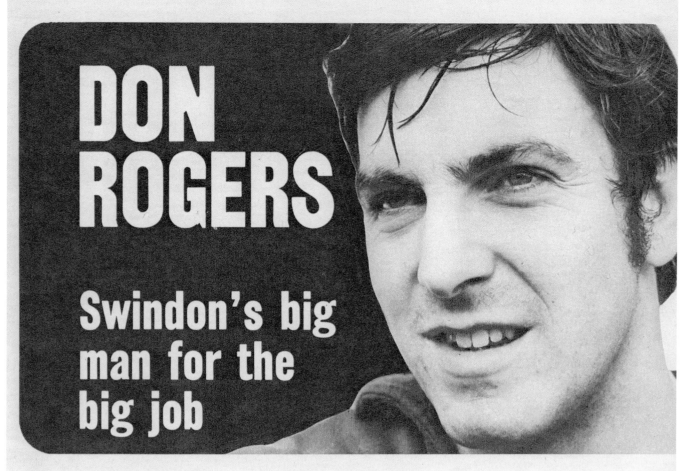

DON ROGERS

Swindon's big man for the big job

THE Football League Cup shock which Swindon Town handed out to Burnley was just another to string along with their giant-killing defeats of Blackburn, Derby County and Coventry City this season...

For the Town, while desperately keen, but unable as yet, to realise their ambition of climbing back to the Second Division, have become the team for the big occasion . . . with the man to go with it.

Ask most Wiltshire folk who is their favourite footballer and the answer will be "Don Rogers", the bulky but ballet-like boy from the deep West.

Rogers fully agrees that the big-time atmosphere does something for himself and his club-mates which is often lacking in the bread-and-butter League games.

"The atmosphere of the big crowds stimulates our players. You cannot compare it with normal Third Division matches, especially in away games where the gates seldom come near those of ours at the County Ground," he says.

And he fully understands the frustration of Swindon fans who know that a reproduction of this "big-time" form would see their club sail through the Third Division . . .

. . . the sort of form which saw them in 1966-67 caning Portsmouth 4-1 in the League Cup, when it took the eventual finalists, West Bromwich, to check their run.

Cup football really took hold of Swindon that season. A score-line for the FA Cup's Third Round which read "West Ham 3, Swindon 3" was a big enough shock for the football world. An even bigger one was the replay result . . . "Swindon 3, West Ham 1". And that, with World Cup acclaim still ringing for those Hammers heroes, Moore, Hurst and Peters!

When Swindon did go out in the Fifth Round it took First Division Nottingham Forest three games, with the second replay at Villa Park, to finally quell these Wiltshire upstarts.

And Don Rogers, by general agreement the best winger in the Third Division but who really plays all along the line where he can be most effective, proved then that he could take higher grade football in his powerful stride.

Spotted by Bert Head, former Swindon manager, at 15, he kept them waiting. He refused Swindon's first offer of a trial because he wanted to join Bristol City. He came up through the Midsomer Norton District team and local Youth clubs.

When Bert Head eventually persuaded him to join Swindon he was just two hours in front of Bristol City who turned up to find the signing completed.

He recalls that his first games with Town's reserves were little to write home about. But six months later he was making his League debut in a 4-1 win for Town which earned him ten outings in that 1962-63 season.

A year later he was in England's Youth team for the "Little World Cup", held in Holland. The trophy was duly won and 18-year-old Don Rogers was accorded the honour of being "Best player of the tournament". He won eight Youth caps against opposition such as Spain, Portugal, Austria and Poland, playing with fellows like Peter Springett, Howard Kendall, David Sadler, Harry Redknapp, John Sissons, Peter Knowles and John Hollins.

So far he has earned two England Under-23 caps, against Yugoslavia, at Southampton, and Wales, at Wrexham, where he scored the winner for England.

This time he really feels that this could be Swindon's year . . . and he is thinking mainly of promotion. "We have a consistency of performance which has been missing too often in the past and team-spirit has never been better than now," he says.

Pin him down to the match he most remembers and he picks that 3-3 draw at Upton Park where he scored twice.

Time and again his name has been linked with bigger clubs. The wonder is that, having proved himself as he has, he has not followed old pals like Mike Summerbee, Ernie Hunt and Bobby Woodruff, into top-class Soccer.

He would still like to take his chance, but will content himself while Swindon get results, and go all out to improve the sports shop he recently opened in the town centre.

IF Don Rogers DID move, as he tried to do last season, he would bring in a near six-figure fee. Would that worry him?

"Quite the opposite," he said. "It would make me a more confident player. No club would part with that sort of money if they didn't think I was worth it."

▲ January 1969

IN all the frantic endeavour, hard work, salesmanship and hard slog—not to mention thousands of dollars—which have been poured into the North American Soccer network over the past 18 months no one step, has to me, more significance than the appointment of Phil Woosnam to coach the United States national team.

Woosnam's initial brief is to get a team together, mould it, and win through the preliminary World Cup rounds they face this autumn against Canada and Bermuda. If he is successful, the long-term benefits of having the United States focus attention in their national team will be of enormous help to a major league still fighting furiously to build a future.

Nothing appeals to an American more than national achievement—particularly in sport. And particularly in international sport. Yet, in the most international sport of them all, Soccer, the United States simply isn't ranked—yet.

But they can, and did, revel in the excitement when the Atlanta Chiefs beat Manchester City on a memorable night late in May, and again when Atlanta won a second game 2-1 on June 16.

Of these games, more later. The biggest factor which came from them was that the non-committed U.S. citizens could, at last, feel and see the extra impact of international sporting conflict, the ingredient which puts the sizzle into Soccer.

Of course, it was wonderful to see my club, the Chiefs, beat Joe Mercer's men fairly and squarely. But the real winner was the first game. The score, 3-2, could not reflect the enthusiasm the game detonated among a crowd of 23,141—at least two-thirds of whom were seeing professional Soccer for the first time.

How could anyone really dispute that, given the time, Soccer could sweep the States when a crowd of this size—enormous by North American Soccer League standards—literally abandoned their seats in this no-standing Atlanta Stadium to stand and yell themselves hoarse for 90 minutes?

The noise at times made Liverpool's Kop sound like a cathedral choir in comparison. It was so great, in fact, that the players "complained" afterwards they could not

IT MADE THE KOP SOUND LIKE A CATHEDRAL CHOIR . . . !

hear the instructions and advice shouted among themselves.

This enthusiasm, this excitement, this exhilarating feeling of achievement the Atlanta public shared with their team, only underlines what will happen when the U.S. National team begins to gain success among Soccer's high society.

And this is what Woosnam's appointment is really all about. He's been given a mandate by the men who control the U.S. national team. James McGuire, Chairman of the International Games Committee and long-time chief flag-bearer for U.S. Soccer in the international network, bluntly told me:

"We're turning professional. We are looking not just to the present, but the future. We want a Soccer supremo, another Ramsey if you like, who can help take us to the mainstream of the game."

Both Mr. McGuire, and Bob Guelker, President of the United States Soccer Football Association, stressed that they will seek international games with far more countries than ever before, to build up experience and know-how among the pool of players who will gradually be developed in the United States.

All this, of course, will take time. It's the biggest single problem facing the entire Soccer project in the U.S. . . . time

to develop the major league network while it is costing so much money, time to develop a national team which can capture the attention of the uncommitted, time for youngsters born in the U.S., to develop into international stars in their own right.

I think Joe Mercer was impressed with the potential of the game in the United States when he visited Atlanta. "I've never seen the game sold so well in my life," he said. He was referring specifically to the first Chiefs-Manchester City clash in particular, but appreciated the soundness of a policy which has attracted 8,500 boys playing Soccer for the first time in their lives in Atlanta over the past year.

The point is that Joe did a great deal of the selling during his visit. He pitched into the missionary atmosphere that Woosnam has generated in Atlanta, talking with Press, radio and TV people with eloquence, passion—and wit.

All three were put to good use on two lengthy "talk" programmes. One station in Atlanta, for instance, deals exclusively in "talk". No music. Just talk, and news —interspersed with commercials.

It is a fascinating formula, particularly when virtually every household in the city has a phone, and they can call the station, get "hooked" on to the programme, and get a direct question-and-answer session over the air.

Mercer and Woosnam went round as a team, completing three weeks of intensive promotional work by the Chiefs. The 23,000 crowd was reward for a lot of effort by a lot of people—and the reaction of that crowd was an extra bonus for those who took part in it.

The result of the game was, without doubt, the biggest boost Soccer in the United States has yet had. It has served as a stimulant for those taking part as pioneers in Soccer within North America. Hopefully, it will also stimulate those based thousands of miles away into taking a longer, deeper look at the whole project than has yet been evident—at least to this writer's eyes.

As the old saying goes . . . it's how you look at it.

Manchester City getting a taste of the American atmosphere—complete with baseball bats.

▲ August 1968

OUR TELE-VIEW

HAMPDEN'S EMPTY BOWL

It's hard to believe it's Hampden! But these were the wide-open spaces when Scotland met Northern Ireland on May 6th, watched by only 7,843!

THAT week of home international Soccer which television spewed out by the hour in May exploded afresh the old TV or not TV sports arguments.

In the battle of words there emerged almost the straight issue of whether the game and the business of football was the better for that week of incessant exposure to the cameras.

Television, mainly the BBC for its greater coverage, was lambasted by well-intentioned people taking the long-term view. They missed the real target—those members of the four home Associations who blessed that May marriage.

THESE are the men who are responsible for the most miserable international attendance in memory at Hampden Park.

THESE are the men to be called to account for allowing the TV platforms at Wrexham to blot out the view of Welsh and Scottish fans who had PAID to see that game.

THESE are the people who made the decision which meant Wembley's smallest international attendance—England v. Wales—this season.

Like so many in sports organisation they snapped up the big purse dangled before them at the possible cost of the long-term interest of their game.

As Amateur boxing, swimming, Rugby League and athletics had done before them.

Don't blame television—although there can be differing ideas on how its operators work, especially after some unseemly incidents following the FA Cup Final which were borne out of the over-zealous competition between the different channels that day. . . .

But in what is an intensely competitive business, the rival TV groups are out for

what they can get. And pay handsomely for it.

The four British Associations could not resist their overtures.

Hampden Park, that ghost stadium of May 6, when a pitiful 7,843 crowd would not have met stretched in single file round a ground which holds 134,000, was grisly testimony to the too eagerly proffered hand of the home Associations.

Wrexham was a scandal.

The scaffolding for the TV crews stretched arrogantly across the face of the main stand and obscured the game for almost 1,000 fans.

The Welsh FA were magnanimously moved to announce that they would consider refunding the admission fee of protesting stand patrons.

But what of the expense incurred, for supposition, of the supporter who travelled from Glasgow or Cardiff? Or the cost of meals and refreshment for what was to be a big day, a day ruined by the mercenary interests of the powers that be?

The Belfast attendance for the Ireland v. England game was down by 35,000 on the previous Windsor Park meeting. . . . Wales v. Scotland dropped nearly 14,000. . . . Scotland v. Ireland was, of course, savagely slashed by 37,000 . . . the England-Wales meeting was clipped by 6,000 on the same fixture in 1966, and Ireland-Wales dipped by 2,500.

Again, to meet the whims of television, we had to have two Saturday evening internationals for the first time, played at night to fit in afternoon transmissions of other games.

So away with tradition—it is not all archaic—and the Saturday night out at the local with the missus. The whip cracked

and everybody had to dance to TV's imperious tune.

To be fair, we have to report a full house for the closing game of the week, England's deadly duel with Scotland. But echo answers . . . when *would* you have difficulty in filling either Wembley or Hampden for this one?

It won't be a popular line, querying the wisdom of this massed TV coverage. Those who had their feet up at home while their screens bounced them from Wrexham to Belfast, to Hampden and Wembley, obviously swallowed the week-long diet whole. And enjoyed the meal.

But as we write, having looked at their gates, Scots and the Irish officials are vowing never again. At least, not the blanket viewing we have just had. Second thoughts are already demanding drastic curtailment next time when the whole show will once more be compressed into a week, in April 1970.

Somewhere along the way the original ideas of clearing the decks for England's summer tour, of not upsetting League clubs with international calls and thus giving the other three countries a real choice of their Football League stars were so lost as to appear that only television mattered.

The Welsh, the Scots and the Irish DID have a greater range of choice. There was the best thing to emerge from it all. With the Welsh and the Irish this certainly showed.

But each time they look at the mournful Hampden scene above we trust that the home Associations get the point.

As the more hard-headed Football League Management Committee have long since done.

▲ July 1969

Macdonald . . .
cheered Haynes
from terraces

I WAS 'FULHAM POTTY' AS A KID . . . NOW LUTON ARE THE GREATEST

says Malcolm Macdonald

HAVING signed for Fulham as a full-back, how would you feel making your debut as a striker?

That's what happened to me soon after joining the club at the beginning of the 1968-69 season. . . . I was flabbergasted to put it mildly!

But don't laugh yet . . . the funniest part is still to come. . . .

In my first ten appearances in the Second Division I notched *FIVE* goals, and I finished as the club's second highest scorer.

How did I come to be given the striker's role? It all started because of a run of unfortunate injuries which left the club weak up front.

Manager Bill Dodgin tried out myself and a few others in the reserves and obviously I must have impressed because the next thing I knew . . . I was *IN*.

I have never wanted to switch back to the defence. Now there is no greater thrill than watching a shot bulge the net. And to think I once tried my hardest to

stop 'em going in!

I have gone from strength to strength, and to prove my goalscoring prowess was no flash in the pan I managed to hit 25 League goals for Luton last season to finish as the Football League's third highest scorer.

Although things never really worked out at Craven Cottage it was the realisation of my boyhood ambitions when I signed for them. . . .

As a kid I was Fulham potty! I was born practically on their doorstep . . . in Finlay Road, which leads to the main entrance of Craven Cottage.

Week after week I stood on the terraces in all sorts of weather cheering on my Fulham heroes—and one player in particular. His name . . . Johnny Haynes of course!

So you can imagine how I felt when asked to join the Fulham staff.

My first taste of organised Soccer was at Sloane Grammar in South London, and I represented London Grammar Schools and the Home Counties.

When I was 16 my family moved to a little village in Sussex called Forest Row—a move which didn't please me one bit! I had to take a two-hour bus-ride to play for a team called Park Juniors.

It was with Park Juniors that I got my first real break . . . and struck up an immediate friendship with Harry Haslam, then manager of Southern League Tonbridge, and now chief scout at Luton.

A Tonbridge scout noticed me one afternoon and recommended me to Harry. After playing in a few practice games I was asked to sign on. I didn't have to be asked twice!

Harry is a great bloke to work with and I feel my game improved tremendously under his direction.

When he quit the manager's chair of the Kent club to become scout to Fulham he recommended me to Bobby Robson, then manager at the Cottage, and he signed me soon afterwards.

It was a bit of a wrench to leave Fulham, but my move to Luton was the best thing that could have happened to me. The enthusiasm, ambition and will-to-win at Kenilworth Road is terrific. I've never enjoyed my football more.

Just to emphasise my point, I started last season with seven goals in seven games!

Mind you, my transfer to Luton nearly killed me with suspense!

I reported to Craven Cottage for what I thought was going to be a normal afternoon's training, just prior to the start of last season, when Bill Dodgin told me that a manager was coming to see me at 2.30 with an offer.

I waited . . . and waited. But still there was no sign of him. Then, around five o'clock, a very apologetic Alec Stock walked through the door . . . he had been delayed because of a burst car tyre!

Although Fulham received £17,500 for my transfer, I don't think my name is a popular one at Craven Cottage. . . . I scored the only goal in each of Luton's games with them—the second match at Fulham really putting paid to their promotion hopes!

Strange how things work out. . . .

Reading were other promotion rivals who brought out the best in me. I scored the solitary goal at Elm Park early in March and took a hat-trick off them in the home meeting on Easter Saturday!

Even stranger is the fact that I hadn't scored in between those two matches!

That we won promotion last season is history now, but let me say right away that this Luton side isn't simply going to be a good one . . . but a great one.

Under our determined and disciplined boss, Alec Stock, who has done such a wonderful job, we feel we can take on anyone in the higher sphere.

We have some fine players, with experienced Graham French, Terry Branston, Dave Court and Roger Hoy alongside promising youngsters like Chris Nicholl and Viv Busby.

It is early days yet and no one at Luton is counting his chickens . . . but I honestly believe I shall achieve my ambition of playing in the First Division in the very near future . . . with Luton!

▲ September 1970

TONY GREEN

▲ August 1970

STEVE KEMBER
Crystal Palace

▲ February 1971

IAN ST. JOHN
Liverpool

▲ September 1970

MIKE CHANNON
Southampton

▲ October 1970

SOCCER SIDESHOW

BY LESLIE YATES

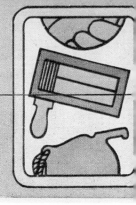

The escape

THE success of Jeff Astle, their 24-year-old striker, had a lot to do with the rise of West Bromwich Albion last season.

Astle joined West Bromwich from Notts County at the end of September, 1964, and now ranks as one of the club's best captures for years.

For Jeff a career in football meant an escape from the mines. After leaving school in the Eastwood district of Nottingham, he worked for four months as an apprenticed fitter at a local colliery.

When the chance came his way to join the ground staff of the Notts club, Astle was quick to grasp it.

They're ready

YEARS ago it was unusual for a footballer to involve himself in business interests before his career had ended.

Nowadays, many players are wise enough to venture into business when at the peak of their playing prime—and, so, are fitted for when the time comes to retire from the game.

Frank McLintock and Ian Ure, Arsenal's Scottish international half-backs, are partners in a property concern controlling a number of flats. They are planning to expand their activities soon.

MICK LAMBERT, the young Ipswich Town forward, has abandoned his cricketing ambitions to concentrate on professional football.

Lambert, a batsman, was on the ground staff at Lords, and has played for the Middlesex and Essex second elevens; in his schooldays he was keener to make good in cricket than in Soccer.

Now he is giving all his attention to football, and hopes to make a name with Ipswich.

He comes from Balsham, near Cambridge, and at one time was rejected by Cambridge United as "not good enough."

THE strange thing about Ian Hutchinson, the young Chelsea forward who made such impact last season, his first at Stamford Bridge, is that he never surfaced as a footballer at Littleover Secondary Modern School, near Derby.

He started an engineering apprenticeship and played for the works team. Nottingham Forest gave him a chance as an amateur in their "A" team, but made no attempt to keep him.

His first big chance came with Burton Albion, who transferred him to Cambridge United. Chelsea noticed Hutchinson while watching another Cambridge player, and he joined the London club a year ago.

Ian's hobby is collecting rare British and foreign coins.

FRANK BLUNSTONE, Brentford's team manager, has no need to emphasise to his players the need to wear shin pads.

Years ago it was unthinkable for any player to step on the field without pads. In modern times many players scorn them.

In mid-season Dick Renwick, the Brentford full-back, had eight stitches inserted in a gash while wearing pads. Without pads he would probably have had a broken leg.

Manager Blunstone pinned the damaged pad to the dressing-room notice-board as a silent warning. His players have taken due note.

RON ASHMAN, Scunthorpe's manager, will watch the progress of Kevin Keegan, the forward he transferred to Liverpool in May, with keen interest.

Scunthorpe were sorry to lose Keegan, but it is never easy for a club in their financial position to turn down a good offer.

If Keegan makes as big a name with Liverpool as Ray Clemence, the goalkeeper they signed from Scunthorpe, there will be plenty of smiles at Anfield.

Keegan was under constant watch by other clubs last season.

JOHN JACKSON, the Crystal Palace goalkeeper, has an ideal way of escaping the tensions of League football.

John lives at Hove, and spends as much of his leisure time as possible fishing off the Sussex beaches.

His biggest catch? An 8-lb. bass, off Shoreham-by-Sea.

Jackson is a West Londoner, who was spotted by Palace when playing for London Grammar Schools.

He planned a career as a teacher, but Palace's offer decided him in favour of football.

IN December, 1954, A.C. Milan visited West Ham for a floodlight friendly and gave a dazzling exhibition to win 6-0.

Malcolm Allison and John Bond, two of West Ham's players at that time, have always associated Milan's display that night with football at its very peak.

It's not surprising, therefore, that Malcolm, Manchester City's assistant-manager, should have introduced Milan's red and black stripes as an alternative strip for his club.

City wore them at Wembley when they won the League Cup last season, and against Leicester when they won the F.A. Cup in 1969.

Now John is manager of Bournemouth, and after many years the club's traditional red shirt has been scrapped for red and black stripes.

That must have been quite a display by Milan at West Ham!

Marksman

THE MOST ACCURATE marksman at Queen's Park Rangers? If the pigeons that hover around Shepherd's Bush could answer that question they would name Les Allen, the club's player-manager!

When Les had more time, he often went shooting on the farms near his Essex home. And he is pretty useful with a 12-bore shot-gun.

This summer he has scared the pigeons off Rangers' playing pitch with an occasional volley of shots. As a result the playing surface is in fine condition for the new season.

DICK KRZYWICKI, the West Bromwich Albion forward, is a Welsh international who cannot remember living in Wales!

Dick, son of Polish parents, was born in Wrexham when his father was stationed there on Army service.

He was only three when the family moved to Leek in Staffordshire, where he attended Mountside Secondary Modern School, and played for the Leek Boys team.

Not long ago Krzywicki made a sentimental journey to North Wales to see where he was born. It was an Army headquarters at the time of his birth, but has since been converted into a library.

Why is the Albion player often called Nick? "When I arrived at West Bromwich the players decided that with a surname like mine, I needed re-christening," explains Krzywicki. "They settled on Nick, but my real name is Richard."

THE 'Chicken Run'—the popular name given to the low cover opposite West Ham United's main stand—has now gone.

For years its humble appearance irritated officials of First Division West Ham, and just before last season ended it was demolished.

A new cantilever stand is now in the course of erection in its place, and by mid-season West Ham will have a ground in keeping with their reputation and status.

To many old-time supporters of the club, however, the passing of the "Chicken Run" has been a sad event. Some have even asked West Ham for bits of wood from the old structure as souvenirs!

No worries

FEW players lead as busy a life as Peter Thompson, Liverpool's English international winger. Thompson has two business enterprises, and takes part in the running of both.

Most days he looks in at the Anfield Service Station, which is behind the Kop end of Liverpool's ground, and from there makes his way to the confectionery and tobacconist's shop he runs in Lark Hill Lane, Liverpool.

Peter has been wise to involve himself in business interests while still in his prime as a player. He now has no worries over his livelihood when his playing days are over.

He joined Liverpool from Preston in 1963 . . . one of the best signings ever made by the Merseyside club.

Selected from 1968–71

It's a snip

WHEN training is over, Terry Mancini, Orient's captain and centre-half, slips quietly into a vastly different role and environment.

He takes over at the reception desk at his wife's hairdressing salon in York-road, Battersea. Terry has no plans to learn the art of hairdressing, but has shown a flair for the business side of the enterprise.

It was the opportunity to open this business that influenced Terry and his wife to return to England from South Africa, where he spent two seasons with the Port Elizabeth club.

Mancini, who came originally from the Camden Town district of London, might have made his mark with Fulham. He spent two months on trial with Fulham, but as nothing came of it, he signed for Watford.

"Now the season's started, I'm spending more and more on toilet-rolls!"

MOST PLAYERS have medals, plaques and pennants among their souvenirs. Jimmy Neighbour, Spurs' young winger, has a memento that is different.

When Jimmy played his first full match for Spurs against Bristol City in the second-leg semi-final tie of the Football League Cup at White Hart Lane this season he kicked the corner-flag, breaking it at its base, instead of the ball!

Neighbour was given the broken flag-pole and it now has a place of honour in his garden at Chingford!

LEAGUE football for Wigan? Officials of Wigan Athletic, members of the Northern Premier League, are optimistic about their chances of gaining election within the next few years.

Wigan have a fine ground at Springfield Park. It was, in fact, the home of the old Wigan Borough club, who resigned from the old Third Division (North) in 1931.

Wigan know they have more support than some clubs at present in the Fourth Division, and feel they would be an asset to the League.

Manager of Wigan is Ian McNeill, the former Brighton and Leicester inside-forward.

It's life!

IF Ron Flowers, the former England and Wolves half-back, had been told a few months ago that he would soon be playing for Telford United, he would have listened in amazement.

There wasn't even a club of that name last season. Telford is the new name for Wellington Town, the Southern League club that has been in existence since 1887.

Flowers was player-manager of North-ampton Town last season, but when the campaign ended he left on a free transfer.

He joined Telford as player-coach, and hopes to bring success to the club in its first season under a new title.

Pauline Hicks is a girl with a difference ... she has just been appointed
secretary to Halifax Town—the League's only woman secretary.

▲ August 1968

here we show the versatile stock range of...

UMBRO

Self Design

Candy Stripe Design

Regular Stripe Design

Trimmed Design

Arsenal Design

Goalkeeper's Sweater

Photos: PAM SALLOWAY

THESE STYLES IN VARIED COMBINATIONS OF THESE STOCK COLOURS ...

555 or 284 AZTEC
WORLD CUP JERSEY
(self)
076 SHORTS
435 SELF HOSE

301 or 302
JERSEY
(candy stripe)
435
BANDED HOSE

294 or 283
JERSEY
(regular stripes)
445
HOOPED HOSE

555 or 284 AZTEC
WORLD CUP JERSEY
(trimmed)
077 SHORTS
445 HOSE (turn over top)

ARSENAL STYLE
555 or 284 JERSEY

450 HOSE (hooped)

359 WORLD CUP
GOALKEEPERS' SWEATER

435 HOSE (banded)

Club Secretaries are invited to send in for 1968 Umbrochure.

▲ August 1968

HONOURS 1968-71

1968-69
Division 1 Leeds United
Division 2 Derby County *(top)*
Division 3 Watford
Division 4 Doncaster Rovers

Scottish 1 Celtic
Scottish 2 Motherwell

FA Cup Manchester City
League Cup Swindon Town
Scottish Cup Celtic
Amateur Cup North Shields

CBFM Readers' Top Ten Players
1. Francis Lee (Man City) 2. George Best
(Man Utd) 3. Bobby Moore (West Ham)
4. Bobby Charlton (Man Utd) 5. Gordon Banks
(Stoke) 6. Billy Bremner (Leeds) 7. Geoff Hurst
(West Ham) 8. Jimmy Greaves (Spurs)
9. Dave Mackay (Derby) 10. Ron Davies
(Southampton)
European Cup AC Milan
Cup Winners' Cup Slovan Bratislava
Inter Cities Fairs Cup Newcastle United

1969-70
Division 1 Everton
Division 2 Huddersfield Town
Division 3 Orient
Division 4 Chesterfield *(centre)*

Scottish 1 Celtic
Scottish 2 Falkirk

FA Cup Chelsea
League Cup Manchester City
Scottish Cup Aberdeen *(bottom)*
Amateur Cup Enfield

European Cup Feyenoord
Cup Winners' Cup Manchester City
Inter Cities Fairs Cup Arsenal
World Cup Brazil

1970-71
Division 1 Arsenal
Division 2 Leicester City
Division 3 Preston North End
Division 4 Notts County

Scottish 1 Celtic
Scottish 2 Partick Thistle

FA Cup Arsenal
League Cup Tottenham Hotspur
Scottish Cup Celtic
Amateur Cup Skelmersdale United

European Cup Ajax
Cup Winners' Cup Chelsea
Inter Cities Fairs Cup Leeds United

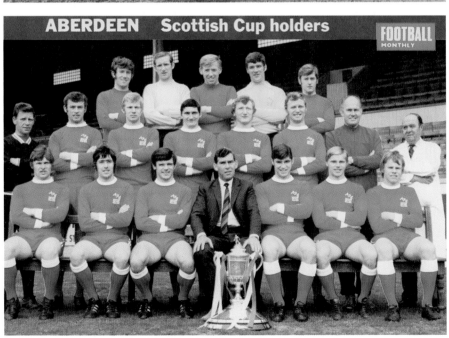

▲ October 1970 | July 1970 | August 1970

Postscript

And what of our heroes? How did they fare after hanging up their boots and returning to the mundanities of everyday life beyond the stadium? If Leslie Yates were around to update his Soccer Sideshow, what tales might he tell of the cover boys and pin ups who inhabited the pages of *Charles Buchan's Football Monthly*?

Certainly Yates and his colleagues would have been amazed, and delighted, at how football's burgeoning heritage sector has commemorated these former stars.

When Stanley Matthews, star of the magazine's first cover in September 1951, died in 2000 at the age of 85, more than 100,000 people lined the streets of Stoke to pay their respects. A statue depicting the 'Wizard of the Dribble' was unveiled the following year outside Stoke's Britannia Stadium. Thanks to support from the Heritage Lottery Fund, his medals and memorabilia are held by the National Football Museum in Preston (itself opened in 2001).

Outside the museum is another statue, to Tom Finney, 'the Preston Plumber' who appeared on the magazine's cover in September 1954 and was knighted in 1998. Jackie Milburn, featured on the November 1951, is commemorated by two statues, in his home town of Ashington, and in Newcastle, close to St James' Park. Milburn and Finney also have stands named after them at Newcastle and Preston respectively, as does Colin Bell at the City of Manchester Stadium and Bobby Moore, at Upton Park. Close by is another statue, depicting Moore and his West Ham and England 1966 team-mates, Sir Geoff Hurst and Martin Peters. Since his death from cancer at the age of 51, a further statue of Moore has been commissioned to stand outside the new Wembley Stadium. Moore's

collection of memorabilia has, meanwhile, been secured for West Ham's club museum.

Other football stalwarts from the magazine's era honoured in bronze are Sir Matt Busby, at Old Trafford, Charlton goalkeeper Sam Bartram at The Valley, Bob Stokoe at Sunderland's Stadium of Light and Billy Bremner at Elland Road. Also at Leeds is a bust of the 'Gentle Giant' John Charles. In Bolton, an image of the 'Lion of Vienna' Nat Lofthouse forms part of a 30m high monument, *The Spirit of Sport*, at the Reebok Stadium.

Most poignant of all are two stained glass windows dedicated to Duncan Edwards at St Francis' Church, in Edwards' home town of Dudley. A statue of the tragic youth also stands in the town centre, where there is a Duncan Edwards exhibition at the Museum and Art Gallery. Munich survivor Bobby Charlton, now a director at Old Trafford, was knighted in 1994. Belfast City Airport was named after George Best, who died in 2005.

Best famously suffered from alcoholism, as did Jimmy Baxter and Albert Johanneson, who died penniless in Leeds. Valeri Voronin died after a drunken brawl in a Moscow back street. Garrincha died in similar circumstances, aged 49, in Brazil, having fathered 14 children with various partners. Arsenal's Jimmy Logie fell prey to gambling and ended up selling newspapers in Piccadilly Circus.

Golden boy Albert Quixall was luckier. His soccer chums rallied round in 2002 to play a benefit match when he fell on hard times. A testimonial match staged by Everton also helped ease the financial woes of 52 year old Tommy Lawton in 1972. Alan Ball was forced to sell his World Cup medal when both his wife and daughter developed cancer.

It fetched £140,000. In contrast, Stan Mortensen sold his medals to help bale out his beloved Blackpool in the 1960s. Also active in saving his former club was Allan McGraw. In the 1990s he became a local councillor in order to help rescue Morton, the club he had served for 36 years.

Many a player paid for his career with arthritic knees, aching joints, and worse. Both Jack Burkitt and Jeff Astle died from a form of dementia exacerbated by constant heading of the old style heavy leather balls. The coroner described Astle as having died from industrial injuries. Tommy Lawton may have suffered similarly, as no doubt did many others. There are now gates dedicated to Astle at The Hawthorns, West Bromwich.

Several others died prematurely: Jeff Hall from polio, aged 30; Grenville Hair at 37; Charlie Tully at 47; Gerry Hitchens at 48; and both Willie Bauld and Jimmy Bloomfield at the age of 49.

To be sure, football could be an unforgiving, and short career. But many players enjoyed long and fruitful careers outside the game. Colin Grainger worked the club circuit as a crooner, once sharing a bill with the Beatles. Charlie Williams emerged as a popular comedian on television. Jimmy Greaves overcame alcoholism to enjoy success with Ian St John as a double act for ITV Sport. Ron Atkinson also found fame and later infamy after giving up his window cleaning business in Oxford.

More typically, Jack Froggatt, Bill Paterson and Joe Baker became publicans. Ted Ditchburn ran a printing business before opening a sports shop and newsagent. Sid Gerrie worked as head storeman with an Aberdeen civil engineering firm. Ron Flowers set up a sports shop in Wolverhampton. Don Rogers did the same in Swindon.

Tommy Cheadle, worked as a postman. John Atyeo and Eddy Brown took up teaching. Ian Ure left coaching to take up social work. Roy McCrohan became a photographer in Florida. Ted McDougall went into business in Canada.

In common with Jackie Milburn, Len Shackleton, Jimmy Armfield and Jimmy McIlroy enjoyed success as journalists. McIlroy has a stand named after him at Burnley. Francis Lee made millions from manufacturing toilet paper. Mick Channon owns racehorses.

Among those who went on to prominent careers as managers and coaches were Syd Owen, Malcolm Allison, Don Howe, Dave Mackay, Tommy Docherty, Bobby Robson, Terry Venables, Brian Kidd and Joe Royle, while Peter Taylor and Brian Clough formed one of modern football's most successful managerial partnerships at Derby and Nottingham, but after falling out in 1983 never spoke again.

Bill Slater rose to prominence in sports education at Liverpool and Birmingham universities, gaining both an OBE and CBE along the way. Bert Trautmann also received an OBE, as did seven other players featured here. Brian Clough, who died in 2004, described his award as standing for 'Old Big 'Ead'.

Professional football has thrust many a great man, and countless more journeymen, into the glaring spotlight of fame. Each has a story.

As do the fans. Three year old Brian Clifford, Sheffield Wednesday's mascot – whom we encountered on the touchlines at Hillsborough in the November 1952 edition – still follows the Owls, as does his mother, his aunt (seen on the left in the photograph), now aged 84, and Brian's son too.

And so the narrative continues. Soccer's sideshow plays on.

Grand indeed!

GOODBYE —THANKS!

The final accolade! Sir Stanley Matthews, C.B.E., of Stoke, Blackpool, Stoke again, and England, age 50-plus, is carried off by two of the world's greatest players, Yashin (left), of Russia, and Puskas, of Hungary and Spain. This was after Matthews's last match—his testimonial.

▲ June 1965

Index

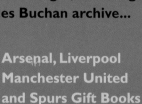

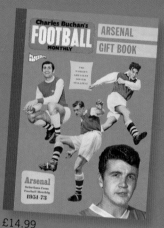
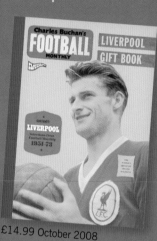
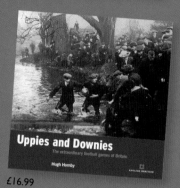

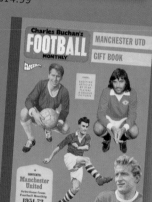
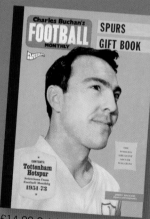

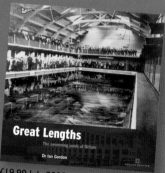